THIRD EDITION

PUBLIC BUDGETING

IN AMERICA

Thomas D. Lynch

Florida Atlantic University

PRENTICE HALL, *Englewood Cliffs, New Jersey 07632*

Library of Congress Cataloging-in-Publication Data

Lynch, Thomas Dexter
   Public budgeting in America / Thomas D. Lynch.—3rd ed.
   p.   cm.
   Includes bibliographies and index.
   1. Budget—United States.   I. Title.
HJ2051.L93   1990
350.72′2′0973—dc19   89-31174
                                                      CIP

Editorial/production supervision and
   interior design: Shelly Kupperman
Cover design: Edsal Enterprises
Manufacturing buyer: Pete Havens

Printed in the United States of America
10 9 8 7 6 5 4 3

ISBN   0-13-737388-0

PRENTICE-HALL INTERNATIONAL (UK) LIMITED, *London*
PRENTICE-HALL OF AUSTRALIA PTY. LIMITED, *Sydney*
PRENTICE-HALL CANADA INC., *Toronto*
PRENTICE-HALL HISPANOAMERICANA, S.A., *Mexico*
PRENTICE-HALL OF INDIA PRIVATE LIMITED, *New Delhi*
PRENTICE-HALL OF JAPAN, INC., *Tokyo*
SIMON & SCHUSTER ASIA PTE. LTD., *Singapore*
EDITORA PRENTICE-HALL DO BRASIL, LTDA. *Rio de Janeiro*

CONTENTS

6 ANALYTICAL PROCESSES   162

7

OPERATING BUDGETS AND ACCOUNTING 206

8

CAPITAL BUDGETING AND DEBT ADMINISTRATION 247

9

REVENUE SYSTEMS   285

10

INTERNAL SERVICE FUNCTIONS   313

GLOSSARY   345

INDEX   365

PREFACE

This edition is primarily an update of the second edition. The major changes are associated with computer technology, debt management, an improving professional literature, and professional developments. The microcomputer is clearly making a difference in budgeting and financial management, and in this edition, I explain its increasingly important role. One subject that needed updating was debt management. The Reagan years brought significant changes in debt management by first opening the Pandora's box of creative financing to government debt managers, and then closing the box due to federal treasury losses. The second edition reflected the first set of changes; this edition reflects the later reforms.

In reflecting on the changes, I believe that most were prompted by remarkable developments in the profession, but that some were prompted by my desire to communicate this complex body of knowledge in a more intelligible manner. Such areas as forecasting and capital budgeting have undergone remarkable changes in recent years. I am still amazed at the rate of change and the increasing sophistication of the subject matter as it evolves. Professional change is not only present but growing. The Government Finance Officers Association (GFOA) is continuing to produce fine additions to the practical literature on budgeting and financial management. However, its most significant recent contribution to the field is its new yearly budget award process. This process is defining "good budgeting" and serving as an incentive to many local governments to prepare "good budgets." In addition, journals like *Public Budgeting and Finance* and the new *Public Budgeting and Financial Management* are producing a steady flow of articles that enhance the professional understanding of our field.

I must acknowledge my appreciation to everyone who has contributed to this edition. I wish to thank the reviewers for their helpful suggestions: Khi V. Thai, University of Maine, and Grace Hall Saltzstein, University of California–Riverside.

Thomas D. Lynch
Boca Raton, Florida

chapter 1

PUBLIC BUDGETING
IN CONTEXT

Public budgeting is a mystery to most people—even to many professionals working in the government. People are aware that chief executives propose budgets to legislative bodies and that these groups in turn make decisions on taxes and what programs will receive financial support. If they work in government, they know that material is prepared to justify "the budget" and that detailed controls exist which often prohibit simple management decisions. In the personal lives of most people, the family budget is a source of tension because of the need to live within one's income. Most people assume that public budgeting must deal with similar matters but that it must involve much more complex accounting techniques.

This chapter examines what public budgeting is and the contextual factors necessary to understand public budgeting in the American context. Public budgeting is an activity and many people view that activity from their own perspectives. Thus, the meaning of "public budgeting" is very much dependent upon perspective. The primary contextual factors in American budgeting are the ideologies of democracy and capitalism, federalism, decision-making theory, and economics. Each helps define how we approach and understand the purpose of public budgeting. This chapter should help the reader understand:

1. the various significant perspectives on budgeting, including that of the public manager;
2. important budgetary and political realities;
3. the nature of the budget cycle (i.e., phases, cycle variations, overlapping of cycles) and the activities associated with each budget phase;
4. the significance of ideology in influencing how we approach public budgeting;
5. the role of federalism as a factor in budgeting;
6. the significance of normative decision-making theory to public budgeting;

7. the major tools of monetary policy, what aspects of the economy they primarily affect, and their significance to public budgeting;

8. the variety of ways in which the federal government can act to stimulate or depress the economy and the theory behind such actions; and

9. an explanation of how economic policy has and has not worked since the 1960s.

WHAT IS PUBLIC BUDGETING?

Perspectives on Budgeting

One can define a term by seeking out the common usages or one can create a definition for one's own intellectual and conceptual purposes. The former approach is particularly useful when one is trying to understand the various perspectives that people bring to a given activity. The latter approach is useful when an author is attempting to establish a reasonably uniform body of thought. Both approaches are used here.

Public budgeting can be viewed from many perspectives, as illustrated by Professor Sydney Duncombe in Exhibit 1 1. Reading the variety of statements helps one to appreciate the various academic and practical perspectives found in the practice of public budgeting. There are many such perspectives, of which none are exclusively "correct." The parable of the three blind men and the elephant helps us understand the significance of perspective. One of the blind men examined the tail and pronounced his description of the animal. Another felt a large foot and leg and then argued that the first man's description was inaccurate. The third man, after examining the beast's trunk, said that the other two were quite wrong in their descriptions. The storyteller was said to laugh at the foolish arguing among the blind men because the storyteller could see all of the elephant. The point of the parable is not the importance of "better" perspective but rather the foolishness of the storyteller for not recognizing that he himself was blinded by arrogance because he was sighted. Each person was correct and each was wrong because our individual perspectives always prevent us from easily understanding another's "truth."

When one works in the world of public budgeting, each perspective is used by various key actors in the budget process. The person trained as a lawyer sees the phenomenon called budgeting as a sort of legal process. The economist and politician describe the phenomenon differently based upon their perspectives. The public manager sees budgeting differently from the others. None are incorrect, because all of them define the phenomenon based upon their educational or professional perspectives. They become incorrect, like the storyteller, when their arrogance blinds them to the significance of perspective when defining and understanding the phenomenon of public budgeting.

For the purposes of this textbook, the more important perspectives are those of the politician, the economist, the accountant, and especially the public manager. Given a democratic society, budgets are the tool used to frame much public policy; thus the politician's perspective is important.

EXHIBIT 1-1   What are the Main Purposes of Budgeting?

I view the budget system as a *means of balancing revenues and expenditures.* Our constitution requires a balanced budget and in preparing our budget we first make careful estimates of revenues for the next year. We then reduce agency budget requests to our revenue estimates for the next year.

I look on the budget process as a *semi-judicial process* in which state agencies come to the Legislature to plead their case just as I plead the case of my clients in court. Our job as a legislative committee is to distribute the available funds equitably among state agencies.

The main purpose of the budget system is *accountability.* The people hold the Legislature accountable through the electoral process. The Legislature holds state agencies accountable by reviewing their budgets, setting the appropriation levels the people want, and letting state agencies know how the people want their money spent through statements of legislative intent.

The most important single reason for a budget system is *control.* State agencies would spend the state bankrupt in two years if there weren't an adequate means of controlling their spending. The appropriations are the first line of defense against overspending. Important second lines of defense lie in allotment systems, position controls, and controls over purchasing.

The executive budget document should be an *instrument of gubernatorial policy.* When a Governor comes into office there are certain programs and policies he would like to see accomplished during the term of office. Many of these program and policy changes cost money, and the Governor will have to either raise taxes or cut expenses to pay for these changes. The people expect the Governor to show accomplishments and the budget is a major means of showing these accomplishments.

Budgeting is *public relations.* I write my budget justifications in the way I think will best gain the appropriations I need. If the budget examiner likes workload statistics, we'll snow the examiner with statistics. If a key legislator would be influenced by how the budget will affect constituents, we put that in the request.

A budget is an *instrument of good management.* Careful use of workload statistics, performance accounting, and standards of performance will tend to insure that personnel are effectively utilized.

A budget is really a *work plan with a dollar sign attached.* As an agency official, I am committing myself to certain levels of program which I promise to attain if I receive my full budget request. When the Governor and the Legislature discuss cutting my budget, I describe as accurately as I can the reduction in program level that will result.

The budget is an instrument for *planning.* A good budget system requires agency officials to project costs and program levels at least several years ahead. Such a system requires agency officials to examine the costs and benefits of alternatives to present programs in order to plan changes in programs where necessary. In short, budgeting should be an annual means for agency heads to reexamine the objectives of their programs and the effectiveness of the means used to accomplish these objectives.

Budgeting is *the art of cutting* the most fat from an agency request with the least squawking.

Source: Prepared by Sydney Duncombe, 1977.

Both economists and accountants have professional perspectives which greatly influence how we understand budgeting and how we believe we should practice it. Economists give us theories and techniques which help us define how we should budget, what factors should be weighed, and how to weigh these factors in making budget policy decisions. Accountants give us conceptual frameworks in which to execute and evaluate budgets. Public managers must understand each of the previous perspectives when managing the affairs of government through the budget process.

Political leaders are often painfully aware that many of the most important policy decisions are made during the budget process. Former New York City Mayor Abraham Beame was reported to have said that "the budget is everything" when that city was undergoing its fiscal crisis during the 1970s. Mayor Beame was quite sensitive to the financial crisis of his city and the resulting policy dilemmas confronting him. Henry Maier, the mayor of Milwaukee, once said, "The budget is the World Series of Government." This mayor in the early 1980s had to support a 20 percent increase in property taxes. Both mayors were aware that many—if not most—of the major political decisions are made when a chief executive proposes the government's budget and a legislative body (e.g., the city council) adopts it.

The budgetary process can be viewed as a political event conducted in the political arena for political advantage. Politics—being a reflection of human nature—has its best and worst sides. In some instances, politicians or individuals who influence politicians are seeking money for themselves. In other instances, the political advantage sought is to further some ethical position or to aid others selflessly. Motivations differ, but the seeking of political advantage is constant. Thus, one signficant perspective on budgeting is political.

Economists view budgetary decisions with the assumptions that budget decisions are made within restricted financial conditions and that economic analysis can therefore help identify the best decision. Every budget decision involves potential benefits which may or may not be obtained; it also involves "opportunity cost." If the available money is spent for one program, then another program is not funded or is funded at a lower level. In other words, opportunities are lost in every budget decision and there never seems to be enough money for every program. When choices have to be made, economic analysis can help one to evaluate the comparative benefits and costs, including opportunity cost. This view of budgeting focuses upon decision-making and places a high premium upon the value of analysis in helping decision makers make "better" decisions.

Accountants stress the importance of capturing accurate financial information. To the accountant, the budget is the statement of desired policy, and information on actual expenditures is compared with the budget to judge whether policy has been followed, as well as to question the wisdom of the original policy. The accountant's view largely defines how public managers understand how they should execute the budget and how some of their evaluators will judge their actions.

None of these views—the politician's, the economist's, and the accountant's—is incorrect. Each perspective is valuable in getting a more comprehensive understanding of public budgeting. Interestingly, the perspective of the public manager most closely approximates that of the storyteller in the parable. Public managers must try to achieve a more comprehensive view, but they cannot fall into the trap of arrogantly believing that such a view is anything more than one valid perspective among others.

A Public Manager's Perspective

Viewed from a public manager's perspective, the budget is often the principal vehicle for developing government plans and policies. There can be a separate planning process, but often such a process develops vague statements without stressing relative priorities. The budget states specific dollar amounts relative to proposed government activities and these decisions reflect the government's plans and policies much more accurately than most planning documents.

The budget also represents the chief executive's legislative program. It states which programs are to be active, emphasized, or ignored given the limited resources available to the government. Other public statements may be made which discuss a mayor's or governor's legislative program, but the comprehensive and detailed presentation is presented in the budget.

There are several different ways to categorize the request for funds to finance a government, but they all outline planned functions, programs, and activities. Program and performance budgets more clearly explain the relationship of money requested and government activities. However, even line-item budgets, which focus upon specific items to be purchased with the budget, provide the knowledgeable reader with a detailed outline of planned government activities.

Most budgets present the planned program for the year against a background of past experiences and future needs. Even zero base budgets normally cite past experience to demonstrate the type of activities likely to be funded in the planned year. In some instances, budgets project future needs beyond the planned budget year in order to suggest the future year implications of budget year decisions. This past and future information is highly useful to decision makers: The past gives them an impression of what the program can accomplish and the future gives them warning of the long-run implications of current budget year decisions.

Strictly speaking, the budget is a request for funds to run the government. The request is normally made by the chief executive to the city council, legislature, or Congress. It also states the revenue and other sources of resources (e.g., debt financing) needed to balance the suggested expenditures. Once the budget is modified or approved, the executive branch develops operating budgets for the budget year. Traditionally, the document sent to the legislature by the chief executive is called *the budget*. In the federal government, Congress receives the budget but passes several appropriation bills which constitute the modified approved federal budget.

An Operational Definition

As can be noticed from the previous discussions, the term "budget" is used in a variety of ways. Each may be quite correct given the perspective of the user of the word. In public administration, the following definition is normally an excellent operational definition:

> "Budget" is a *plan* for the accomplishment of *programs* related to *objectives* and *goals* within a definite *time* period, including an estimate of *resources required,* together with an estimate of the *resources available,* usually compared with one or more *past periods* and showing *future requirements.*

The budget always represents what someone wishes to do or have someone else do. It is a tool to help us control our affairs. Once the money is spent, it can be contrasted to the plan but it no longer represents something called a budget; rather it represents actual obligations or expenditures. Prior to that time, the budget may change many times. The document sent to the legislature by a chief executive is normally considered to be "the budget," whereas the plan used by the bureaucrats during the budget year is normally called the "operating budget."

People writing budgets have programs and program accomplishments in mind. Admittedly, those people may have rather vague notions of the exact nature of each program and their desired goals and objectives. Dealing with and avoiding vagueness is one of the major challenges of public budgeting. But in spite of vagueness, people preparing budgets do believe that the requested funds will be used for some set of activities and that those activities will result in accomplishments.

Budgets are focused upon a specific time period called the budget year. In some instances, the year used corresponds to the calendar year, but normally an arbitrary year called fiscal year (e.g., October 1 to September 30) is defined. The money is planned to be spent or obligated in the budget year. Years prior to the budget year (BY) are called prior or past years (PY) and the current time period in which the government is operating is called the current year (CY). Future fiscal years beyond the budget year are referred to as budget year plus one (BY + 1), budget year plus two (BY + 2), and so on. For example, let us say we are preparing the budget for the fiscal year (FY) 1990 but we are actually in FY 1989. The BY is 1990. The CY is 1989. The PY is 1988. The BY + 1 is 1991.

Budgets are planned for a specific time period and an estimate is always made of the resources required during that time period. The estimates include the revenue as well as the expenditures. Estimating is another challenge of budgeting as one can never be certain that a specific dollar sum will be raised or that the government can live within its proposed expenditures. The latter is more easily controlled, but unexpected emergencies or problems do occur.

In order to facilitate a better understanding of the requested resources, the budget usually compares the BY requests against the PY and CY actual obligations or expenditures. This provides a basis for comparing and permits the decision maker to focus upon the difference or increment between the CY and the BY. This is called incremental budgeting. In zero base budgeting, one ignores the differences and demands that the whole BY amount be justified. As will be explained later in more depth, this distinction between incremental and zero base budgeting is overstated. Increasingly, budgets also go beyond the BY and show BY + 1, BY + 2, BY + 3, BY + 4, and BY + 5. This showing of future requirements helps the decision maker realize that BY decisions have an effect beyond one budget year. Thus, a policy maker may decide that a given set of decisions may be affordable for the budget year but not wise, given the likely future requirements. Unfortunately, policy makers often ignore future implications and this situation represents yet another challenge of public budgeting.

Budget Realities

If you examine a budget, there will be many tables and charts. If you work in government, there will be many forms that must be completed so that a budget can be prepared, executed, and evaluated. The details in the forms and tables are an essential part of budgeting, but you can never understand public budgeting by examining those forms and tables *per se.* The numbers and the formats used to present the numbers are merely some of the means and not the ends of public budgeting.

Budgeting is a good reflection of actual public policy and often a better reflection than formal speeches or written statements. Politicians must get elected to hold office, and clarity of expression may be dysfunctional because it makes needless enemies. Also, it is often difficult to verbalize policy. The budget states the planned priorities and the programs in a meaningful way to the people who must carry out the policy. This is not to say that all policy is reflected in the budget, because some important policy matters have no fiscal implications. Nor is it to say that all budgets clearly present policy. But an expert can read the message which will be operationalized by the bureaucracy.

A budget focuses upon a given year (the budget year), but its preparation, execution, and evaluation take place over a period of several years (the budget cycle). Going back to the FY 1990 example, the preparation and approval of the 1990 budget year should have been finished just prior to the beginning of the fiscal year (October 1, 1989). In order to have an approved budget on time, the preparation and approval process must begin much earlier. Sometimes the preparation begins a full year or more before the beginning of the budgeted fiscal year. During FY 1990, the operating budget is used to guide obligations and expenditures, but after FY 1990 no more money can be obligated, though some money can be spent to fulfill the FY 1990 obligations. The period in which to fulfill obligations can be open-ended, but sound practices place a one- or two-year limit so that the books can be closed. The final stage in the budget cycle is auditing and evaluating the program resources obligated in the earlier budget year. This can take place one to several years after the completion of the fiscal year. In other words, the FY 1990 budget cycle can start as early as 1989 and end as late as 1993.

Budgeting is highly emotional, detailed, and a great deal of work. When policy makers decide to fund or not to fund programs, people are profoundly affected, lives are changed. Not surprisingly, budget decisions evoke strong emotions because the stakes are high and the consequences are important. Budgets are also detailed. The one cardinal sin for a budget officer is to make an arithmetic error because that is one mistake everyone can catch and criticize. The budgets are often hundreds and thousands of pages long, filled with tables. Each number is usually important to someone and mistakes are not treated lightly. The preparation of this mass of information requires much work. Deadlines drive the process and require intensive 50- to 60-hour-plus work weeks, especially prior to a major deadline such as submission of material to a legislative committee. The work is consuming and requires almost complete devotion. The work is also extremely interesting because of the interrelationship of budgeting and politics.

Students of public budgeting must use concepts developed in political science, economics, accounting, the behavioral sciences, finance, and other disciplines. Political science helps the budget person understand the political nature of government and the public policy-making process. Economics provides useful analytical tools and highly influential theories. Accounting provides the means to keep track properly of the complex array of dollars. The behavioral sciences help the budget person understand the human as a part of the budget process. Finance gives the practitioner some conceptual tools to use, especially relative to the revenue aspects of budgeting. Public administration helps bring this information together and adds some concepts of its own. Students of public budgeting should be able to draw upon a broad interdisciplinary background so that they can more easily deal with their challenging problems.

Public budgeting does require highly specialized knowledge, critical behavioral patterns, and important skills. These can be learned through experience and the learning process can be facilitated through formal education. This text sets out the primary knowledge useful to those involved in public budgeting as well as those wishing to better comprehend government by understanding public budgeting. Public budgeting requires more than knowledge. To be effective, certain important behavioral patterns should be mastered and that requires a learning laboratory or experience. Also, certain skills must be acquired, such as being able to translate possible policy positions into dollars and cents almost instantly in order to deal effectively in active political bargaining situations. Public budgeting is one of the most professionally challenging and often most emotionally rewarding activities in public administration.

Budgeting is a constantly changing field and some of the significant public administration reforms took place in the 1970s. In later sections of this chapter and in chapter 2, the history of budgeting will be explained in more depth. A major Congressional budget reform took place in 1974 and two years later another major reform was considered. In the federal executive branch, Presidents Johnson, Nixon, and Carter each have sought major budget reforms. Debates at the highest level continue to occupy public attention in spite of the complexity of the subject.

One last public budgeting reality should be stressed. Public budgeting is very big money. The 1987 federal budget outlay was over $1 trillion. In 1985 the government sector was 20.6 percent of the Gross National Product.

State and local government is also huge today. For example, in 1929, the combined federal, state, and local expenditure was $10.4 billion; in 1977, the New York State budget alone exceeded that combined 1929 amount. Bureaucrats often round off their working tables in the thousands, and they commonly prepare and execute budgets for billions of dollars.

Political Realities

Budgets are decided through politics; analysis is only ammunition in the decision-making process. Sometimes the politics are crude and unethical; sometimes reason and ethical views prevail. Often the decisions involve complex, conflicting values supported by minimal analysis, but they are decisions which must be made. The analyses used in public budgeting are only significant to the political actors if those actors use the analyses in their deliberations. Even when used and not ignored the analyses are merely some of the ammunition used to persuade other political actors. In some cases, an appeal, such as to the nation's pride, may be more significant than an elaborate analysis. In other situations, an analysis can be the key to persuading political actors how they should vote on a major policy matter.

Budgets are proposed plans. The budget presentations sometimes can make the difference for a program but in some instances the presentation will make no difference because the program is politically weak. In other instances, the program may be so politically strong that even a bad budget presentation will not defeat the program. Often the proposed plan or budget of the executive is a significant factor in the public decision-making, and the quality of the presentation is considered to be a reflection of the managerial competency of the program.

Political sacred cows do exist. An influential congressman or political executive can successfully demand a specific project or program. The appropriateness of the project or program is irrelevant, but the power of the political actor is very relevant. In public budgeting, the professional must learn to tolerate this unless a moral or legal question is involved. The nature of the American political system almost insures the existence of sacred cows. Some of them are prompted by campaign promises and some by less desirable motivations. The percentage of programs and projects that are sacred cows will vary, but normally they are the exception. If the program decisions are dominated by sacred cows, then public management will suffer as foolish programs or projects cannot be stopped except by highly political and time consuming debate.

Public budgeting is strongly influenced by the political causes of the day. The causes vary over time but some contemporary causes include national security, energy, environment, poverty, recession, and inflation. Policy makers, who decide on budgets, are keenly aware of the political causes because their positions on those causes influence people to vote for or against them. Therefore, politicians wish to know how budgets relate to those causes. Not surprisingly, budget justifications are often cast in terms of those causes or, at a minimum, the agency is prepared to answer questions involving the program and the politically sensitive topic. For example, in a time of recession, with large numbers of people unemployed, a major defense project will be justified first on the basis of providing jobs and secondly on the basis of national security.

THE BUDGET CYCLE

The Nature of the Cycle

The budget cycle takes place in four phases which can extend over several years. The first phase is *planning and analysis*. Here, the issues are explored and the agency budget is prepared. The second phase is *policy formulation*, which involves extensive executive and legislative reviews and decisions. The third phase is *policy execution* and *reinterpretation* when the budget becomes operational. The final stage involves *audit and evaluation*. The beginning of the third phase is a key date. On that date, the operating budget goes into effect, to end in one year. Prior to that date, enough time must be provided to consider the issues, conduct analysis, prepare the budget, and permit various executive and legislative groups to modify the evolved budget. After the end of the operating budget, time is needed to close accounts and to audit and evaluate the programs. This latter phase can take place in a few months, but often involves several years.

Cycles vary from one government to another and from one agency to another. If the government or agency is small, then the smaller numbers of people normally require a briefer budget cycle. In a large agency with many field units, coordination is difficult and more time is needed to prepare the document.

The federal budget cycle is particularly important because state and local governments sometimes use the federal government as a model and—more importantly—local and state governments are dependent upon federal transfer payments, such as revenue sharing and grant programs. If the federal government delays, many other groups are affected.

One confusing reality of public budgeting is that the budget person and agency must operate with overlapping budget cycles. On the same day, a budget person may have to review the evaluations covering last year's program, prepare readjustments on the current year or operating budget, and answer Congressional questions on the budget year covering the next fiscal year. This can be and is confusing. Not surprisingly, people working in budgeting learn to refer to their work by specific fiscal years to minimize confusion.

Budget Phases

Planning and analysis.   The planning and analysis phase was popularized by PPB in the 1960s, but the phase was not original to PPB reforms. The New York Bureau of Municipal Research encouraged planning and analysis at the turn of the century. Almost all budget preparation did and does involve some analysis, but the amount and sophistication were greatly increased during the PPB reform era. Planning and analysis can take many forms, but most of the techniques were developed in the disciplines of economics, operations research, and systems analysis. Techniques including modeling, sensitivity analysis, and survey research are used, but are not covered in this text because they are not closely associated with budgeting. Other techniques, such as forecasting and cost-benefit, cost-effectiveness, and marginal utility analyses, are introduced in various sections of this text.

The planning and analysis phase takes place at the beginning of the budget cycle, but analysis does occur at other periods in the cycle. In the policy formulation stage, time is a key factor so there is not the luxury of being able to prepare elaborate analyses. Only quick original analysis or reapplication of earlier analyses can be used in this phase. There is little analysis, except for forecasting, done in the policy execution phase. A great deal of analysis is done in the audit and evaluation phase. The techniques, analytical problems, and focus of analysis do change somewhat when this budget phase occurs relative to other budget activities.

Policy formulation.   In the policy formulation process, the budget is developed and approved. Policy positions become operationalized as the budget is prepared. The agency is the preparer and significant advocate of the budget. The agency's clientele group and elements in the legislative and the highest levels of the executive branch may also support the agency's budget or aspects of the budget, but the agency is the advocate. The reviewers and modifiers of the budget include the department, the chief executive and his or her staff, and the legislature. A variety of conflicting influences converge on the budget process from various levels in the executive branch, the legislature, clientele groups, the media, and even sometimes the judiciary branch.

The federal process is elaborate, but it does illustrate the complex steps in the policy formulation process. Prior to this phase, the agency has submitted quarterly program financial plans which give budget reviewers initial indications of likely fund requests five years beyond the budget year. At the beginning of the phase, the central executive branch budget office (i.e., Office of Management and Budget) issues guidelines to the departments and agencies for the development of the new budget. Then the various agencies issue their budget calls to agency personnel in order to compile the necessary information for the budget. The agency uses this information to prepare its budget.

The remaining portion of the policy formulation phase involves budget reviews and eventually decisions on the budget. The agency submits the budget to the department budget office. The format can vary in style from a line-item to a program budget to decision packages. The department budget office and the highest officials review the budget and decide upon the department's recommended budget. The agency makes the necessary changes and the revised budget is submitted to the Office of Management and Budget. Again the budget is revised, OMB arrives at its recommendations, and the president revises and eventually approves the budget. In some cases, the president permits an appeal from the department. In the federal government, a current services budget is submitted to Congress with the president's budget in January. The Congress then reviews the submission and passes appropriate bills prior to the beginning of the new fiscal year.

Policy execution.   In the policy execution phase, the budget is used as guidance for specific decisions by bureaucrats. This phase takes place during the current year, and all obligations must be made in this year if they are to be attributed to the fiscal year. The executive branch can sometimes reinterpret policy during this phase by not spending the planned resources or by shifting funds from one activity to another. As a general practice, the latter does not occur at the federal and state levels, but does occur sometimes at the local level. The executive policy not to spend appropriated funds is an impoundment. The nonspending can take the form of a delay in spending in the intended budget year or of a recision from the budget. On the state level, some executives have the power of line-item vetoes or impoundment, depending on the state constitution.

At the agency and department level, the rate of obligation and disbursement of resources can be controlled by allotment. This power is intended to assure that funds are available when needed for proper economic and managerial purposes. With the greater emphasis upon macroeconomics, the federal government is more carefully controlling the rates of both obligation and disbursement. Sometimes the allotment power is used for political purposes, such as insuring maximum and timely obligations on key programs at the correct moment in a political campaign. The allotment power might be abused and treated as an illegal impoundment, but no evidence of such abuse has been publicly raised yet. Normally, allotments are used entirely for economic and managerial purposes.

Authorizations and appropriations are often phrased in technical budget language. The technical wording can be significant to the operating budget. The normal appropriation is for the budget year only, but the language need not be so limiting. For example, the appropriations may be for no-year funds, thus permitting the agency to obligate the funds in subsequent fiscal years if the money is not entirely obligated in the current year. Other technical devices are contract and bond authority. The Congress can also place special conditions on appropriations. For example, the appropriation can read, "$150 million is appropriated under section 204 of XYZ legislation but none of this money can be used to build a flag pole in front of the Bureau of Standards building nor can any money be spent on the ABC project." Often such detailed conditions are not included in the appropriation language, but are included in the nonlegally binding report which accompanies the appropriation bill. Agencies are sensitive to such requests and normally will comply unless some very unusual circumstance exists. Another technical budget device is for the appropriations committee to negate yearly contract authority by saying that no more than a specific amount can be obligated during the budget year.

The federal and state government use of the authorization and appropriation distinction is extremely useful, given the complex budget decisions which are made. Many local governments do not make the authorization and appropriation distinction because a two-stage process is not as useful to them. There are normally fewer city councilors or county supervisors, so a more elaborate two-stage process is not needed to coordinate decision-making.

Once the allotments have been made, the agency can prepare its operating budgets. Normally, the operating budget is not the desired sophisticated managerial tool which has proper linkages to accounting, management-by-objectives and progress reporting, and program evaluation. The operating budget should inform the agency's units how much and at what rate resources can be obligated and disbursed. The operating budget should reflect the decisions made in the MBO process. The recording of progress and accounting of actual obligations and disbursement should be used in a classification scheme so that management can verify that budget and MBO decisions were executed. Also, proper program evaluations can be done only if the program direction is understood and necessary cooperation exists among the evaluators, managers, and budget persons.

Audit and evaluation.   The final phase takes place after the current year is complete. Some audit and evaluation work can and should be started much earlier in the cycle, but the focus of the work and the preparation of the final reports take place in this final phase. Audit and evaluation activities are conducted by such groups as the agency, the department, the General Accounting Office, and the Congress itself through its oversight function. Audits are often addressed to checking if the agency properly recorded its transactions and obligated resources legally. Increasingly, auditing has been expanded to include program evaluation, especially by GAO. However, program evaluation is often done in separate agency and departmental program evaluation units. To a limited extent, legislative bodies conduct oversight hearings and investigations which can be considered program evaluation.

Laws are sometimes quite specific in requiring audits and evaluations. States have audit agencies, and states require auditing in and of local governments. States often require a local government to submit its annual audit to the state. The audit is often examined by the state itself. States sometimes have legislative review commissions which perform program evaluation. Often, audit agencies are staffed by accountants who are reluctant to perform program evaluations because they are not trained in that activity. However, the trend is for audit agencies to become more involved in program evaluation and for new evaluation groups to be established. In the federal government, many programs are now being required to set aside and use a portion of program funds for program evaluation.

Local Government Budget Cycles

There are some differences between federal and state government and local government budget cycles. Revenue estimation is very important in local as well as state government, particularly in the planning and analysis phase. The estimation is normally done by the finance or central budget office. Budget formulation practices vary in local government, but often there is a small central budget staff. Procedures are much more informal, but sometimes state law or local charters require more formal practices such as public hearings. Often the budget is prepared by a budget office receiving input from the city agencies and guidance from the city manager or mayor. The chief city executive sometimes serves as the person who resolves outstanding issues and as a court of appeals. The exact procedure depends upon each local government, with some having the agency heads reporting directly to the city council or county elected board of supervisors.

Local governments vary greatly in their review and power over the budget. Normally, budgets are detailed line-item documents which part-time nonexpert board members must review and approve in a short time. Not surprisingly, budgets are confusing and frustrating to board members. They usually focus their attention upon small comprehensible items or pet projects rather than conducting a comprehensive review of the submitted budget. Often, local governments conduct public hearings in connection with the legislative deliberations on the budget.

Once the budget is approved, the focus of the budget is upon control. In some local governments, almost every change in the line-item budget must be approved by the legislature. In other local governments, almost any change can be made by the city manager or department head. The money is controlled, but the ability to make changes in the budget during the operating year varies.

CONTEXT OF AMERICAN BUDGETING

Ideology

Public budgeting is best considered in the context of the ideological culture of a nation. Budgeting practices in Canada, the United States, France, Panama, Israel, Yemen, India, the USSR, Japan, and the People's Republic of China are not identical because the budgeting process relates to the fundamental political and economic value schemes of each society. Techniques and concepts can be similar across societies, but how those techniques and concepts are meaningfully applied depends upon the society's culture.

Ideas are powerful, especially when shared by many people, because they can guide behavior by discouraging "bad" and encouraging "good" activities and actions. Ideas can be and often are used to place a value on people, things, activities, and even other ideas. Sometimes ideas can be logically consistent or nearly consistent and form belief systems. These systems in turn can be shared by many people and can guide entire civilizations. These belief systems are called ideologies and every culture has them.

In the United States, two important ideologies, both of which influence the way public budgeting is conducted, are democracy and capitalism. Other belief systems and subsystems are important, but are not central to this simplified sketch. "Democracy" is a term that can have many meanings, as illustrated by its use in American and many Communist societies. Democracy as defined in the United States evolved from a desire to have a limited representative government which respected the political rights of minorities. In the agriculture-oriented colonies, certain rights, such as freedom of the press, were considered essential and were built into the Constitution. These rights were viewed as a means to prevent tyranny and permit the peaceful change of government. In time, the definition of "voter" extended from white male adult landholder to an adult citizen of either sex and any racial or religious background.

The American democratic system of government evolved into a pattern partially explained by the Federalist Paper No. 10 of the 1780s. Parties and groups interact to influence government in a manner deliberately designed to decentralize and diffuse political power. People continually learn that they can best influence government by acting in groups and directing their political efforts at partisans in the political process. The partisans interact and adjust policy based upon the relative strengths of lobbying forces and varying influential ideologies. The strength of policy in some instances may be due to economic interests, but often that strength rests upon shared and effectively argued belief systems.

In America, the notions of partisan bargaining, minority and fundamental human rights, diffusion of power, and the influencing of partisans through collective action over time together constitute the meaning of *democracy*. The activity called public budgeting tends to reflect that ideological culture. Thus, budget decisions are made through partisan bargaining in a system of diffused political power. Decisions made by partisans are influenced over time by a process called lobbying. Public agency clientele groups (i.e., those affected directly by the agency's activities) can and do lobby the legislature and the executive. The agency's actions are thus largely determined by the complexly combined influence of executive, legislature, and clientele; and the mechanism of that influence is often the budget. Freedom of information and sunshine legislation, logical extensions of minority and fundamental human rights, are taken seriously; and discussion of these issues opens up much budget detail to the media and the general public. In America, budget decisions require a melding of executive and legislative will to achieve the necessary policy mandates as prescribed in the Constitution. Often the influence of democratic ideas has even extended to requiring public hearings on budget decisions. The belief system called *democracy* does greatly influence the way Americans think public budgeting should be conducted.

The second major American ideology is *capitalism*, which does not exist in the strictest sense of the term. Unlike democracy, capitalism is subject to active ideological challenge, which has led to a blending of logically conflicting belief systems. Strict capitalism evolved from a reaction against the extensive English-government-dominated mercantilism of the 1760s and was reinforced by the Social Darwinism of the late 1880s to the 1930s. The desire was to limit the role of government in the economic activities of society.

The capitalist ideology does have a role for government, but it is limited to "public goods" like national defense, and possibly could be extended to include:

1. coping with public allocations for the general good, like public education and pollution control; and
2. avoiding inconvenient private monopolies on such things as highways, bridges, and water systems.

Advocates of capitalism raise severe protests when subjects such as redistribution of wealth and the use of government control to achieve economic stabilization and growth are raised.

From the 1890s to the present, contrary economic (and related political) belief systems arose. One advocated a predominantly guiding role for government over society. Another argued for total governmental control over society. The guiding role was advocated by the Progressives. They felt that government should intervene in the social and economic conditions in society in order to insure that national concerns were being met. Progressives were quite successful politically and their accomplishments included child labor laws, the income tax, the Federal Reserve System, social security, a national park system, and other landmark legislation.

Communists and some Socialists advocated a total role for government in society. They felt that government should run the society and curb the economic abuses of the wealthy elites. The most visionary advocates of this belief system expected that a classless society would eventually evolve, eliminating the need for government to act as the people's trustee. In over a third of the world, that belief system is dominant. In the United States, the Socialist belief system challenged the social consciences of the nation and aided in the passage of many Progressive reforms such as the reduced workweek and worker safety requirements.

After 1932, the Progressives and many of the less radical American Socialists merged politically into the liberal movement. They have played an active role in such matters as the advocacy of consumerism, the protection of the environment, the fight for equal opportunity, and the implementation of workplace and product safety.

The correct mix of the public sector and the private sector in the United States continues to be the major issue dividing partisans in many major political battles. For purposes of public budgeting, the important point to understand is that this ongoing ideological debate is taken very seriously and affects budgeting. The very size and scope of government is at issue; thus the question of what is and should be budgeted is also at issue. Attitudes about how government can and should influence the overall national or regional economy are critical to the way budgeting is conducted. The stress on economy, efficiency, and productivity arises out of capitalism and its economic doctrines. The use of enterprise funds and government corporations also evolved from the ideological debate. A later unit in this chapter will discuss current economic thinking and its influence on budgeting.

Federalism

The United States is a federated government and budgeting differs on each level. The scope, size, and different nature of programs lead to the differences in budgeting. In public budgeting, the similarities are more striking than the dissimilarities. However, the differences are important and are discussed here.

In the national government, more effort is focused on the expenditure as opposed to the revenue aspects of budgeting. Taxes are important, but more effort is channeled into controlling, managing, and planning expenditures. The state of the economy and the role of the budget in stimulating the economy are actively debated and are very significant in shaping both presidential and Congressional budgets. The revenue side of the budget is considered in terms of its influence on the economy. The typical agency budget officer does not consider the revenue aspects of the budget. At the highest levels in OMB and Congress, attention is addressed to macroeconomics and the analysis of proposed expenditures. There is a strong desire to improve the analysis associated with public budgeting; productivity is considered important.

The national government manages many of its programs in cooperation with state and local governments. Sometimes the federal government interacts directly with citizens, as in the case with veterans' programs. In many programs, categorical and block grants are provided to state and local governments, which manage the programs. The government also has a significant revenue-sharing program with local governments. The result is that many federal activities are really intergovernmental in nature, with the actual services being provided by local government.

Unlike the federal government, state and local governments must balance their budgets. Sometimes that legal requirement is not met, but it does exist. Revenue and expenditure forecasts are thus important for state and local governments in developing balanced budgets.

State governments have a great deal of potential power over local governments. States commonly focus their efforts upon highways and education, with increasing interest being addressed to health, environmental control, and welfare. Like the federal government, state governments provide assistance to local governments, often acting as pass-through agents for the federal government. Unlike the federal government, state governments can directly control local governments. Many local budgeting requirements are established by state law.

The form of local government varies from large cities to small villages and townships. Each unit of government has a budget process. Each is concerned with balancing revenue and expenditure. Local governments provide direct services, including public safety, education, and sanitation. Many local government activities require large expenditures for capital items like schools and roads; thus debt administration is an important aspect of local government. Transfer payments in the form of grants and revenue sharing are an important source of revenue.

The complex overlapping jurisdictions, economy of scale, and the growth of suburban areas and decline of cities are important to local gov-

ernment budgeting. The overlapping of jurisdictions means that tax collection is more complex and coordination of services is difficult. The existence
of small governments means that many services are provided without the
advantage of economy of scale. The declining tax base for cities is putting
extreme pressure on city budgets. The increased population of suburban
areas has strained the expertise and capability of the suburban governments
to cope with the challenge. They must develop budgeting expertise while
dealing with massive program growth. Each problem is significant and helps
explain the challenge of local budgeting.

Decision-Making Models

Public budgeting is a decision-making process. Not surprisingly, there
are several theories as to the way public policy decisions should be made.
These theories or conceptual models are important because many people
take them seriously and try to reform public budgeting using one of the
theories as their guide. To better understand contemporary public budgeting reforms, these theories must be understood. But first, a criterion must
be developed to judge the conceptual models, and the concept of conceptual models itself must be explained.

A conceptual model can be viewed as a tool which enables the user to
understand and deal with complex phenomena. A tool can be judged
"good" or "bad" in terms of the user's purpose. A hammer, for example,
may be a good tool for building a shed, but it is bad for chopping wood.
Professionals should judge conceptual models or theories in terms of the
model's usefulness in helping them accomplish their tasks. Those tasks must
be accomplished within a decision-making context largely induced by the
ideologies of the culture.

Public budgeting in the United States must be conducted in a political,
human, and often practical environment. The democratic ideology has
helped to define the political environment. Consensus and partisan adjustments best explain the political context. Public budgeting is conducted by
humans and it affects humans; thus emotional drama, error, pride, and
other human characteristics help define the context of budgeting. In public
budgeting, the practical is often a significant factor because decisions must
be made. Even a so-called nondecision often represents an allocation of
resources in budgeting. If the data or analyses are not available, then the
decision maker must make do with conventional wisdom or personal biased
judgment. Thus the "do-able" or practical is significant.

Decision-making models can be judged in terms of their applicability
to the decision-making environment of the public budget person. If the
model is not in harmony with the decision-making environment (which is
unlikely to be changed) then the model is "bad." That is, the model is not
appropriate to the user's purposes. This value judgment must be limited to
the decision maker discussed here.

Some major and commonly noted decision-making models are the incremental change model, the satisficing model, and the ideal-rational

model. To this list, a provocative but little-cited model called the "stages of problem solving" can be added. The incremental model is used for descriptive and normative purposes, but just because something exists in a certain way does not mean that it should continue to exist. The focus in this and subsequent paragraphs shall be on the normative use of the model. In the incremental model, major public policies evolve through cautious incremental steps; political forces mutually adjust their positions and, over time, public policy changes. This is an inherently conservative approach and it biases the decision makers against more radical innovative alternatives.

An agency develops a budget which it advocates to its department, to the Office of Management and Budget, and to Congress. In the major phases of the budget approval process, the agency takes the role of an advocate; the reviewer (e.g., Office of Management and Budget) questions the wisdom of the proposal; and the reviewer makes a tentative decision, which is often appealed to the secretary, the president, or the Senate. This model is consistent with the incremental change model in that policies are mutually adjusted because someone advocates and someone accommodates.

The satisficing model points out that decision makers develop a criterion to judge acceptable policy alternatives for a given problem. They then search the alternatives and select the first acceptable alternative they discover. Time is significant in the satisficing model. Alternatives are considered but the ideal is not sought. The acceptable is the standard for judgment. Like the incremental change model, the satisficing model is used for both descriptive and normative purposes; but the consideration here is only on the normative use. The reasons for the limited search are the lack of time for an exhaustive search and the opportunity costs of such a search.

The rational model is most commonly cited as the ideal way to reach decisions, especially major public policy decisions such as those in public budgeting. Its assumptions are deeply rooted in modern civilization and culture. The model systematically breaks decision-making down into six phases:

1. establish a complete set of operational goals, with relative weights allocated to the different degrees to which each may be achieved;

2. establish a complete inventory of other values and resources with relative weights;

3. prepare a complete set of the alternative policies open to the policy maker;

4. prepare a complete set of valid predictions of the cost and benefits of each alternative, including the extent to which each alternative will achieve the various operational goals, consume resources, and realize or impair other values;

5. calculate the net expectations for each alternative by multiplying the probability of each benefit and cost for each alternative by the utility of each, and calculate the net benefit (or cost) in utility units; and

6. compare the net expectations and identify the alternative (or alternatives, if two or more are equally good) with the highest net expectations.

In fewer words, using the rational model is merely defining one's goals, analyzing the available alternatives, and selecting the alternative that best meets the goals.

Although similar to the rational model, the "stages of problem solving" model is amenable to observation and analysis, but it too can be a normative model. Exhibit 1-2 presents the model visually. The starting point is the perception that a problem exists—not the formulation of goals. Perception permits the possibility of multiple value perspectives, whereas in formulating goals one tends to ignore the possibility of multiple or conflicting values. Either formally or informally, the decision maker defines the

EXHIBIT 1-2   Stages of Problem Solving

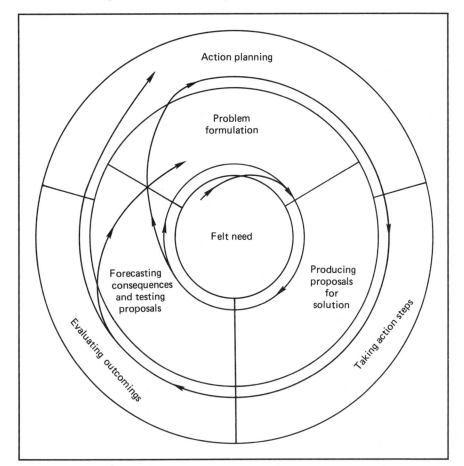

Source: Richard Wallen in Edgar H. Schein, *Process Consultation: Its Role in Organization Development.* Reading, Mass. Addison-Wesley Publishing Co., Inc., 1964, p. 46. Used by permission.

problem, considers the solutions, and analyzes the alternatives in a manner similar to someone using the rational model. A key decision is then made either to reconsider the nature of the problem or to plan to resolve the problem. (This reconsideration step is not a part of the rational model.) If the decision is to proceed, the necessary action steps are taken and outcomes are evaluated. (This second reconsideration is also absent from the rational model.) From evaluation, the decision maker may either start over by reconsidering the problem or replan his or her action steps.

The incremental change model is an excellent tool for understanding the political environment of public policy making, but it is not useful for explaining the more technical difficulties associated with analysis. On the other hand, the rational model helps us comprehend the technical difficulties of analysis, but is relatively useless in explaining the highly important political environment.

With the incremental change model, the public budget person can better understand how the budget process is dominated by the strategies employed by and the conflicts that arise among the participants (clientele groups, agencies, departments, the Office of Management and Budget). Definable strategies exist that require such practices as agency cultivation of an active clientele, the development of confidence among other reviewing government officers such as budget examiners, and skill in following tactics that exploit temporary opportunities. Analysis in the budget process must serve to aid the key factors involved in making public policy. Reasoning from the incremental change model, program and budget analysis must be timely, must be able to be used to seize political opportunities, and must be comprehensible to those who must use the analysis in partisan bargaining situations.

The satisficing and ideal-rational models are useful for understanding the difficulties associated with decision-making. The satisficing model dramatically emphasizes that decisions are made under pressure, and severe limitations make achieving even a satisfactory alternative a significant accomplishment. The problem with the model is that one is often not satisfied that the best alternative has been selected. On the other hand, the desire for deciding on the best alternative is reflected in the ideal-rational model. The problem with that model is that the best alternative often cannot be achieved because of practical concerns such as a lack of time. We seem to be trapped between our desire for quality and the necessity to cope with our daily pressures.

The stages-of-problem-solving model can be contrasted to the ideal-rational model. In the problem-solving model, the starting point is the perception that a problem exists, thus permitting one to consider the significance of culture, time, and perspective. By contrast, in the rational model the starting point is the definition of one's goals. Next in the problem-solving model, the person formulates the problem, defines alternatives, gathers information, and tests proposals. In the rational model, the next steps cited are defining alternatives and gathering information. In the problem-solving model, the last steps are planning action, taking action steps, and evaluating outcomes. Again in contrast, the rational model is limited to deciding a given matter with the intention of maximizing goals. The rational model does not extend to taking action steps and evaluating outcomes. Another distinction is that the rational model does not have reconsideration as a factor, whereas the problem-solving model does.

The problem-solving model can help people working in public budgeting understand the nature of analysis. The rational model serves as the primary theoretical explanation of how analysis should be conducted, but the rational model cannot be attained. The problem-solving model serves as an alternative theoretical explanation of how analysis should be conducted in the budget process. The problem-solving model permits cycles of defining one's problem, producing alternatives, and testing alternatives. It implicitly recognizes that any given analysis will depend upon the ingenuity of the analysts, the kind of data available to them, the amount of resources at their command in undertaking the analysis, and other factors. Also the problem-solving model helps the public budgeting person relate budgeting, management-by-objectives, progress reporting, accounting, auditing, and program evaluation.

None of the models by themselves is adequate. The problem-solving and the incremental change models help the bureaucrat to understand the role of program and budget analysis in the budget-making process. They can be significant, but there are some constraints in using them. The problem-solving model helps the bureaucrat to understand the context in which intelligence, knowledge, and analytical techniques must be used. Together, the models meet the criteria.

The rational model, the theoretical basis for some budget reforms, can lead individuals to make false and naive expectations. That model ignores the political context and demands the impossible in terms of analysis. This can encourage some individuals in the budget process to neglect timeliness, seek needlessly expensive data, search for needless alternatives, and quest for clarity in objectives which will not be forthcoming. The rational model can be useful, but not in the manner commonly assumed. The usefulness is more to point out the impossible rather than serve as an ideal for the possible.

ECONOMIC INFLUENCES ON BUDGETING

Twin Evils

As noted earlier in this chapter, capitalism as modified by socialism provides the ideological economic climate for the United States. The dispute between capitalism and socialism centers on the role of government in society and thus on the appropriateness of what should be included in a public budget. Today there is a belief that government can make a difference in the overall economy, but disagreement exists on the question of what government should and should not do to help the economy achieve the desired condition of minimum unemployment with minimum inflation.

The agreed-upon twin evils are *severe unemployment* (mild unemployment is called a recession and a severe recession is called a depression) and a *sustained increase in price without an equal increase in value* (a mild increase is called inflation and a radical increase is called hyperinflation). Both result in significant hardships for the people of the world. Unemployment means that many people in the economy who want jobs cannot find them. Usually, during a recession, the economy is not growing or is growing very slowly; as a result, families do not receive adequate money for a decent existence. Inflation often means that people can buy fewer goods and services with the same amount of money. People on fixed incomes or slow-rising incomes are more likely to be hurt by inflation.

Exhibit 1-3 shows the U.S. employment rates from 1929 to 1982. The reader can easily understand why the 1930s are called "The Great Depression" since more than 5 percent unemployment is normally considered unacceptable and the unemployment rate in that era reached a high of 24.9 percent. Some inflation is common, but the rate of inflation can rise to hyperinflation levels. Prices can rise so fast that no one is willing to receive or hold money. In Germany in 1923, the rate of hyperinflation was so high

EXHIBIT 1-3   Unemployment Rates for Selected Years 1929–82 (% of Civilian Work Force)

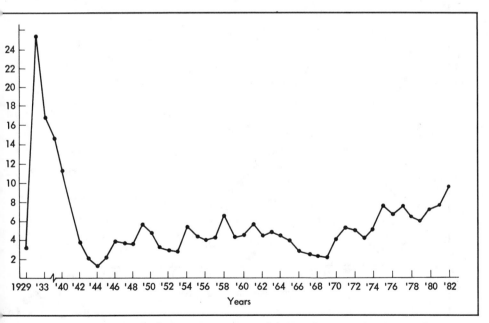

Source: U.S. Department of Labor, *Economic Report of the President;* U.S. Department of Commerce, *Statistical Abstract of the United States.* Washington, D.C.: Bureau of the Census, 1983.

that paper currency became almost worthless and was used as wallpaper; barter reasserted itself as the principal method of trade. However, Western civilization has evolved to the point where it cannot sustain itself with a barter economy. Hyperinflation exists when a government enormously expands the money supply to finance large-scale expenditures. Mild inflation exists for reasons which will be discussed later.

Recession and inflation have been with us throughout modern society. Economic theory largely addresses these twin problems: How do they occur? What can be done to avoid them? In the last quarter of the twentieth century, our tools to deal with these problems are monetary and fiscal policy. Both involve public budgeting.

Exhibit 1-4 is a Phillips curve which helps describe the relationship between the unemployment rate and the rate of inflation. Note that there is an inverse relationship. In the exhibit, as unemployment goes down, inflation goes up. Also note the odd locations of the points for 1970 and 1971, which reflect a different pattern than those for the 1960s.

EXHIBIT 1-4   Phillips Curve

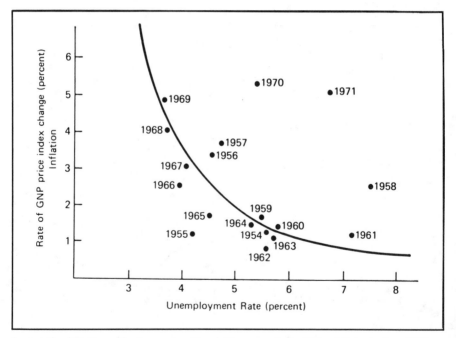

Source: Lloyd G. Reynolds, Economics, 4th ed. Homewood, Ill.: Richard D. Irwin, Inc., 1973, p. 174. Used by permission.

Influence of Economics

When Franklin D. Roosevelt became president of the United States, the country was in the Great Depression. He advocated and the Congress strongly agreed that action was necessary and that jobs had to be created. FDR was not motivated or influenced by economic theory. He was influenced by the large number of unemployed people, as cited in Exhibit 1-3.

The Great Depression was a political turning point for the United States. Before that time, social and economic thinking called for minimum or laissez faire government. The works of Adam Smith, Herbert Spencer, and Charles Darwin were highly influential prior to 1929. The least government was considered the best government. Nature and business should take their courses without interference as if they were guided by invisible forces or laws which would enable society to evolve into a higher, improved state. The Great Depression was a harsh awakening. In 1933, 24.9 percent were unemployed. This was not an improved state. Voters and many intellectual leaders felt the old theories were unacceptable.

The idea that government could and should be used as a positive instrument in society gained widespread approval. No longer was the least government the best government. FDR launched massive public works programs for the times. Today, most economists agree that he was not bold enough. The spending for World War II is probably what got the United States and the world out of the depression. FDR's New Deal programs convinced many Americans that a strong, active federal government was "a good thing." World War II and the subsequent Cold War convinced even more Americans that the United States must remain a strong military power. Thus, the public's view of the role of government in American society has been greatly altered since 1929.

In the mid-1960s and 1970s, economic theory guided some of our most significant government decisions, and a variety of government units have arisen as the institutional means to consider and implement economic policy. Especially at the national level, economic theory has become the context in which major decisions are made.

The institutional mechanism is complex. In the executive branch, there is the Council of Economic Advisors, the Office of Management and Budget (OMB), and the Department of the Treasury. Each helps consider economic policy, and the OMB is the major implementer of fiscal policy once decisions are made by Congress and the President. In the legislative branch, the Congressional Budget Office (CBO), the Joint Economic Committee, the House and Senate Budget and Appropriations Committees, the House Ways and Means Committee, and the Senate Finance Committee all play important roles. The CBO and the Budget Committees are particularly important in setting overall fiscal policy. Partly independent of both Congress and the president, the Federal Reserve System largely establishes the nation's monetary policy. The detailed workings of each group are beyond the scope of this text, and readers are encouraged to take economics courses to pursue these subjects.

For both the legislative and executive branches, the primary device to establish fiscal policy is the federal budget. The primary device to establish monetary policy is the Federal Reserve System.

MONETARY POLICY

Central Bank

The Federal Reserve System is the central bank for the United States. It attempts to control the economy's supply of money and credit. This supply in turn affects unemployment and inflation. The Federal Reserve tries to expand money and credit to foster greater employment and to contract money and credit to combat inflation. The Federal Reserve banks have tools which influence member banks, and they in turn influence business and the public. These tools are based on the facts that banks maintain a reserve-to-loan ratio and borrow money from the Federal Reserve System banks. The three main Federal Reserve tools are as follows:

1. open-market operations;
2. discount-rate policy; and
3. changes in the legal reserve requirement of the member banks.

Two other less significant tools are (4) moral suasion and (5) selective controls over "margin requirements" for loans made to buy stocks.

The most frequently used tool is open-market operations. The Federal Reserve's Open Market Committee frequently meets to decide to buy or sell government bonds or bills. Selling results in tightening, and buying results in expanding, the money supply. For example, selling $10 million in government bonds depresses the overall money supply. The buyers of the bonds will draw checks at a member bank, and the Federal Reserve will present the checks to the member bank for payment. That bank will then lose an equivalent amount of its reserve balance. This will contract the money supply, often by $50 million. This anti-inflationary tactic results in decreasing the total money supply.

Another tool is the discount rate, which is the interest the Federal Reserve (Fed) charges member banks for short-term loans. An increase in the discount rate increases interest rates, which makes money more expensive, thus discouraging people from borrowing. This contracts the economy. The reverse Fed action will stimulate the economy.

The third tool, changing the reserve requirement, is the most powerful, but most clumsy, tool. In a previous example, a 20 percent reserve requirement was assumed. The Federal Reserve Board has the limited power to raise or lower that required legal ratio within Congressionally established limits. The Fed can tighten the money supply by requiring a greater reserve to be maintained, thus shrinking the loan amount available. The converse increases the money supply. Changing reserve requirements is the most powerful tool, but it is used infrequently because of its clumsy nature.

The minor tools are also useful. Moral suasion (e.g., "jawboning") might mean merely appealing directly to key banks. The appeal alone may be sufficient. Selected credit controls are another important tool, as they involve stock margin requirements. The Federal Reserve establishes how much credit a person is allowed to use in the buying of common and preferred stocks. This selective control acts in the same manner as the reserve requirement.

Effectiveness

The major advantages of monetary policy are as follows:

1. decisions can be reached and applied rapidly due to the less political nature of the Federal Reserve; and
2. monetary policy does work if the proper vigorous action is taken, especially in combating some types of inflation.

The advantages are significant, but the use of monetary policy should be understood in terms of its effect on society. Federal Reserve policy severely affects companies in industries such as housing which depend heavily upon external credit. When banks are forced to restrict loans, the higher credit groups will have preference; thus smaller and newer businesses will suffer. Therefore, tight monetary policy will affect certain sectors of our economy more than others and certain groups (e.g., the young and the minorities) more than others. The events of fall of 1966 illustrate the dangers of restrictive monetary policy. At that time, the policy:

1. brought the capital market to the brink of crisis;
2. caused a radical decline in home construction;
3. threatened the solvency of intermediaries (e.g., banks), and
4. left banks reluctant to make long-term loans.

Monetary Policy and Public Budgeting

Monetary policy is significant to public budgeting in at least two important ways. First, all levels of government borrow and invest. Monetary policy affects available credit and especially interest rates. The interest paid and earned is important to any government. This shall become more apparent in subsequent chapters. Second, many government programs (e.g., housing, environment) are heavily influenced by monetary policy. Budget justifications and intelligent budget reviews would not be possible without a thorough understanding of the effects of monetary policy on those programs.

FISCAL POLICY

Policy Goals

The principal macroeconomic or fiscal policy goals are as follows:

1. *Full employment:* Practically, this means about a 4 percent unemployment rate in the United States. At this rate, there are about as many people looking for jobs as there are jobs available.
2. *Maintenance of price stability:* Inflation increases prices. This brings a shift in the distribution of real income from those whose dollar incomes are relatively inflexible to those whose dollar incomes are relatively flexible. Thus, those on fixed incomes such as the elderly are hurt by inflation.
3. *Steady constant economic growth:* As the population increases, economic growth is essential, not only to maintain the past standard of living but to improve that standard.
4. *An adequate supply of collectively consumed goods:* Some activities are public in nature and involve services for the good of the society. These include police protection, national defense, highways, schools, and so on.

In macroeconomics, there is an assumed relationship between the total spending level in the economy and the existence of either unemployment or inflation. Total spending can be thought of in terms of the gross national production of the society. The gross national product (GNP) equals personal consumption plus gross private domestic investment plus government purchases of goods and services plus net exports of goods and services. The GNP is the total productive activity in a country during a certain period of time.[1] If GNP is at the target level, then the unemployment rate and the inflation rate are at acceptable levels. In Exhibit 1-4, the reader will notice the inverse relationship between the unemployment rate and inflation. The best possible rates in the United States are debatable but many consider them to be about 4 percent unemployment and about 3 percent inflation. These optimal rates occurred in 1966 and 1967. All the macroeconomic or fiscal policy goals were being achieved. In the other years, the goals were not met.

Role of Government

How does a society reach these goals each year? This is the challenge of macroeconomics. Examine again the definition of GNP. Notice the key ingredients are both private and public. Exhibit 1-5 defines the ingredients of the GNP in billions of current dollars.

Today, the GNP is well over $1 trillion, but the key relationships are the same. The private sector is the most significant (about 67 percent), but the public sector is large (33 percent). The key is total GNP. If the private sector is inadequate, then the government can act positively by changing its

---

[1]Economists commonly define GNP as "the sum of final products such as consumption goods and gross investment (which is the increase in inventories plus gross births or productions of buildings and equipment)."

EXHIBIT 1-5   1985 Gross National Product (in billions of dollars)

Personal consumption expenditure	2,601
Gross private domestic investment	661
Net exports	−79
Government purchases	815
Gross National Product (GNP)	3,998

Source: U.S. Department of Commerce, *Statistical Abstract of the United States.* Washington, D.C.: Bureau of the Census, September 1986, p. 417.

level of spending or influencing the private sector. If the level is too high, the economy will probably suffer inflation; and if the level is too low, the economy may suffer unemployment. The fiscal powers can be viewed as operating in pairs.

GOVERNMENT POWERS	EXAMPLES
1. Buy or sell	1. Purchase of goods or sale of stockpiles
2. Take or give	2. Taxes or rebates
3. Lend or borrow	3. Surplus or deficits in the budget

The economy can be influenced by government action. Buying as a consumer stimulates the economy. Selling depresses prices. Increasing taxes depresses the income because consumers and corporations have less to spend. Giving tax rebates stimulates the economy. A budget surplus will depress the economy and deficit spending will stimulate it. Fiscal powers exist through government action because the federal government is a major actor in the economy.

There is no one fiscal policy solution to an economic problem. An examination of the paired powers of government listed above implies that policy makers reasoning from macroeconomic theory can disagree on the appropriate fiscal solution. This does not imply that all methods or techniques will give the same results. For example, if faster consumer stimulation is desired, then rebates are probably better than deficit spending because the latter takes much longer to be felt in the economy. On the other hand, if the problem is chronic, then deficit spending may be the best solution. Possibly the economic problem is temporary and concentrated in one major product such as steel. Then the solution may be to stockpile the goods to stimulate jobs or to sell the stockpile to depress inflationary price increases.

Macroeconomic theory does not necessarily condemn the existence of a public debt or a national budget deficit. If the debt can be easily serviced, then there is no difficulty in having a public debt (as pointed out in a later chapter). Having a chronic national debt may lead to serious difficulties. The debt payments may interfere with the government's ability to finance other useful projects. Large interest payments can mean an equitable or nonprogressive redistribution of income. Note that these problems are manageable and do not speak against a deficit in one or more particular years. Also, there are beneficial aspects of a large national public debt:

1. the public debt provides the means for the Federal Reserve to increase or decrease the money supply in connection with reserve requirements;
2. it provides needed liquidity for all the financial and nonfinancial businesses; and
3. it provides a safe investment for the unsophisticated and unwary investor.

There are built-in fiscal stabilizers in the U.S. economy. Several fall outside the scope of this text, but one that is important for public budgeting is transfer payments. These payments rise substantially during periods of recession and fall during prosperity. When people are unemployed, they receive unemployment compensation and eventually they may receive welfare and food stamps. Farm prices are likely to fall so agriculture price supports programs automatically start working. Today, emergency public works programs also begin automatically. During prosperity, these transfer payments shrink. These are commonly referred to as entitlement programs, and they constitute a large share of the national budget.

Using Fiscal Policy

In the early 1960s, the unemployment in the nation was excessive. In fiscal terms, the actual GNP was less than the desirable GNP level but prices were stable. The fiscal policy adopted was a tax cut. The Investment Tax Credit of 1962 and later the Revenue Act of 1964 were passed. The former stimulated the private sector to increase investment, thus stimulating income, employment, and the economic growth rate. The latter reduced tax liabilities, thus stimulating consumption. The policy was successful. In 1965, further tax reductions were enacted and the fiscal policy seemed sound.

By early 1966 unemployment fell below 4 percent, and predictably (see Exhibit 1-4), the price level (inflation) was rising. Only modest steps were taken to increase taxes, but government purchases rose sharply. This was a period of guns and butter—a war in Vietnam and a war on poverty. In 1967 President Johnson did ask for a temporary tax surcharge, but Congress took no action. The Fed acted as noted earlier. The excessive use of monetary policy tools caused a credit crunch with high interest rates and a recession in the home building industry. In early 1968 the situation was getting worse. President Johnson requested another "war tax," but the Congress refused to enact this politically unpopular tax. Finally, in June 1968, a compromise tax surcharge was passed, but it proved ineffective.

President Nixon inherited an economic problem. Monetary policy continued to be quite restrictive. The U.S. role in the Vietnam war began to diminish and government purchases were cut. The Vietnam war boom ended by late 1969, and a recession started by 1970.

The 1960s experience with using fiscal policy indicates that it is not a flexible policy easily applied. Quick action might be desired, but Congress is slow to act, especially on unpopular tax increases. Thus, a significant lag occurs.

Look again at Exhibit 1-4 and notice 1970 and 1971. Unlike the other years, they are not on the Phillips curve. We experienced both relatively high unemployment and inflation. The Phillips curve seems to have shifted to the right. In other words, we experienced a time in which both unemployment and inflation were at unacceptable levels at the same time. Economists call this stagflation—stagnation accompanied by price inflation.

Economists and political leaders are arguing about this phenomenon. In August 1977, a Treasury Department official was quoted as saying of President Carter: "I don't think that he understands why there's high inflation and high unemployment at the same time. But, then neither does anyone else."[2]

Some facts can help us to understand the phenomenon, but confusion on this subject continues. The recession fell disproportionately on narrow groups—particularly the young and blacks. Monetary policy curbed economic activity in the sectors of the economy dependent on borrowing, but the nation has evolved into a service economy which is not as affected by monetary policy. Inflation originated most in food and oil price increases which rippled throughout the economy. The new labor and industry custom of applying automatic cost-of-living increases prevents the traditional groups from absorbing the inflation loss, thus lengthening the inflation effects. In other words, the American economy after 1975 is more complex than before, and the aggregate monetary and fiscal policy actions of the 1960s were apparently not as effective as they once were.

President Reagan approached the stagflation economy with a new economic theory largely developed by Professor Arthur B. Laffer then of the University of Southern California. The heart of this theory is the relationship between tax rates and tax revenues. The Laffer curve is presented in Exhibit 1-6.

In this exhibit, the vertical line represents tax rates and the horizontal line represents tax revenues. The two extremes of zero tax rate and 100 percent tax rate produce no tax revenue. In between, the curve demonstrates that at some point an increase in tax rates actually reduces tax revenue. This is because at the higher rates individuals reduce their taxable work effort, spend more time seeking ways to reduce tax liabilities, and engage in more nontaxed activities. The implication for budgeting is that if marginal tax rates have exceeded that key point, then, ironically, a reduction in tax rates will actually lead to an increase in tax revenues.

President Reagan and his economic advisors felt that the way to get the American economy out of stagflation was to cut the tax rates. Because such a cut would result in higher budget deficits, they advocated cutting government expenditures (with the exception of military expenditures, which they increased). The immediate result was lower inflation, higher unemployment, and a larger federal debt. Given the automatic fiscal stabilizers

[2]Robert J. Samuelson, "The Enemy Among Us," *National Journal*, 9, 42 (October 15, 1977), 1619.

EXHIBIT 1-6   Laffer Curve

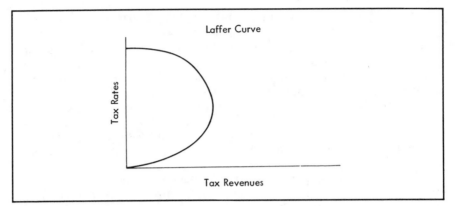

Source: Dom Bonafede, "Reagan's Supply-Side Policies Push Economics Writers into the Spotlight," *National Journal*, 1337 (September 26, 1981, p. 1723).

built into the government programs, the federal budget expenditures grew to offset rising unemployment and revenues fell because there were fewer taxpayers. The larger federal debt, coupled with a monetary policy of high interest rates and with other factors, resulted in high interest rates which retarded economic growth and recovery.

Fiscal Policy and Public Budgeting

At the national level, fiscal policy largely influences federal budgets. Once policy is determined, using macroeconomics, then those policies influence the following budget concerns:

1. the overall size of the budget, including revenue and expenditure totals;
2. the types of spending, such as capital investment versus direct payments;
3. the timing of spending programs;
4. the balance of activities—federal programs do work at cross purposes, and it must be decided which to emphasize and which to deemphasize;
5. the size of entitlement programs, and the amount available for the controlled programs;
6. the building or selling of stockpiles;
7. jawboning big labor or big corporations; and
8. tax policy.

A federal budget professional and most state and local budget officers must understand fiscal policy. Macroeconomics is the theory used to make many key budget decisions. Budget justifications and reviews are often done using macroeconomics. With the CBO and budget committees, Congress is likely to be more effective in using fiscal policy than it was in the 1960s, but political forces will still discourage the use of tax increases.

OTHER ECONOMIC TOPICS

In a text of this nature, all aspects of economics important to public budgeting cannot be covered in a single chapter. Subsequent chapters use various economic concepts, but the important contribution of economics to public budgeting is still not stated fully. Students are encouraged to read various economics texts, especially public finance books. The following subjects are worth investigating at greater length:

1. multiplier effect;
2. economic growth;
3. balance of payments;
4. regional economics;
5. public interest, including Rawl's "justice is fairness" implication to economics;
6. pareto-optimum;
7. welfare economics;
8. labor economics;
9. public goods theory; and
10. public choice theory.

REVIEW QUESTIONS

1. Explain the various perspectives one can have on public budgeting and how the definition of public budgeting can be affected by each perspective.
2. Assuming policy is defined as "a guide to action," explain how budgeting is policy. Why and in what way is this understandably significant to policy makers and public managers?
3. What is the budget cycle? How does the local budget cycle differ from the federal one?
4. In what ways are American ideologies significant in shaping public budgeting?
5. Explain the federal context of American budgeting and the significance of that context.
6. What are the major normative decision-making theories and how do they affect public budgeting as a practice?

7. Explain why inflation and unemployment rates act in inverse relationship.
8. What happened in 1970 and 1971 which cast doubt upon macroeconomic theory?
9. Why does the shift in the American economy from an industrial to a service economy have significance to the effectiveness of monetary policy?
10. How can liberals and conservatives disagree on fiscal policy but still base their thinking on macroeconomic theory?
11. Why is public debt not bad *ipso facto?* Explain why entitlement programs are consistent with macroeconomic theory.
12. Explain the economic theories which Reagan relied upon in making his economic recommendations. Contrast them to the other, more accepted macroeconomic theories.

REFERENCES

BAKKER, OEGE. *The Budget Cycle in Public Finance in the United States.* The Hague: W. P. Van Stockum, 1953.
BARTIZAL, JOHN R. *Budget Principles and Procedures.* Englewood Cliffs, N.J.: Prentice-Hall, 1942.
BRUNDAGE, PERCIVAL FLACK. *The Bureau of the Budget.* New York: Holt, Rinehart & Winston, 1970.
BUCHANAN, JAMES M. *The Demand and Supply of Public Goods.* Chicago: Rand McNally, 1968.
BUCK, A. E. *Public Budgeting.* New York: Harper & Row, 1929.
BURKHEAD, JESSE. *Government Budgeting.* New York: John Wiley, 1965.
—— and JERRY MINER. *Public Expenditure.* Chicago: Aldine, 1971.
CENTER FOR THE STUDY OF AMERICAN BUSINESS. *The Supply-Side Effects of Economic Policy.* St. Louis, Mo.: Washington University, 1981.
DAHL, ROBERT A. *A Preface to Democratic Theory.* Chicago: University of Chicago Press, 1956.
DAVID, JAMES E., JR. (ed.). *Politics, Programs and Budgets.* Englewood Cliffs, N.J.: Prentice-Hall, 1969.
DORFMAN, ROBERT. *Measuring the Benefits of Government Expenditures.* Washington, D.C.: Brookings Institution, 1965.
DUE, JOHN F. and ANN F. FRIEDLAENDER. *Government Finance.* 5th ed. Homewood, Ill.: Richard D. Irwin, 1973.
HAVENMAN, ROBERT H. and JULIUS MARGOLIS. *Public Expenditure and Policy Analysis.* 2nd ed. Chicago: Rand McNally, 1977.
LEE, ROBERT D. and RONALD W. JOHNSON. *Public Budgeting Systems.* Baltimore, Md.: University Park Press, 1973.
MILLER, RODGER L. E. *Economics Today.* 4th ed. New York: Harper & Row, 1982.
MOAK, LENNOX L. and ALBERT M. HILLHOUSE. *Local Government Finance.* Chicago: Municipal Finance Officers Association, 1975.
Municipal Performance Report, 1, 4 (August 1974).
MUSGRAVES, RICHARD A. and PEGGY B. MUSGRAVES. *Public Finance in Theory and Practice.* New York: McGraw-Hill, 1973.

NICHOLS, DOROTHY M. *Modern Money Mechanics.* Chicago: Federal Reserve Bank of Chicago, 1975.
RABIN, JACK and THOMAS D. LYNCH. *Handbook on Public Budgeting and Financial Management.* New York: Marcel Dekker, 1983.
REYNOLDS, LLOYD G. *Economics.* 4th ed. Homewood, Ill.: Richard D. Irwin, 1973.
SAMUELSON, PAUL A. *Economics.* 10th ed. New York: McGraw-Hill, 1976.
SWAN, WALLACE K. "Theoretical Debates Applicable to Budgeting" in Jack Rabin and Thomas D. Lynch (eds.), *Handbook on Public Budgeting and Financial Management.* New York: Marcel Dekker, 1983.
TRUMAN, DAVID. *The Governmental Process.* New York: Knopf, 1951.

chapter 2

TOWARD MODERN BUDGETING

This chapter examines public budgeting, reflects upon how it has evolved into its present condition, and reflects upon its significance in the larger context of public administration. Some attention is given to explaining what knowledgeable people define or characterize as public budgeting. Particular attention is focused on the critical issues which shaped the evolution of public budgeting. This chapter should help the reader understand:

1. the major historical reforms which have shaped public budgeting in America, and how the issues implicit in those reforms are still influencing what we perceive to be the "proper" role of budgeting in our government;
2. the executive focus on contemporary budget reforms;
3. the legislative focus on contemporary budget reforms; and
4. the state of modern budgeting in America.

PRELUDE

Parliament versus the King

Public budgeting in the United States is very much influenced by early English history. The word "budget" seems to have originated in the Middle English *bouget*, meaning bag or wallet. A great leather bag was used by the king's treasurer—later called the exchequer—to carry the documents explaining the king's fiscal needs. That bag was called the budget. Over time the document came to be called the budget, and the system used to prepare and execute the document came to be called budgeting. The bag was used primarily when the king's treasurer went to Parliament seeking funds for the king.

English history is largely a story of struggle between the king and the Parliament over the control of the nation. To a greater extent than other feudal realms, the newly established Norman kingdom of England in 1066 stressed the power and authority of the king over all others, including the important nobles. In England, the elite barons, who controlled large landed estates, actually held their estates as tenants-in-chief of the king rather than being actual property owners, as the concept is understood today. By 1215, the kingdom was ruled by King John—a descendant of William the Conqueror. King John lost the continental portion of his kingdom, which included Normandy, and he engaged in a civil war with many of his English barons and other nobles. In an attempt to achieve peace, the king signed the Magna Carta. The twelfth article of that document stated that no taxes could be imposed "unless by the common council of the realm." The "council of the realm" became Parliament.

In the important Reformation period, the power of the king versus that of Parliament was tested to its utmost. By 1649, not only had the Parliamentary forces prevailed over King Charles I in battle, but also King Charles had been beheaded. From the Parliamentary forces, Oliver Cromwell emerged as a military leader and became dictator of England, Scotland, and Ireland. A few years after his death, key elements of the army rebelled against Cromwell's son and supported the restoration of King Charles II in 1660. The tension between the Crown and Parliament continued. Charles II and the other Stuart kings favored a divine-right-of-kings interpretation of power and seemed to consider adopting Catholicism as the state religion. In 1688, James II was forced from the throne, and King William and Queen Mary (the sister of James) were asked to share the throne. A key product of that era was the English Bill of Rights of 1688. It established that no man could be compelled to pay a gift, loan, or tax "without common consent by Act of Parliament." The concept of a shared legislative and executive power was established. By 1770, the king even agreed to an annual specified grant of funds that were controlled by the Parliament.

This struggle, or tension, between the legislative (the Parliament) and the executive (the king) is also one of the most important characteristics of public budgeting in the United States. At the time of the American Revolution in 1776, the stress was upon legislative supremacy, and the use of executive power was greatly suspect as a principal of proper government. The Revolution was fought against the "tyranny" of the king. From the end of the Revolution to 1789, the country was run under a weak executive system as established by the Articles of Confederation.

With the adoption of the Constitution in 1789, the principles of proper government shifted away from a weak central government, with a weak executive, toward a strong executive authority and a national government. James Madison was particularly influential in arguing for continued legislative-executive tension. He believed that such tension was not only functional, but even necessary. He argued that power should be separated, especially between the legistlative and executive branches. This separation of powers would prevent an executive abuse of power yet still permit strong executive leadership to exist.

Since the beginning of the Republic, almost every budget reform addresses or affects this intended tension and balance of power between the legislative and executive branches of government.

Colonial America

In colonial America, the revenue was generated within the colonies, and the various state houses had a great deal of control over revenues and expenditures. The king's representatives administered the government. The legislatures became the place where the leading colonists gathered. They became accustomed to exercising power with a separate group actually administering the government programs. The separation from England, abetted by the primitive means of transoceanic transportation, fostered independence. But the need to live within their own resources and to decide how to apply their own resources using a locally elected legislative body were the important factors leading to self-reliance.

Many of the causes of the American Revolution relate directly to public budgeting issues. England decided to impose taxes (e.g., the Stamp Act) on the colonies largely because of the expensive French-Indian War. This unilateral act seemed unfair given the legislative authority over tax matters and the reasoning of such documents as Magna Carta and the Bill of Rights. Of course, many other reasons as well explain the emotions leading to the American Revolution, but issues concerning public budgeting were some of the most emotionally charged subjects of that era.

Not surprisingly, those strong feelings helped shape the U.S. Constitution. For example, Article I, Section 9 of the Constitution requires that all matters dealing with revenue must originate in the House of Representatives. The founders of the United States were not content to say that Congress had to act on revenue matters, as the English Bill of Rights had said of Parliament a century earlier. Rather they stated that this matter had to start with the chamber of Congress which was to be *the* representative of the people. Today, the president presents his budget somewhat as the king's treasurer did. The House passes the appropriation bills first. The Senate often acts as an appealing body and eventually the two chambers agree upon the appropriations. However, the House is still considered the leading chamber on matters concerning revenue and appropriations.

Budgeting in the 1800s

For the first few years of the federal government, Alexander Hamilton was the influential secretary of the Treasury. He viewed his role as being much like that of the English exchequer, and his department was the most significant nonmilitary department. The national government's revenue source was customs duties, and the Coast Guard was an important force in ensuring their proper collection. Hamilton also effectively had the very large Revolutionary War debt retired.

Hamilton, a leader of the Federalist faction, argued in favor of strong executive in government. He not only felt that government was responsible for the welfare and defense of the country but also that the nation's leaders should act as trustees for the people. To Hamilton, strong executive leadership was important, and the government's budget and financial affairs were primary tools of his leadership. The Federalist view was influenced by contemporary England, where the ministers dominated the Parliament and the executive activities.

Thomas Jefferson came to be the leader of the anti-Federalist faction which opposed Hamilton. Jefferson thought not only that the separation of powers was critical, but also that policy matters, including budgetary decisions, were the dominion of the Congress. Executive leadership on comprehensive budget matters was considered improper by some presidents, but, interestingly, Jefferson's administration was characterized by the strong leadership by Secretary of the Treasury Albert Gallatin.

Congress started with a unified and comprehensive approach to public budgeting. The Ways and Means Committee was extremely powerful, as it made decisions on revenues and appropriations. With few exceptions, the executive branch did not have a unified approach. The Treasury Department did compile the expenditure estimates from all the agencies, but it did not edit or analyze the estimates. Such activities were considered to be legislative in nature.

As the nineteenth century evolved, the Congress eroded its unified approach to the budget, and the executive did not attempt to assert itself. By 1865, a separate House Appropriations Committee was established so that revenue and expenditures were considered separately. By 1855, there were eight separate committees·which recommended appropriations. This disunity lessened the budgetary focus of power; but, except for periods of war or depression, the federal government was not concerned about tight budgets. In this era, there was a constrained view of what government should do in society, so budgets tended to be small. Also the major revenue source—the customs—was providing more revenue than was needed by the demands for expenditure, so that Congress had the unusual problem of dealing with large surpluses.

Progressive Reform Movement

What is commonly considered "modern budgeting" started in the Progressive era with the Progressives' reactions against corruption in local government. Largely due to the efforts of popular newspapers and book writers, called "muckrakers," the Progressive political movement gained popular support, which included demands for municipal reforms to curtail corruption. The political views of the Progressives were similar to those of Alexander Hamilton, but much of their political philosophy was influenced by German political philosophers such as Georg Wilhelm Friedrich Hegel and conservative English philosophers such as Edmund Burke. The most effective municipal reformers were the National Municipal League (founded in 1899) and the New York Bureau of Municipal Research (1906).

The latter group is one of the most remarkable in American history. One of the leaders was Charles Beard, who was a noted historian and founder of the academic discipline of political science. Luther Gulick and other members of that Bureau were also instrumental in founding public administration as a study and practice. The research arm of the Bureau moved to Washington, D.C., and evolved into today's Brookings Institution. The training arm was moved to Syracuse University in 1925 and became the Maxwell School of Syracuse University. The Bureau served as a model and "mother house" for many other bureaus throughout the country. The members of the Bureau led and staffed almost every major governmental reform committee between 1910 and 1950.

Not surprisingly, the New York Bureau of Municipal Research was highly influential in budget reforms. One year after its creation, it prepared the first detailed report demonstrating the need for adopting a municipal budget system. In that same year, the Bureau produced an object classification budget for the New York City Department of Health. By 1912, the reforms of the Bureau were reflected in the Taft Commission report, which called for object (line-item) classification budgeting in all federal departments and agencies. By the 1920s, most of the budgets of major American cities were reformed. In 1929, A. E. Buck, a staff person of the Bureau, wrote the first (and very influential) text on public budgeting.

Budget reform was stimulated by a desire to strengthen the executive authority. Influential reformers such as Woodrow Wilson believed that executive authority could be strengthened if citizens could vote for candidates who had the power to carry out their promises. Wilson argued against a government dominated by the Congress. He felt the chief executive should be stronger and that budget reform was one of the best ways to strengthen the executive. Wilson, like other Progressives, argued for a professionalization of the career administrators who would report to elected decision makers.

EVOLUTION

Prior to 1921

In the early 1900s, the federal government started to experience large federal expenditures and budget deficits. The customs revenue was not adequate and a federal income tax was passed. This new tax solved the fundamental revenue problem, since the tax rate could be increased to provide the necessary revenue. This tax also attracted the keen attention of the business community, as they now had a vested interest in minimizing the money that the government took from them as corporations and individuals. Business interests dominated the times. Business and many citizens stressed the importance of economy, efficiency, and government retrenchment. Many felt that the least government was the best government.

President Taft issued a report prepared by the Commission on Economy and Efficiency Goals titled "Need for a National Budget." The report stressed that the president should be responsible for preparing a unified executive budget. The rationale was motivated by two themes: (1) economy and efficiency, and (2) strengthening democracy. A budget would better enable the president to plan government activities so that maximum economy and efficiency were achieved. A president's budget would also strengthen the president's power—thus citizens could vote for or against a person who had the power to fulfill campaign promises. President Taft was not successful in his reforms and Woodrow Wilson's income tax temporarily took the pressure off.

Prior to 1921, agencies still followed the Jeffersonian tradition of preparing their estimates and transmitting them to the Treasury Department, which passed them on to Congress. Treasury conducted no analyses. The various Congressional committees considered the estimates with minimum coordination among themselves. The agencies did sometimes overspend the appropriations and Congress felt obligated to appropriate the overspent amount. The president did not participate in the budget process and there was no overall Executive Branch Plan.

Budgeting and Accounting Act of 1921

President Taft's reforms were largely enacted in 1921. Pressures for budget reform continued, especially with the expense of World War I. The Budget and Accounting Act of 1921 provided for a national budget and an independent audit of government accounts. The law specifically required the president to submit a budget, including estimates of expenditures, appropriations, and receipts for the ensuing fiscal year. The new legislation created the Bureau of the Budget (BOB) in the Treasury Department. Section 209 of the legislation states:

> The Bureau, when directed by the President, shall make a detailed study of the departments and establishments for the purpose of enabling the President to determine what changes (with a view of securing greater economy and efficiency in the conduct of the public service) should be made in (1) the existing organization, activities, and methods of business of such departments or establishments, (2) the appropriations, (3) the assignment of particular activities to particular services, or (4) the regrouping of services. The results of such study shall be embodied in a report or reports to the President, who may transmit to Congress such report or reports or any part thereof with his recommendation on the matter covered thereby.

This landmark legislation greatly strengthened the president and created the powerful BOB as an arm of the president. The agencies were required to submit their estimates and supporting information to BOB. Agencies were not allowed to initiate contacts with Congress. Also legislation established that all recommended legislation from agencies had to be sent to BOB for review and clearance. This clearance function greatly increased presidential power because it allowed the president to insure the executive branch was in step with presidential policy. The Bureau could and did prepare the president's budget, which was the executive branch (president's) proposal to the Congress. The agencies and departments in the executive branch were and are required to support the president's budget.

Budgeting is largely a story of relative legislative-executive strength. With Hamilton, executive strength was asserted but short-lived. After Jefferson, legislative strength in the budget area dominated but was diminished by the nonunified approach which evolved in the Congress. With the passage of the 1921 legislation, executive branch strength started to grow in spite of the fact that the Congress largely initiated the legislation. The power of the Congress was not diminished, but the 1921 Act did increase the power of the president.

The Budget and Accounting Act of 1921 also created a Congressional agency called the General Accounting Office (GAO) to audit independently the government accounts. This agency is headed by the comptroller general, who is appointed to a 15-year term by the president. The purpose of the audits is to verify that government funds are being used for legal purposes. The independence of the agency prevents improper pressure being exerted upon it by members of the executive branch.

The president's 1937 Committee on Administration Management (Brownlow Committee) recommended the strengthening of BOB's management activities. The 1921 legislation had given the bureau certain managerial responsibilities, but they were not exerted. The Brownlow Committee's report eventually led to the Reorganization Act of 1939. This in turn led to the establishment of the Executive Office of the President and the transfer of BOB to that new office. President Roosevelt defined the duties of the Bureau as follows:

1. to assist the president in the preparation of the budget and the formulation of the fiscal program of the government;

2. to supervise and control the administration of the budget;

3. to conduct research in the development of improved plans of administrative management, and to advise the executive departments and agencies of the government with respect to improved administrative organizations and practice;

4. to aid the president in bringing about more efficient and economical conduct of the government services;

5. to assist the president by clearing and coordinating departmental advice on proposed legislation and by making recommendations as to presidential action on legislative enactment, in accordance with past practices;

6. to assist in the consideration and clearance and, where necessary, in the preparation of proposed executive orders and proclamations;

7. to plan and promote the improvement, development, and coordination of federal and other statistical services; and

8. to keep the president informed of the progress of activities by agencies of the government with respect to work proposed, work actually initiated, and work completed, together with the relative timing of work between the several agencies of the government, all to the end that the work programs of the several agencies of the executive branch of the government may be coordinated and that the monies appropriated by the Congress may be expended in the most economical manner possible with the least possible overlapping and duplication of effort.

The Bureau became the right arm of a strong president.

Post-1940 Reforms

During World War II, the Bureau became even more important with all activities directed toward the war. Taxes were increased and record deficits were incurred. The Bureau assumed added duties, including supervision of government financial reports and establishing personnel ceilings. In 1945, the Bureau's budget function was extended to include the government corporations. Also accounts had to be maintained on a program basis and full cost information was required. The Government Corporations Act of 1945 also directed the GAO to appraise the corporations in terms of their performance rather than merely in terms of the legality and propriety of their expenditures. This provision was eventually extended to all GAO reviews.

The Full Employment Act of 1946 called for economic planning and a budget policy directed toward achieving maximum national employment and production. The late 1940s saw the addition of more duties to BOB. The Classification Act of 1949 required the director to issue and administer regulations involving agency reviews of their operations. The Travel Expense Act of 1949 assigned the director regulatory functions on travel allowances.

President Truman appointed the Hoover Commission in 1947 and a report was submitted in 1949. The Commission recommended that

1. a budget based on functions, activities, and projects, called a "performance budget," be adopted;
2. the appropriation structure be surveyed and improved;
3. the budget estimates of all departments and agencies be separated between current operating and capital outlays; and
4. the president's authority to reduce expenditures under appropriations "if the purposes intended by the Congress are still carried out" be clearly established.

Several reforms resulted from the Hoover Commission, but the Budget and Accounting and Procedures Act of 1950 was particularly important. It recognized the need for reliable accounting systems and the president was given the authority to prescribe the contents and budget arrangements, simplify the presentations, broaden the appropriations, and make progress toward performance budgeting.

The Second Hoover Commission (1955) led to more technical but equally important budget reforms. Agency accounts were to be maintained on an accrual basis. Cost-based budgets were encouraged. Synchronization between agency structure and budget classifications were encouraged. The President's Commission on Budget Concepts in 1967 did not address any fundamental budget reforms but concerned itself with smaller technical issues. In summary, the post-1940 period saw many reforms which continued to strengthen the executive budget process.

Approaches to Budgeting

By the 1950s, there were three accepted formats for budgeting—line-item, program, and performance—with two underlying philosophic perspectives on budgeting—incremental and rational. In line-item budgeting

EXHIBIT 2-1 Hennepin County Line-Item Budget

MAJOR PROGRAM: COMM. SERV. & ECON. ASST.	PROGRAM ACTIVITY BY LINE ITEM	BUDGET YEAR 1980

PROGRAM: COMMUNITY SERVICES SUBPROGRAM: MANAGEMENT & PLANNING ACTIVITY:	DEPARTMENT COMM. SERVICES	PROGRAM CODE 8831

ACCOUNT NO.	DESCRIPTION	1979 BUDGET	1979 ACTUAL & ESTIMATED	1980 DEPARTMENT REQUEST
	Personal Services (8000)			
8002	Salaries & Wages-Reg	$1,586,573	$1,673,696	$1,763,765
8004	Salaries & Wages-Temp	14,137	25,000	24,000
8006	Overtime	11,117	12,000	13,000
8008	Intern Stipend	—	—	—
8014	On Call	—	—	—
8016	Emergency	—	—	—
8020	Shift Differential	—	—	—
8022	Sunday Differential	—	—	—
8048	Long Term Disability Insurance	14,694	15,308	11,789
8052	Life Insurance	1,456	1,422	1,489
8054	Health Insurance	70,401	80,619	77,388
8060	FICA	82,649	91,050	102,421
8062	PERA	106,810	111,275	104,828
8064	MERA	—	2,658	2,951
8066	Severance	—	—	—
8068	Stability	37,242	37,242	40,330
8070	Supplemental Retirement	13,236	13,789	11,851
8072	Unemployment Compensation	6,915	3,400	3,600
8074	Worker's Compensation	4,872	4,872	5,424
8080	Other Personal Services	10,000	10,000	10,700
8099	Personal Services-Contra	—	—	—
	Subtotal	$1,960,102	$2,082,331	$2,173,536
	Commodities (8100)			
8012	Office Supplies	$ 38,557	$ 43,000	$ 49,000
8103	Photocopying	22,181	15,000	16,500
8104	Film & Photographic	33,900	25,000	27,500
8110	General Supplies	6,000	2,000	2,200
8120	Food & Beverages	—	500	500
8130	Clothing & Linens	—	—	—
8134	Kitchen & Dining	—	—	—
8140	Surgical & Medical	—	—	—
8142	Drugs & Medicine	—	—	—
8150	Laboratory	—	—	—
	Subtotal	$ 100,638	$ 85,500	$ 95,700

Source: Hennepin County, Minnesota, Budget.

(Exhibit 2-1), the items necessary to run a government process (e.g., salaries, supplies) are identified for each government unit, and the sum of money required for each item is identified by year. Program and performance budgeting are more sophisticated approaches. In the former, a logical grouping of government activities is defined and money is allocated to these activities. Performance budgeting goes one step further, identifying specific program outputs which are associated with specific program money requests. Exhibit 2-2 illustrates performance budgeting.

Those working in budgeting in the 1950s tended to follow either the incremental or the rational philosophic perspective. The former stressed that budget decisions should be viewed as essentially incremental, with the last fiscal year serving as the base upon which the new year is judged. This is why budget formats often show the PY, CY, and BY (and, normally, BY-

EXHIBIT 2-2   Hoover Commission Performance Budget Model

MEDICAL CARE

Summary: This appropriation request in the amount of $43,648,008 is to provide for the care of a daily average of 18,696 sick and injured, maintenance and operation of 34 hospitals, 2 medical supply depots, 2 medical storehouses, 6 medical department schools, 11 research facilities, operation of 432 other medical activities ashore, instruction of personnel in non-naval institutions, and care of an estimated 1,859 dead; and for Island Government—6 hospitals, 80 dispensary beds, and instruction of native practitioners. Specific programs are as follows:

1. Medical and Dental Care Afloat—to provide technical medical and dental equipment, supplies, and services for an average of 232,485 personnel at sea, and initial outfits for 4 new naval vessels to be commissioned in 1948	$ 2,822,923
2. Medical and Dental Care Ashore	48,419,168
3. Care of the Dead—to provide services, supplies, and transportation for an estimated 1,859 deaths in 1948	502,700
4. Instruction of Medical Department Personnel	2,645,347
5. Medical and Dental Research—to provide civilian employment of 328 and supplies and equipment to operate and maintain 6 research facilities and 5 field research units in 1948	2,519,742
6. Medical and Dental Supply System	2,936,396
7. Island Government	1,910,463
8. Departmental Administration—to provide civilian employment of 550, travel, telephone, telegraph, supplies, and equipment for the departmental administration of the responsibilities of the Bureau of Medicine and Surgery in 1948	1,432,100
Appropriation Request, 1948	$43,648,008

Source: Hoover Commission, 1949.

CY)—so that the incremental difference can be examined. The latter perspective, popularized by economists, stresses that rational decision-making requires examining budget decisions for a set of objectives, using analytical techniques to help discern the best decision possible.

Critics of incrementalism stress that the CY numbers may remain the same in the BY, but that significant policy shift can occur even if the numbers remain constant. Agencies may focus their arguments on the BY-CY difference, but their success rate on such requests is low. Incrementalists agree that this is true, but insist that it does no harm to their original arguments, because decisions still focus upon the current services in the CY and the proposed difference in the BY. Critics of the rational philosophic perspective argue that it is a logical absurdity and is inconsistent with a pluralist political system which accepts a multiple-value culture. A counterargument used by rationalists is to stress that the analytical techniques associated with the perspective do help executive branch decision makers.

There are three common purposes behind the budget activity: control, management, and planning. If control is the main purpose, then budget formats are designed to insure that the money is spent according to established policy and that no resources are used for illegal purposes. If management is the purpose, then budget process stresses directing people in the bureaucracy and achieving efficiency and economy in those programs. If planning is the purpose, then the process emphasizes improvements in the political decision-making process. These three stresses are not mutually exclusive. All of them exist in most budget processes, but the three-purpose distinction is conceptually useful. Reformers in various eras tended to emphasize one budget purpose over the others, but the other purposes did not cease to exist.

If reformers are stressing control, they wish to guarantee fiscal accountability. They are fearful of corruption and of leaving the decisions of public employees unchecked. Those arguing for greater control are supported by arguments to increase the strength of the chief executive (which will also achieve greater economy and efficiency in government). Strong chief executives can enhance their strength through improved budget control mechanisms. Strong control can also mean that inefficient and uneconomical activities are increased because not enough management flexibility is permitted to deal with changing situations. The added procedural requirements can result in more workers and less productivity.

Early American public budget literature stressed the control function. Given the well-publicized political corruption of the era, the stress on control is certainly understandable. The reforms included such well-known budget features as the following:

Annual budget: revenues and expenditures presented for one fiscal year period;

Comprehensive budget: all revenues and expenditures included in the budget;

Detailed line items: presenting the exact amount planned to be spent for every separate thing or service to be purchased;

Identification of all transactions: recording every obligation and transfer of money and liquidation of obligation; and

Apportionments and allotments: an executive branch mechanism to regulate the rate and actual spending of authorized funds.

Stress on budget control comes with a price tag. Extreme control limits management flexibility, which might be essential in many situations. Interestingly, the reform for efficiency can lead to inefficiency because management cannot easily adapt to more efficient procedures. Budget control is a high administrative cost activity. Recording all transactions and every line item requires many people even in this era of the computer. Another cost of budget control is more subtle in its effect upon government. By stressing control, the emphasis is upon detail and the big policy decisions tend to be ignored. Thus government becomes less responsive to the problems of society.

If reformers are stressing management, they view the budget as a tool of the executive to achieve effective operational direction with greatest efficiency. The budget can be used as a mechanism to guide the massive bureaucracy. Reforms like performance budgeting (i.e., categorizing the planned activities to stress the relationship of money to achievement) and productivity improvements (i.e., getting greater results for relatively fewer resources) are stressed. Often reformers decentralize the details to the agency level while stressing means to achieve greater centralized direction. Normally those reforms are more conservative and business-oriented, and, not surprisingly, these reforms were stressed more in the 1920s, early 1930s, 1970s, and 1980s, when conservative Republicans were president.

If reformers are stressing planning, they view the budget as a way to bring greater rationality into the public policy-making process. These reformers are appalled at the poor decision-making situation of top policy makers and the noncoordinated nature of many decision-making processes. They believe that coordinated and rational decision-making is important and that more planning and greater use of analysis will improve the decision-making process. Those reformers stress the importance of analysis, data, and categorizing the budget to facilitate analysis. In the 1960s, PPB (planning-programming-budgeting) and the use of analysis was stressed in public budgeting. In the 1970s, ZBB (zero base budgeting) also stressed analysis.

AN EXECUTIVE FOCUS

Planning and Analysis

Planning-programming-budgeting (PPB) was an attempt in the federal government—continuing today in some state and local governments—to institutionalize analysis in the executive branch decision-making process. The advocates of PPB believed public budgeting was the key to most of the important decisions made in government and that public policy-making lacked enough analysis for top level decision makers. They believed that procedural reforms could insert essential analysis into the public budgeting process, thus improving public policy-making.

PPB was not a new creation in the 1960s. In 1907, the New York Bureau of Municipal Research developed the first Program Memorandum. The Hoover Commission advocated performance budgeting and budgets were organized into programs in the 1940s. In the 1930s, welfare economics developed many of the same techniques later associated with PPB. In the 1950s, operations research and systems analysis also developed techniques later associated with PPB.

PPB was popularized in the 1960s by Secretary of Defense Robert McNamara and spread by President Johnson to the whole federal government. Secretary McNamara had a strong analytical background and asked Charles Hitch to apply the concepts developed at Rand Corporation to the Defense Department. Most people, and especially President Johnson, were impressed with the McNamara management of the Department of Defense. In 1965, President Johnson ordered that PPB be used in every federal department and agency. In time, PPB also spread to many state and local governments as well as to governments around the world.

The era of PPB was one of guns and butter. The United States was fighting a war on poverty and a war in Vietnam. There were strong, intelligent people (then called the "best and the brightest") running the country, but the goals outmatched the available talent and resources. This was true with PPB because the goals were visionary, but the resources, including talented people, were inadequate for the challenge.

PPB was an attempt to embody the rational model of decision-making into the executive branch's policy-making process. The attempt and PPB were declared dead in the Nixon administration, but the verdict was too harsh. PPB was officially deleted from the U.S. Office of Management and Budget (the renamed Bureau of the Budget) official guidelines, but federal agencies continued to use it. In some federal agencies PPB worked, in many others it was never really tried, and in some agencies it just didn't work.

A common misunderstanding of novices about budgeting is to equate PPB and analysis. PPB was and is an attempt to institutionalize analysis into the public budgeting process. PPB is not analysis or a form of analysis. It does encourage the application of marginal utility analysis, cost-benefit studies, cost-effectiveness analysis, sensitivity analysis, pay-off matrix, present values, and other techniques.

Analysis can be characterized as various art forms—many would argue sciences—which examine alternatives, view them in terms of basic assumptions and objectives, and test as well as compare alternatives. All this is done with a purpose of finding "useful" information or conclusions concerning policy questions. The techniques vary and were developed in several different disciplines.

PPB was operationalized through the use of several mechanisms. The use of analysis was stressed, particularly in the early stages of the budget cycle. A categorization of government programs called a "program structure" was required to facilitate analytical comparisons. A greater use of data associated with the programs was encouraged. Output measures and five-year projections beyond the budget were considered essential. Analysis was further encouraged by the use of mandated special studies and analyses addressed to specific major program issues.

What are the lessons which can be learned from the PPB experience? They can be summarized as follows:

Theoretical and Conceptual Issues

1. Program budgeting, policy analysis, and other related concepts are vague, and thus present a difficult challenge to the practitioner who wishes to apply the concepts. A great deal of effort and creative talent is necessary to tailor and operationalize these concepts.
2. The rational model, as an ideal for practitioners, can result in serious mistakes.
3. The use of one program structure does not strengthen but rather limits policy analysis. Subjects of analysis vary and one categorization greatly limits the necessary range of analysis.
4. Government programs often do not have and may never have logical, consistent operational objectives. Policy makers recognize the value of vagueness in achieving necessary political consensus and know that vagueness often hides conflicting views on the proper direction of a program. Public administrators inherit this confusion and must deal with it even though most analytical techniques cannot work with such ambiguity.
5. Analysis normally is helpful only for relatively narrow but often important policy questions. The use of analysis is constrained by such things as the ability of the analyst and the nature of the subject being examined. Analysis is often most useful on technical questions.

Implementation

1. A significantly large amount of money and many talented people must be devoted to making a reform like PPB work.
2. A phased implementation plan should be adopted so that agencies and portions of agencies most likely to accept the change can be introduced to the innovation first, and resisting agencies can be introduced to the change last. As a matter of realistic strategy, one can expect resistance from some top management which will effectively prevent successful implementation. Training and hiring policies can minimize the problem, but such effective resistance cannot be avoided entirely.
3. The key person for insuring effective policy analysis is the agency head. A desire and ability to use policy analysis effectively should be one criterion for hiring a person for this position. Then a tailor-made brief orientation course could be given new agency heads which could include the use of policy analysis in public policy making.
4. One particularly difficult problem is to achieve coordination of policy among the policy analysts and planners, the budget officer, the accountants, the lawyers, the public affairs officer, the analysts preparing the agency's progress reports, and the program managers within an agency.

Political Factors

1. The use of plans covering five years does not appear to limit the political options available.
2. Policy analysis rarely addresses the political costs and benefits of a program

to specific key individuals such as legislators, but good analyses do address analytical questions which set out political costs and benefits in general.

3. The political advantages of not using analysis with explicit objectives may be critical to reaching some decisions in some specific political situations, but there is no reason to believe there is a common circumstance.

Human Factors[1]

1. People in an agency must believe that the reform is a significant and legitimate undertaking. The real test for them will be how seriously key people (like the agency head) and key agencies (such as the Office of Management and Budget) treat the reform. If these people and groups continually demand and use the products of this reform, then significance and legitimacy will be established.

2. Positive and politically practical recommendations must be the products of the reform. If they are not generated, the people directly responsible for operationalizing the reform in the agency will lose effectiveness both among organizational peers and also among the key decision makers who use the products.

Management

1. Systematic attempts to institutionalize policy analysis do tend to centralize governmental decision-making.

2. Reforms like PPB do not greatly influence government reorganization.

Management by Objectives

At the beginning of the second term of the Nixon administration, the White House and the Office of Management and Budget strongly encouraged the federal departments and agencies to use management-by-objectives (MBO). The technique called MBO is the setting out of specific objectives for agencies and requiring regular high level periodic reports on the progress toward achieving those objectives. The Nixon administration's use of MBO varied from the conventional MBO, especially by not stressing lower level participation in the formulation of objectives. Also the adoption of MBO was not done through OMB regulations, as PPB had been, but was required through the use of the informal memorandum from OMB to the various departments and agencies requesting information to a specific MBO format.

Serious government-wide presidential use of MBO was short-lived and died with the Nixon administration. The reform did have a significant influence on many federal departments and agencies as the technique was integrated into their standard operating procedures.

In a few agencies, there was an attempt to link MBO and public budgeting. Such a linkage is theoretically possible but is rarely done. The linkage is accomplished by using a matrix table with MBO objectives and budget activities. The matrix table squares contain the amount of money needed

[1]Some items were covered under "Implementation."

to carry out the objective during the budget year. A given program may have multiple objectives; therefore the money cited would not be placed in mutually exclusive categories. Also, not all program activities would be covered by the objectives used in MBO. The advantage of the linkage is to insure that resources are available to meet the high-priority objectives of the government.

Zero Base Budgeting

Zero base budgeting is an approach to public budgeting in which each budget year's activities are judged in a self-contained fashion, with little or no reference given to the policy precedents of past years. ZBB is contrasted to incremental budgeting, in which the budget justification is focused upon the difference between the current year (CY) and the budget year (BY). In making the distinction between ZBB and incremental budgeting, a false impression can be given of both concepts as they are practiced. In ZBB, the analysts normally will want information on past funding levels and past accomplishments, but the analysts could also ignore such data. In incremental budgeting, the analysts normally will want information on all activities being planned in the budget year but their focus will be upon the program changes from the current year. The analysts already know much of the program information from reviewing last year's budget.

In 1964, the U.S. Department of Agriculture used a ZBB approach to prepare its budget. It was an additional exercise on top of the normal budget process. ZBB required voluminous documentation and a great deal of departmental time and energy. Critical evaluators of the approach concluded that, except for a few small decisions, the department reached the same conclusions as it would have reached with the less expensive incremental approach. The higher level officials did feel that they gained a much fuller understanding of their organization because of the ZBB experience. However, ZBB was abandoned.

Peter A. Pyhrr used ZBB in the private sector and popularized its wider use. Mr. Pyhrr used it successfully in Texas Instruments and wrote a book titled *Zero-Base Budgeting*, and also authored an extremely influential 1973 article in *Harvard Business Review*. The then governor of Georgia— Jimmy Carter—read about ZBB and invited Mr. Pyhrr to help him apply the approach to the state of Georgia. Presidential candidate Carter talked a great deal about the virtues of ZBB and President Carter required its adoption by the federal government.

The use of ZBB in the private sector has been confined primarily to overhead activities (i.e., expenses needed to maintain the organization versus expenses needed to produce the product). There is a great deal of difference between public and private budgeting, but they are the most similar in the area of overhead. In private budgeting, revenue comes from sales, which can fluctuate due to a variety of factors. If sales are up and unit costs are constant or lower, then the company has more money to spend or give back to the investors. In public budgeting, revenue comes from taxes, which normally are intended to buy certain services. The focus is upon the services which are sometimes difficult to define, such as national defense preparedness. In the private sector, overhead is meant to be a service to the organization, much as government is a service to the society. Not surprisingly, the private sector has had little difficulty budgeting for its major functions, but has had greater difficulty budgeting for its overhead functions. ZBB has proved to be a useful budgetary approach for the private sector's overhead activities.

The use of ZBB in the public sector is a recent development, with the exception of the Department of Agriculture experience. ZBB was adopted by a few cities and several states (including Georgia, New Jersey, Idaho, Montana, and Illinois). The assessment of its success and failure is unclear, but its initial advocates were enthusiastic. Problems have arisen similar to the ones experienced with PPB but conclusions are unclear, with the few empirical studies generally negative.

There are several different ZBB approaches. This is appropriate, as ZBB should be tailored to each government's unique circumstances. Normally, the ZBB consists of preparing budget proposals and alternative levels of spending grouped into "decision packages." Program and higher level managers then rank those decision packages in the order of priority. The lowest levels don't get funded.

Decision packages are self-contained units for budget choice containing input and output data (i.e., resources needed to operate the program and the products of the program) as well as the expected levels of performance for each defined level of expenditure. These packages are prepared by the manager responsible for each discrete activity at the lowest level of an organization capable of formulating a budget request. Alternative decision packages are prepared and ranked, thus allowing marginal utility and comparative analyses. Often the guidelines stipulate that a package should be prepared for the minimum cost essential to carry out the activity effectively, but some guidelines recognize the extreme latitude given the manager using that type of guidance. Some states have selected arbitrary percentages to insure that an amount smaller than last year's request is considered. They do this by stipulating that one alternative must be 50 or 80 or 90 percent of last year's request.

Decision packages are then ranked by managers and executives by priority. Other, lower cost packages within each activity are necessarily given higher priority over the more costly packages. The packages are ranked by the managers preparing the packages and by executives at each level above the manager. A chief executive can and does establish a cutoff point for the government as a whole, as well as for each agency. Only the packages above the cutoff are included in the executive branch budget submitted to the legislature.

There are some serious problems in using ZBB. The most obvious is that ZBB can be a paper monster which buries executives in an avalanche of documents. ZBB necessarily means thousands of decision packages. For example, in Georgia there were 10,000 decision packages, and no chief executive can review each one. Mechanisms must be created to manage the paperwork, limiting it to only the critical decisions. Another problem is dealing with programs which are effectively uncontrollable in the budget, such as veterans' benefits, social security, interest on the debt, retirement, and food stamps. ZBB cannot address them, yet they represent over 75 percent of the federal budget and are significant in many state and local budgets as well. The technique does not help judge priorities between budget activities such as defense, welfare, and environments. Also the technique does not lend itself to demanding responsive grant programs (e.g., grant-in-aid programs), which are designed to let communities largely define objectives and priorities. Marginal analysis of the budget packages cannot be used in those programs because the granting agency cannot accurately forecast benefit. The agency does not know who will qualify or what the funds will be used for and therefore what benefits should result. Also a very serious question still exists: Are government decisions different from private-sector decisions or is there something to which government decisions are being compared?

There are some apparent advantages to ZBB. In programs involving clear operational missions, such as highways, recreation, and public works, the technique is analytically relevant to the program analysts and decision makers. The approach shifts budget attention away from adding to the current year program and focuses consideration upon increases to the minimum level of operational support. The approach is successful in educating higher level executives and their staffs on the nature of government programs. Also the approach may stimulate redirection of resources within budgets and programs into more productive activities.

TBB and Envelope Budgeting

There is a nonrational approach to budgeting which rejects PPB and its foundations; it is called target base budgeting (TBB) in Cincinnati and Tampa and envelope budgeting in Canada. In sharp contrast to PPB, envelope budgeting is a top-down rationing process which is concerned with establishing priorities and limits at the top as a means to force choice among alternatives at the bottom. It does not stress economic rationality but rather political rationality by:

1. permitting the Canadian Committee on Priorities and Planning to establish ceilings—priorities and envelope expenditure levels—for each ministry;
2. delegating authority to Policy Committees to fund new proposals from established envelope resources; and
3. permitting additional funding for new proposals through a limited policy reserve.

TBB is quite similar to envelope budgeting. Both rely heavily upon BY revenue forecasting, with most of the projected revenue assigned to city agencies or national departments according to their proportion of current year budget allocations. In envelope budgeting that linkage is not stressed as heavily as in TBB. The remainder is put in a "discretionary reserve" in Cincinnati and Tampa; in Canada it is put in a "policy reserve." In both situa-

EXHIBIT 2-3   Executive Legislative Clearance Process

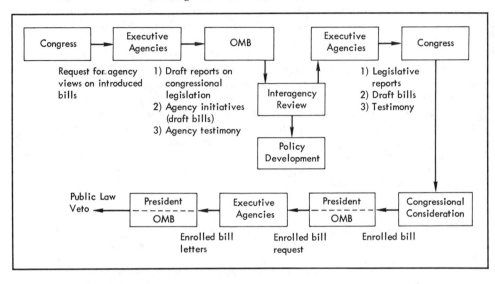

tions, the major government units are required to submit their budgets within the targets or envelope ceilings. Requests upon the discretionary reserve or policy reserve are considered.

Reagan

President Reagan advanced and strengthened the executive in terms of the budget process by adding a third important executive power. The first power was the pulling together of the agency budget requests and their organization into the President's budget recommendation. The second was the OMB legislative clearance process (see Exhibit 2-3), which covers agency legislative proposals, agency reports and testimony on pending legislation, and enrolled bills. OMB insures that proposals, reports, and testimony conform to presidential policy and coordinates agency recommendations on presidential vetoing of enrolled bills. The third power was added in 1981 by Executive Order 12291. All federal agencies which have proposed regulatory changes must send them to OMB for its clearance on regulatory budget and economic implications. This greatly strengthens OMB's influence, especially over entitlement programs.

A LEGISLATIVE FOCUS

The 1974 Budget Reform Motivations

The Congressional Budget and Impoundment Control Act of 1974 is one of the landmark pieces of budget reform legislation in this century. The law's passage is dramatically related to the events surrounding President

Nixon's resignation. The 1974 legislation created a unified congressional budget reform and it made the Congress a coequal branch with the executive on budgetary matters.

President Nixon and the Democrat-controlled Congress were constantly in battle. Nixon wished to decrease the role of government in society and Congress passed legislation seeking government action to redress various societal problems. Nixon had the advantage because it is much easier to redress various societal problems. Nixon had the advantage because it is much easier to defeat programs than it is to initiate them. One tactic employed by President Nixon was to use the disputed presidential impoundment powers on a wide range of programs, including those he had vetoed with the veto being overridden. Another tactic was to stress that the Congress was acting in an irresponsible manner because of its piecemeal and uncoordinated approach to appropriations. As Herbert Jasper—an important actor in developing the legislation—pointed out, the Congress was most upset at Nixon's charge of reckless Congressional spending.

The Watergate crisis weakened President Nixon and strengthened the Congress. The 1974 Act was one of several reforms directed toward strengthening the legislative branch. The Congressional Research Service and the General Accounting Office were expanded. Various reforms were passed to improve the Congressional oversight activities. The important legislation was to achieve a unified Congressional budget approach and neutralize the presidential impoundment powers. There was a great deal of difficulty in drafting the Act because it affected the strength of some of the most powerful legislators in both the House and Senate. Congress was able to overcome its internal struggles and passed the legislation in 1974 so that it could deal more effectively with President Nixon.

The 1974 legislation should be viewed in the context of the historical tension between the executive and legislative branches built intentionally into our system of government. After the Jefferson administration, the purse strings were clearly controlled by Congress, but Congress itself fractionalized the power over the years. This was not particularly significant as the executive did not attempt to exercise leadership in this area. With the passage of the 1921 legislation and a series of strong presidents, the power of the executive greatly increased against a fractionalized Congress. With the 1974 legislation, Congress once again focused its purse string powers and could deal with a strong executive.

Unified Congressional Budget Reforms

The 1974 legislation made several changes. It created the new Senate and House Budget Committees, created a new Congressional Budget Office, required a current services budget, and required various reforms addressed to the presidential budget. The new Congressional committees' duties included drafting overall budget targets. They could prepare reconciliation bills between budget resolutions and appropriation bills. Also the new committees were intended to, and have, put pressure on Congress to meet established budget deadlines.

Linda Smith, a former House Budget Committee staffer, pointed out in *The Bureaucrat* that the concept of a unified budget approach to Congressional budgeting was challenged, but the process worked, at first. However, the unified approach has not resulted in a balanced, or even a nearly balanced, yearly federal budget. One hope was that the annual appropriation bills would be passed prior to the fiscal year in which they were to become effective. This has rarely occurred. The process has resulted in a comprehensive examination of the budget, but the comprehensive treatment has made it easier for single issue oriented groups to threaten the whole budget to further their policy aims.

The Congressional Budget Office (CBO) is a source of nonpartisan budget expertise for both chambers of Congress. The office is charged with presenting the Congress with respectable and viable alternatives on aggregate levels of spending and revenue. The office must also make cost estimates for proposed legislation reported to the floor and provide cost projections for all existing legislation. The Act requires CBO to prepare an annual report covering "national budget priorities" and "alternative ways of allocating budget authority and budget outlays." One last important duty is to keep score on administration and Congressional actions related to the budget. See Exhibit 2-4 for a complete list of responsibilities.

The CBO has proven to be a successful policy aid to the Congress. Its economic forecasts have proven to be more accurate than those produced by executive branch agencies. The scorekeeping reports have proven particularly useful. CBO is not the Congressional counterpart to the executive branch OMB. That type of power rests with the budget and appropriation committees. CBO provides essential information so that the Congress knows the fiscal implications of various proposals and can act in a deliberate manner on fiscal policy matters.

Another innovation of the 1974 legislation was to require a "current services budget." In judging budget requests, normally reference is made to how much money was requested or spent for the same item in last year's budget. This is useful information, but it is still difficult to assert what exactly is the change in the budget. Last year's expenditures do not reflect accurately how much the program will cost in the budget year, given a maintenance of current services. To get that information, Congress has required the executive branch to prepare a current service budget. Some argue that the effort involved is not justified, given the small analytical advantage over merely using last year's expenditures. This still remains an open question.

The 1974 Act changed some of the previous requirements in the presidential budget development. The president's budget is still due in mid-January but the detailed backup information supplied by the agencies is due with the presidential budget. Given the president's normal habit of delaying decision until the budget is distributed, and given the time needed to prepare the agency backup material, this requirement is unrealistic, but it does accelerate the agency submissions by several weeks. This earlier information is made available to CBO, the Budget Committees, and the Ap-

EXHIBIT 2-4   CBO Responsibilities

Budgetary Estimates

Scorekeeping.   Each spring, the Congress formulates and adopts a concurrent resolution on the budget, setting expenditure and revenue targets for the fiscal year to begin on the coming October 1. In September, the Congress reviews the detailed spending and taxing decisions it had made during the summer in the form of individual bills. It then arrives at and adopts a second concurrent resolution, reconfirming or changing the totals in the spring resolution. While the first resolution sets targets, the second establishes an actual ceiling for spending and a floor for revenues. CBO keeps score of Congressional action on individual bills, comparing them against targets or ceilings in the concurrent resolutions. The Office issues periodic reports showing the status of Congressional action.

Cost Estimates.   Four types of cost estimates are required of CBO by the Budget Act.

CBO prepares, to the extent practicable, a five-year estimate for what it would cost to carry out any public bill or resolution reported by Congressional committees (except the two appropriating committees).

CBO furnishes to a reporting committee a report on each committee bill providing new budget authority. Each report shows: (a) a comparison of the bill with the most recent concurrent resolution, (b) a five-year projection of outlays associated with the bill, and (c) the amount of new budget authority and resulting outlays provided for state and local governments.

CBO also furnishes to a reporting committee an analysis of each bill providing new or increased tax expenditures. The reports cover: (a) an assessment of how the bill will affect levels of tax expenditures most recently detailed in a concurrent resolution, and (b) a five-year projection of the tax expenditures resulting from the bill.

As soon as practicable after the beginning of each fiscal year, CBO prepares a report that analyzes the five-year costs of continuing current federal spending and taxing policies as set forth in the second concurrent resolution. The purpose of these projections is to provide a neutral baseline against which the Congress can consider potential changes as it examines the budget for the upcoming fiscal years.

Fiscal and Programmatic Analysis

Fiscal Analysis.   The federal budget both affects and is affected by the national economy. The Congress thus must consider the Federal budget in the context of the current and projected state of the economy. To provide a framework for such considerations, CBO prepares periodic analyses and forecasts of economic trends. It also prepares analyses of alternative fiscal policies.

Inflation Analysis.   Beginning in 1979, CBO prepared estimates of the inflationary effect of major legislative proposals and, more generally, identifies and analyzes the causes of inflation. These estimates are intended to provide the Congress

(continued)

EXHIBIT 2-4 *(continued)*

with guidelines, as it undertakes new programs, of the cost in terms of inflation that these programs might entail.

Program and Policy Analysis. CBO undertakes analyses of programmatic or policy issues that affect the federal budget. These reports include an examination of alternative approaches to current policy; all reports are nonpartisan in nature. These reports are undertaken at the request of: (1) the chairman of the committee or subcommittee of jurisdiction of either the House or the Senate; (2) the ranking minority member of a committee of jurisdiction of either the House or the Senate; or (3) the chairman of a Task Force of the House Budget Committee.

Annual Report on Budget Options. By April 1 of each year, CBO furnishes to the House and Senate Committees on the Budget a report that combines many aspects of the functions outlined above. The annual report presents a discussion of alternative spending and revenue levels, levels of tax expenditures under existing law, and alternative allocations among major programs and functional categories.

CBO's analyses usually take the form of published studies comparing present policies and programs with alternative approaches. The responsibilities of CBO are (1) budgetary estimates, and (2) fiscal and programmatic analysis.

Source: 21.S. Congressional Budget Office, 1982.

propriations Committees, thus providing them with more time to conduct essential analyses. The Act also stipulates that the following data is required:

1. a list of existing tax expenditures, including revenue lost through preferential tax treatment and proposed changes;
2. funding projections on all *new* legislative proposals of the president;
3. budget figures presented in terms of national needs, agency missions, and basic federal programs;
4. five-year projections of expected spending; and
5. requested authorizations (procedures for obligation including ceilings) for legislation a year in advance of appropriation (budget year specific guidance on obligations and expenditures) legislation.

The required data in the 1974 legislation reflected a thorough knowledge of the budget process. By requiring a list of tax expenditures and projecting funding of new added legislation, presidential surprises can be minimized. The requirement that budget figures must be presented by national need, agency mission, and basic federal programs permits the Congressional analysts to conduct program analyses. The timing for authorization is essential to prevent preferential treatment of new presidential legislation rather than the desired Congressional comprehensive and unified approach to the budget.

The drafters of the legislation carefully designed budget procedures and timing to insure a unified appropriations consideration (see Exhibit 2-5). The final action on appropriations is prohibited until after the budget committee action. Not one of the thirteen appropriations bills can be considered until all have been marked up in committee. A deadline is established on final action for the appropriation bills. The deadlines and other requirements establish clear Congressional standards for responsible committee action, and the budget committee chairpersons have not been reluctant to use that standard in prodding Congressmen and Senators. There is a two-stage budget reconciliation: The first stage sets initial targets by resolution; the second stage permits reconsiderations and face saving. The use of House and Senate resolutions places a heavy burden on both the Appropriations and Ways and Means Committees to act within the consolidated-unified approach or appear irresponsible. In the House, the Budget Committee uses an interlocking directorate with the other key powerful committees in order to facilitate consensus. Finally, the 1974 legislation guarantees a unified approach by calling for a reconciliation bill on all spending and revenue measures with the second concurrent resolution.

The Congressional budget reform also changed the federal fiscal year from July 1 through June 30 to October 1 through September 30. This was realistic. The Congress always had difficulty approving a budget by the beginning of the July 1 fiscal year and the new reforms anticipated even more

EXHIBIT 2-5   Budget Timetable

Late January: President submits budget (15 days after Congress convenes).

March 15: All legislative committees submit program estimates and reviews to Budget committees.

April 15: Budget committees report first resolution.

May 15: Committees must report authorization bills by this date.

May 15: Congress completes action on first resolution. Before adoption of the first resolution, neither house may consider new budget authority or spending authority bills, revenue changes, or debt limit changes.

May 15 through the seventh day after Labor Day: Congress completes action on all budget and spending authority bills.

Sept. 15: Congress completes action on second resolution. Thereafter, neither house may consider any bill, amendment, or conference report that results in an increase over outlay or budget authority figures, or a reduction in revenues, beyond the amounts in the second resolution.

Sept. 25: Congress completes action on reconciliation bill or another resolution. Congess may not adjourn until it completes action on the second resolution and reconciliation measure, if any.

Oct. 1: Fiscal year begins.

Source: 21.S. Congressional Budget Office, 1982.

Congressional deliberation. Everyone agreed that public management would be improved if Congress were timely in its passage of appropriations, so the fiscal year had to change. Exhibit 2-6 is a summary of the federal budget process.

Backdoor Spending

One of the concerns of the advocates of the 1974 reform was the use of backdoor spending (the commitment of federal funds outside the effective control of the appropriation process). Reformers argued that backdoor spending is contrary to the concept of a unified consolidated Congressional budget because some activities cannot be balanced against the competing claims of other activities. The 1974 legislation outlaws or tries to control backdoor spending, with some major exceptions. The major exceptions were necessary or the legislation would not have passed.

There are various forms of backdoor spending. One is permanent appropriations, by which the program is allowed to spend whatever is necessary. This blank check is theoretically possible but is not found in practice. Another is contract authority, by which government officials can obligate the government through legal contracts and Congress must pass subsequent appropriations to fulfill the obligation. Borrowing authority is similar except the government official can borrow money and the Congress must pass subsequent appropriations to liquidate the debt. Yet another method is mandatory for entitlement spending, such as unemployment compensation, welfare, food stamps, payment on the national debt, veterans' benefits, and so on. The payment levels are established by programmatic rules set down in legislation and administrative regulation. If there is a recession, the government will *automatically* pay more in unemployment compensation, welfare, and food stamps, and the Congress must pay appropriations to fulfill the obligation. Earmarked revenue is considered by some to be backdoor spending because funds from a specific source (e.g., gasoline tax) can be spent only for a specific activity (e.g., highways). This earmarking prevents a unified consolidated consideration of the budget. Use of the unexpended balance (i.e., money appropriated but not spent in the last fiscal year) by carrying it over to the budget year is also contrary to the unified approach, but it is allowed in many programs.

The backdoor spending exceptions cover about 75 percent of each year's budget. The 1974 prohibition applies only to *new* contract authority, budget authority, and entitlement programs. Other major exceptions are as follows:

1. all Social Security trust fund programs;
2. all trust funds that receive 90 percent or more from designated taxes rather than from the general revenue (e.g., highways);
3. general revenue sharing;
4. insured or guaranteed loans;
5. federal or independent public corporations; and
6. gifts to the government.

THE FEDERAL BUDGET PROCESS

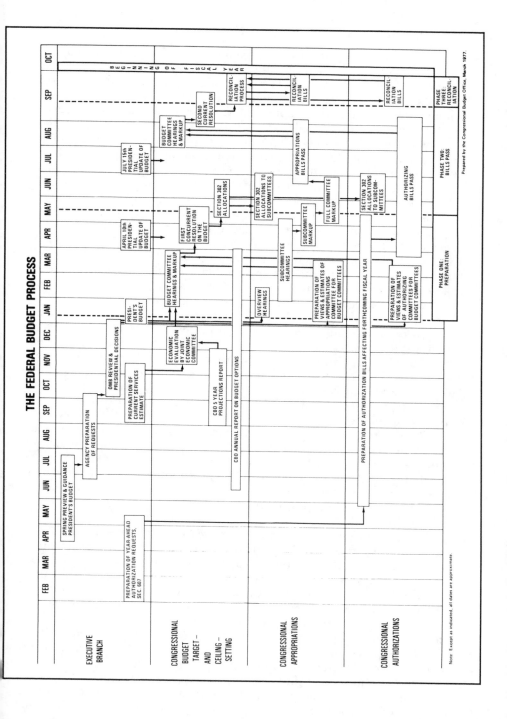

Note: Except as indicated, all dates are approximate.

Prepared by the Congressional Budget Office, March 1977.

61

Impoundment

As was pointed out earlier, the extensive use of impoundment by President Nixon was quite upsetting to the Congress. Nixon impounded large sums of money because he did not favor the programs which Congress had enacted and funded. The impoundment was not used because the executive branch found it could accomplish the Congressionally mandated purpose with less money. It was used because it was a type of veto which could not be overridden by Congress. Interestingly, in some cases the Nixon administration impounded funds for programs which had been preserved by the Congress only by overriding a presidential veto. Congress felt that Nixon violated the spirit if not the letter of the Constitution.

The judicial branch concurred with the majority of Congress. In every instance that someone took the expense and time to battle the Nixon administration on impoundment, the president lost and was forced to spend the money. Court challenges take months and often years, so the delay tended to *de facto* establish the impoundment. The program administration was crippled by this executive-judicial decision-making process because of the extreme delays.

The 1974 legislation redefined the impoundment powers. The Congress and the courts pointed out that neither the Constitution nor the law granted the president the impoundment power. The executive branch argued that ample precedent existed over the many years of the nation's history. Congress recognized the best solution was to redefine the impoundment powers so that the president could not cripple a program regardless of the true validity of the impoundment powers. Congress pragmatically wanted to prevent a president from overruling the will of Congress on government spending issues.

Today there are two types of impoundments, each handled somewhat differently. If the impoundment is to defer the spending appropriated by Congress, then *either* the House *or* the Senate can force the release of funds by passing a resolution calling for their expenditure. If the impoundment is to cut or rescind the appropriations, then *both* House *and* Senate must pass recision resolutions within 45 days of the recision or it is not valid.

The deferral type of impoundment has been challenged successfully on constitutional grounds. In *Immigration and Naturalization Service v. Chadha*, the Supreme Court struck down the one-house legislative veto as unconstitutional. Thus, the implication is that there was no way to overturn presidential deferrals except by passing a law which the president could then veto. This left the president with a *de facto* line-item veto. At first the Reagan administration did not attempt to use this apparent advantage, but it was eventually employed. Not surprisingly, the reaction was a legal suit. The plaintiffs argued that the Congress had never intended to give the president the deferral power that resulted from the Chadha case. At the district level, the federal courts agreed and found in favor of the plaintiffs.

One technical problem in writing the 1974 law was how to deal with a president who might not inform the Congress of an impoundment. The threshold of trust between the Congress and the president was at a low ebb in 1974. The legislation required the president to send a message to Congress requesting impoundment and setting forth the rationale for it. The legislation then stated that if the president did not comply with the law, then the comptroller general (a Congressional branch employee) would report the impoundment to the Congress. If the president did not comply, the comptroller general was directed to go to the courts to get a court order forcing compliance.

The ultimate strategy involved is complex. The Constitution provides for a means to impeach the president and requires the president to execute faithfully the laws of the nation. If the courts rule against the president after the new procedure has been applied faithfully, then the president has an extremely weak defense against the argument that he refuses to execute the law faithfully. Under the procedure, both the Congress and judicial branch would have said he must comply. The Congress would be in an excellent position to impeach the president under such circumstances.

The first minor test of the impoundment process occurred in the Ford administration. The president did send the required impoundment messages to Congress and did comply with the will of Congress except for one situation. On April 15, 1975, the comptroller general of the United States filed a lawsuit in U.S. District Court for the District of Columbia. Named as defendants in the suit were Gerald Ford, president of the United States, James T. Lynn, director of the Office of Management and Budget, and Carla A. Hills, secretary of Housing and Urban Development.

The new legislation was being tested. On October 4, 1974, President Ford transmitted his impoundment messages, including the deferment of approximately $264 million in contract authority for the section 235 housing program, but the legislation was due to lapse on August 22, 1975. The comptroller general reasoned that this would permit only 52 days to obligate the money, thus it was a *de facto* recision, and under the law the comptroller general reported the error in a formal message to Congress. This meant that Congress had 45 days to act or the money had to be spent; it did not act, nor did the president release the funds. The comptroller general then notified Congress of his intention to bring a lawsuit and the Senate passed a resolution in support of the comptroller general. The Ford administration challenged the 1974 legislation on the grounds that (1) the comptroller general was improperly carrying out an executive function by instituting the lawsuit, and (2) the Constitution provided means other than the courts for resolving disputes between the branches of government. The legal arguments continued, but the case came to an abrupt end without a court resolution. On October 17, 1975, Carla Hills announced that the section 235 program would be reactivated and there was no longer a need for the suit. The Congress had won.

Reconciliation

The major architect of the 1974 Budget Act, Richard Bolling, was surprised by the ploy that was tried in the Congress by the Republicans and the conservative Democrats (called "Boll Weevils") soon after President Reagan took office. Although the reconciliation provision of the 1974 Act clearly says that a concurrent resolution on the budget may "determine and recommend changes in laws, bills, and resolutions . . . ," the Democratic Congressional leadership had carefully avoided serious confrontation with their powerful committee chairmen. With Ronald Reagan's election in 1980, the Republicans not only captured control of the White House and the Senate, but also gained a working majority in the House of Representatives by joining forces with Democratic conservatives. President Reagan and his aides worked with their Congressional allies to use effectively the reconciliation power stated in the 1974 Act but not previously used.

The confrontation and its success were a surprise to the House leadership, as illustrated in Exhibit 2-7. The Republican-controlled Senate concurred with President Reagan's budget suggestions (e.g., increased national defense, reduced taxes, and a huge cut in domestic spending). It passed the necessary instructions to other committees in its first concurrent budget resolution. The real confrontation occurred in the House, where the Democratic budget resolution was dramatically overturned on the House floor by a Republican/Boll Weevil coalition which supported the president's views. This monumental budget resolution, called Gramm-Latta I, contained instructions for budget reductions in fifteen House committees and fourteen Senate committees, required very large outlay reductions (i.e., of $56 billion), and provided reconciliation saving of discretionary and entitlement programs. The Congressional committees responded as called for by the 1974 Act, but the result was unacceptable. The next ploy was a quickly fashioned, massive reconciliation bill called Gramm-Latta II. This extraordinary law (see Exhibit 2-8) changed eligibility rules for entitlement programs (e.g., food stamps), limited programs earlier authorized, and rewrote major parts of substantive law. No hearings were held on the law; amendment possibilities were strictly limited; debate lasted only two days; and the law was passed in a single vote rather than a section-by-section vote. Speaker O'Neill's reactions are not surprising. Reconciliation was clearly demonstrated to be a powerful budget tool.

EXHIBIT 2-7   House Speaker Thomas P. O'Neill, June 25, 1981

I have never seen anything like this in my life, to be perfectly truthful. What is the authority for this? Does this mean that any time the President of the United States is interested in a piece of legislation, he merely sends it over? You do not have any regard for the process, for open hearings, discussions as to who it affects, or what it does to the economy? But because a man, who does not understand or know how our process, sends it over, are we to take it in bulk? . . . Do we have the right to legislate? Do we have the right to meet our target or can he in one package deregulate, delegislate, the things that have taken years to do?

Source: Congressional Record, June 25, 1981, #3383–85.

EXHIBIT 2-8   Final Reconciliation Savings

The final version of the reconciliation package (HR 3982) altered existing programs to achieve the following budget savings (by House committee jurisdiction, in millions of dollars).

Committee	FISCAL 1982 BUDGET AUTHORITY CUTS	FISCAL 1982 OUTLAY CUTS	FISCAL 1983 BUDGET AUTHORITY CUTS	FISCAL 1983 OUTLAY CUTS	FISCAL 1984 BUDGET AUTHORITY CUTS	FISCAL 1984 OUTLAY CUTS
Agriculture	$ 2,449	$ 3,264	$ 3,042	$ 3,878	$ 3,930	$ 4,661
Armed Services	846	882	767	731	374	374
Banking, Finance and Urban Affairs	13,566	481	15,954	1,154	18,402	2,115
District of Columbia	39	40	56	58	72	69
Education and Labor	10,088	7,297	12,414	10,749	14,261	13,881
Energy and Commerce	7,955	7,115	7,457	7,710	6,686	6,961
Foreign Affairs	376	286	524	463	538	515
Interior and Insular Affairs	820	736	+236[1]	111	68	5
Judiciary	72	30	70	71	59	66
Merchant Marine and Fisheries	242	106	242	212	265	253
Post Office and Civil Service	4,706	5,163	6,253	6,690	7,214	7,555
Public Works and Transportation	6,606	1,411	5,070	3,136	6,371	5,418
Science and Technology	1,395	828	961	1,016	1,209	1,065
Small Business	504	823	540	517	527	506
Veterans' Affairs	110	116	122	127	124	128
Ways and Means	4,140	8,981	4,455	9,822	4,763	10,803
Total Cuts[2]	$51,900	$35,190	$55,734	$44,033	$61,721	$51,353

[1]Increase in budget authority attributable to an increase in the cap on Interior Department funding; conferees' elimination of a provision to increase the price of government uranium enrichment services; and increased funding for the Naval Petroleum Reserve, requested by the administration.

[2]Adjusted for jurisdictional overlap.

65

The future effective use of the reconciliation process is open to question. President Reagan was much less successful in his second term using that process. A precedent has been established for its sweeping use to write comprehensive legislation by a coalition of key legislators in cooperation with the president. However, such enactments of law are antithetical to the traditional process of slow deliberation by the committees of Congress. The use of the reconciliation process will largely depend on the voting blocks and political skill of a president and the Congressional leadership.

Sunset Legislation

In many states and in the federal government, sunset legislation is being considered and implemented. The sunset concept is that government programs should automatically expire unless positive action is taken to renew them every few years. The form of the legislation varies. In most instances, the sunset provisions permit the program to remain on the law books but the authorization for funds expires. In other words, the program technically exists but no money can be spent on the program unless the legislature reenacts the authorization section of the law. The cycle for renewal varies, but often a staggered five-year cycle is used.

The states of Colorado and Florida have taken the lead in sunset legislation. Colorado was the first state to enact major sunset legislation, but it is limited to the state's regulatory agencies. In June 1976, Florida also passed sunset legislation directed toward regulatory agencies, but it set termination dates for both the agencies and substantive laws.

The federal government considered enacting sunset legislation. In fact, many authorization bills were approved with sunset provisions in them. Comprehensive sunset legislation has not passed the Congress. In sunset legislation, the termination schedule is staggered so that programs within a budget function can be reviewed at the same time. Some programs are exempt, such as interest payments on the national debt, retirement, health care, and disability programs. The review process is controlled on a day to day basis so that Congress can decide the form, scope, and time allotted for each review appropriate for the subject.

Sunset legislation is misleading. The title and the first explanation lead people to believe that there will be wholesale terminations of government programs. This is unlikely. If there is a strong enough reason to create and fund a program, then there is strong enough reason to reenact the authorization section of the legislation. Some programs will expire, but not on a wholesale basis. The legislation will mean a great deal more paperwork addressed to justifying programs, and, potentially, to a situation in which Congress may not be able to handle the generated volume of justifications.

Gramm-Rudman-Hollings

The Gramm-Rudman-Hollings Act (also called the Balanced Budget Act of 1985) has been somewhat effective, but it is fundamentally flawed. The act addresses the federal deficit problem by requiring that it be reduced by $36 billion a year until it vanishes in 1991. This is to be done by the following:

1. setting yearly total deficit targets;
2. using an across-the-board sequestration process if the Congress does not meet the yearly targets; and
3. tightening up on the procedural rules related to the budget process.

The Act ran into immediate difficulty with a question about its constitutionality. A court case brought by Alan Morrison (a Ralph Nader lawyer) and Representative Mike Synar (D-Oklahoma) questioned the constitutionality of the new law. The Supreme Court ruled that assigning an executive function to the Comptroller General (a legislative official) violated the separation of powers concept of the Constitution. This left the law operative but significantly weakened. In 1986, the law was amended to remedy the Supreme Court objection by assigning this executive function to the Office of Management and Budget—an office already reporting to the President.

If there is a deficit beyond the limits set in the legislation, Congress has 45 days to accomplish the necessary reduction of spending, the necessary increase in taxes, or both. If it fails to act, or acts but cannot overcome a presidential veto of its decision, then the law requires automatic spending reductions to take place following a formula written into the law. The formula calls for an across-the-board cut, with major exemptions for debt service and social security. Thus, both domestic and military programs would be cut in an arbitrary manner. Of course this procedure is established in law, and Congress could void the whole process by amending the law at any time. However, there is the threat of a presidential veto that would prevent Congress from passing an amendment. The across-the-board cuts with their harsh or foolish implications are the threat in a legally established game of "chicken" between Congress and the President. Such threats do not always work.

The revisions to Congressional procedure related to the budget seem to be resulting in greater Congressional budget discipline, particularly in the Senate. A Senate rule says that any legislation, amendment, or budget resolution is out of order if it would breach the Balanced Budget Act's deficit ceiling. Thus, to add money over the ceiling is almost impossible because any Senator could kill it by merely raising a point of order. Under the rule, the only way a program can get more money is for the proponent of additional funding to also propose cutbacks equal to or greater than the additions. This rule is only applicable if the yearly figures are over the ceiling, but Congress tends to work right up to or even over the deficit ceiling.

The result of the new procedural rules is that Congressional budgeting decisions are a zero-sum game. If a congressman wishes to suggest additional appropriations, the suggestion must include specific suggestions for cuts equal to or exceeding the extra appropriation amount. This discourages action because additional political enemies are made when cuts are proposed. Politically, achieving support for more money and specific cutbacks is very difficult. Thus, there is a whole new way that budgets are decided upon in the Senate. Budget committees now have more leverage, and more budget discipline exists in Congress. Supplemental appropriation bills, in particular, have become more difficult to pass as they must also be deficit neutral.

On the surface, the Balanced Budget Act seems sound, but it is fundamentally flawed. The act is based on the assumption that it will take a budget reduction of $36 billion a year until the deficit is eliminated in 1991. The act is based on assumed projections of the deficit and not on reality; these important assumptions bring us to an unfortunate, but likely, chain of events. The most noted fact about federal budget and deficit forecasting is that it is always wrong and often significantly wrong. Unfortunately, forecasts are always wrong by underestimating the yearly budget deficit. Traditionally, the OMB estimate is off more than the CBO estimate. If the economy makes unforeseen shifts, the projections are off not in the magnitude of $32 billion but as high as $95 or more billion. As the time for final budget decisions draws near, Congress and the president can normally manipulate enough to find $10 billion without significantly altering policy. When the numbers reach the level of $32 billion or higher, then difficult budget-cutting decisions must be made or the across-the-board cuts come into effect.

At some point, the real deficit and the target deficit assumptions in the Act will not only be different, but also the real numbers will be significantly higher. The only way to remedy the problem will be to rewrite the law with a mechanism to update the deficit targets that were not placed in the original law. Congress will then start an annual charade of updating the targets, much like the annual games played to update the limit placed on the national debt. Much is said at that annual "ceremony" of the debt ceiling, but, realistically, Congress must raise the debt limit because there is no other choice. In all likelihood, a parallel "ceremony" will exist on raising the deficit ceilings.

This divergence from reality and the Congressional use of fiction has already begun. The forecasting agencies of OMB and CBO cling to an optimistic view of economic growth. Given that such a view makes it easier to meet the immediate deficit ceilings of this year's budget, such optimistic forecasting is not surprising. However, when reality proves the forecasters wrong, then the next year's deficit ceiling becomes politically impossible to meet. Something would have to give and the most likely candidate would be the ceilings in the Balanced Budget Act. The brutality of large across-the-board cuts makes that option practically and politically impossible.

Federal Budgetary Madness

Clearly, the current federal budget process is widely considered to be inadequate. In a 1983 article, this author questioned the process and made specific recommendations for significant change.[2] Naomi Caiden called for

---

[2]Thomas D. Lynch, "Federal Budgetary Madness," *Society*, 20, 4 (May/June 1983), 27–32.

reform and described the current process as "preventing consistent policy making, and encouraging deadlocks, blackmail, and symbolic voting."[3] Thirty states have called for a constitutional convention to address an amendment that would mandate a balanced budget. The Congress's General Accounting Office has published a report, "Federal Budget Concepts and Procedures Can Be Further Strengthened,"[4] which calls for reform. Civil servants have called for reform (see Exhibit 2-9) and the National Capital Area Chapter of the American Society for Public Administration has called for reform (see Exhibit 2-10).

There should be continued interest in budget reform. High yearly deficit budget levels will exist unless politically difficult policy changes occur. The Reagan administration made commitments in the mid-1980s to defense which tended to obligate future administrations to larger defense spending. In addition, a significant political demand for increased domestic programs continues to exist. Thus, any president will find budget related decisions as well as the budget process itself politically difficult to handle. There will not only be pressure to enact new types of taxes but also strong views to not raise them. Without a major new revenue source, policy makers will have to say "No" to new programs or expanded programs. If an emergency occurs, then raising the national debt may be politically acceptable, but there will be strong political pressure to not raise the debt as was done in the Reagan years. This political tension will make the already faulted federal budget process an even more likely target for extensive reform.

Federal budget decision-making, as it is currently practiced, can be said to have the following characteristics: (1) it is concerned more with many special political interests to the disadvantage of the larger public interest, (2) it is fragmented—with little appreciation shown for the connection between programs and money, (3) key officials do not take the necessary time to familiarize themselves with budgets, (4) key officials are willing to accept less than the best from the process, and (5) key decision-making takes place in unreasonably and unrealistically short time frames.[5]

State and Local Challenges

Unlike the federal situation, state and local governments are passing balanced budgets and are improving their budget processes. Nevertheless, state and local governments have faced and will continue to face difficult budget challenges. Especially at the medium and small government level, more professional expertise is needed to meet the challenges of improved forecasting, capital financing, financial managing, and properly using the

[3]Naomi Caiden, "The Myth of the Annual Budget," *Public Administration Review,* 42, 6 (November/December 1982), 516–523.

[4]"Federal Budget Concepts and Procedures Can Be Further Strengthened" (PAD 81–36) (Washington, D.C.: U.S. General Accounting Office, 1981).

[5]Carl Grafton and Anne Permaloff, "Budgeting Reforms in Perspective," in Jack Rabin and Thomas D. Lynch, eds., *Handbook on Public Budgeting and Financial Management* (New York: Marcel Dekker, 1983), pp. 89–124.

EXHIBIT 2-9   Agenda for the Budget

1. Observations
   a. The budget is the primary management system, partly because it is the only action-forcing process. It can be expected to remain the chief arena for policy debate, program planning, and execution.
   b. Its six phases are often confused. They are: long-range planning based on analysis of program/policy issues; setting out concrete objectives and short-term goals; costing out resource allocation decisions; winning support of OMB, Congress, and the public; budget execution/monitoring effectiveness and controlling the pace; and program evaluation (which completes the circle and links to planning).
   c. Certain factors affect the current atmosphere: breakdown in trust and confidence between executive and legislative branches, sometimes for good reason; growth of congressional staff and consequent interstaff competition; growing influence of single issue interest groups; more congressional control; and too much yielding by executive agencies.
   d. The budget process is overextended, dysfunctional. It serves too many purposes; focuses on detail at the expense of thinking; takes too much time; frustrates and exhausts managers and political leadership. All recognize the need for a better way.
   e. The overcontrol and inflexibility in budget execution promotes waste through rigidities. The execution process often does not track plans well.
   f. Recommendations should: shift the focus to front-end analysis and planning; make room for time and energy for concentrating on the most important issues; stabilize the system and allow more certainty on the part of managers; and simplify the process and reduce workload while allowing the appropriate degree of control.
2. Major Recommendations
   a. Reemphasize the planning and analysis function at the presidential level.
      (1) One way of establishing a focus on planning is to change the name of OMB to the Office of Planning and Budgeting (which would be symbolic).
      (2) If focused on the future, OMB can be a valuable resource to any president as a source of dispassionate analysis and by virtue of its cross-cutting, interagency responsibilities.
      (3) OMB is now deteriorating. It has too many jobs to do, some inconsequential; too little staff; good people overwhelmed and burned out; is politically top-heavy; and seems to be in competition with, rather than complementary to, the White House staff.
      (4) Access to the president is the key, which might also be achieved by securing more management strength in OMB or by the establishment of a separate office in the executive establishment.
      (5) Establish a president's management agenda to function as a driving force.
   b. Allow more opportunity for analysis and planning by shifting to a two-year budget and appropriations cycle. It would allow:
      (1) more front-end loading (e.g., planning, learning about programs, opening up the process to affected groups before going into the budget stage, tying evaluation to planning);

(2) more time for OMB and congressional staff to think about programs, interact with agencies, and operate in a more relaxed manner;
(3) more stability and certainty for the executive and managerial staff;
(4) cutting down the problems in budget execution; and
(5) emphasizing the need for flexibilities and adjustments because of lead time in making estimates.

3. Other Recommendations
   a. Find better techniques for dealing with program cuts than the arbitrary, unthinking approaches so often used.
   b. Find better ways to work things out with congressional staff, as an alternative to earmarking funds.
   c. Reestablish programming flexibility.
      (1) The president should push for some governmentwide tolerance, such as five percent programming authority.
      (2) Give executives the leeway to move dollars to where they can be better used, as a means of reducing potential spending waste.

Source: The Bureaucrat, Fall 1981, p. 81. Used by permission.

computer in preparing and monitoring budgets. Even today many local governments do not have program budgets, and most do not use performance measures to judge the programs' effectiveness and efficiency. Many budget staffs are not able to conduct sophisticated budget and program analyses.

The professional challenges of budgeting and financial management are significant, as demonstrated by the illustrations in this book. However, budgeting is an activity which can be done with a minimum of professionalism. Thus, governments can "get by" with yearly balanced budgets. Unfortunately, the loser is government, the image of government, and the taxpayer, who receives fewer and poorer services for the tax dollar. A good budget and finance office will not solve all of government's problems, but more services and a higher quality of performance should be the results of such an office. If forecasting is improved, then idle cash will produce more revenue and disruptive financial emergency controls need not be used. If capital financing practices are good, then less interest will be paid on the government debt and more capital improvements will be possible for the same tax dollar. If creative financial management of enterprise funds is used, governments will have more revenue available at a time when taxpayers are hostile to tax increases. If budget and financial offices can make more effective use of the rapidly improving computer then time-consuming, routine "numbers crunching" can be replaced with more sophisticated analyses designed to improve the quality of government management. The professional challenges are exciting, but they will not easily be confronted and conquered. The highest levels of professionalism will be required.

The Government Finance Officer's Association (GFOA) has developed a local budget awards program which is having an impact on the quality of budgeting in local government. Governments voluntarily submit their annual budget document to GFOA. They send them to GFOA member reviewers who use evaluation criteria adopted by GFOA. If the government's bud-

EXHIBIT 2-10   NCAC Position on Budget Reform

1. Problems With the Current Budget System. The current Federal budget and financial management systems contain a number of problems which are having
   increasingly serious effects on Congress, Federal managers, recipients of Federal
   funds (including State and local governments and private sector contractors),
   and private financial markets. As a result, these problems are affecting not only
   the internal workings of the Federal government, but also the national economy
   and the general public. These problems can be described as follows:
   a. The detailed, iterative Congressional budget process has produced a cum-
      bersome, repetitive process which results in heavy workloads for both
      Congress and the Federal agencies. This process is based in current law,
      which requires Congress to go through an authorization and appropria-
      tion process, with statutory deadlines and requirements, every year. The
      resulting workload, in turn, produces:
      (1) a tremendous waste of Federal labor hours in the formulation, pres-
          entation, and implementation of sometimes three budgets a year;
      (2) inadequate time for Congressional policy setting and oversight;
      (3) delays in action on appropriations bills.
   b. The frequently delayed action on appropriation bills results either in con-
      tinuing resolutions or a shutdown of the Federal government. Both result
      in:
      (1) Uncertainty for program managers, causing program delays, disrup-
          tions and other inefficiencies, and reduced cost-effectiveness.
      (2) Funding disruptions cause instability and incoherence for recipients
          of Federal funds. These disruptions are especially harmful for capital
          outlays (such as highways and defense items), R & D and the planning
          processes of State and local governments.
   c. Both the workload and disruption problems increase the costs of oper-
      ating the government. Manpower costs are high and funding stretch-outs
      usually increase the total costs of contracts and grants. Relatedly, costs
      are increased by iterative annual authorizations, without overall funding
      commitments, for multiyear programs (e.g., capital outlays).
   d. The overwhelming amount of detail to be prepared by the agencies and
      reviewed by Congress prevents officials of both from concentrating on the
      larger policy issues. This situation results in:
      (1) an inadequate link at all levels between planning and budget for-
          mulation;
      (2) lack of adequate Congressional supervision.
   e. The vast number of Executive Branch financial management and other
      information tracking systems (planning, budget formulation, budget exe-
      cution, accounting, auditing, evaluation, MIS, etc.) increase the difficulty
      of program management by:
      (1) increasing managers' information overload;
      (2) being unable to provide adequate feedback to managers about de-
          cisions made by others, causing them to be "in the dark" about their
          own programs;
      (3) producing program-specific rather than policy-oriented information;
      (4) segmenting rather than integrating useful facets of information.
2. NCAC Objectives for Budget Reform
   a. To reduce the time and paperwork required in the budget process.

(1) To allow more time for policy making and planning and less time for detailed microbudgeting;
(2) To allow more time for Congressional oversight and evaluation;
(3) To minimize delays on appropriation bills.
b. To increase the stability of Federal activities and funding.
(1) To improve the efficiency of government procurement and program management;
(2) To provide consistency for projects and entities being funded.
c. To reduce unnecessary Federal operating and funding expenses.
d. To increase the policy and planning role and capability of Congress and of agency officials.
(1) By improving the link between policy and budget formulation;
(2) By moving from specific manpower planning to general workforce planning.
e. To streamline and integrate the Federal financial management and related information tracking systems.
(1) To provide better feedback to managers;
(2) To enhance oversight and program review.

Source: National Capital Area Chapter, American Society for Public Administration. Newsletter. February 1983. Used by permission.

get document is given a passing grade, then the government budget office will get an award from GFOA, which the local government normally places in next year's budget document. The process has been sufficiently rigorous and the comments constructive enough to influence the profession. This peer group review process is upgrading the local budget processes.

REVIEW QUESTIONS

1. The roots of the executive/legislative struggle go back as far as 1215, but the struggle greatly influences how budgeting is done in the United States today. Explain those roots and how that struggle helps us understand modern budgeting. In what ways do we see that struggle taking place in modern budgeting?

2. Compare and contrast the rationalist approaches to budgeting (e.g., PPB, MBO, and ZBB) with the incrementalist approaches. Explain how the role of analysis varies—if it does—in each approach.

3. Compare and contrast line-item budgeting, program budgeting, and performance budgeting.

4. Explain the 1974 Congressional budget reforms. What was meant to be accomplished and what means were devised to accomplish those ends?

5. The current federal budget process is said to be inadequate. Why? What reforms could help resolve the identified problems?

6. The professional challenges of state and local budgeting are significant. What are those challenges? What should be done by professionals to meet those challenges?

REFERENCES

Advisory Commission on Intergovernmental Relations. *ACIR State Legislative Program*. Vol. 4. *Fiscal and Personnel Management*. Washington, D.C.: Government Printing Office, November 1975.

ALYANDARY-ALEXANDER, MAND (ed.). *Analysis for Planning, Programming and Budgeting: Proceedings of the Social Cost-Effectiveness Symposium*. Washington, D.C.: Washington Operation Research Council, 1968.

ASPIN, LES. "The Defense Budget and Foreign Policy: The Role of Congress," *Daedalus* (Summer 1975), 155–74.

BAKKER, OEGE. *The Budget Cycle in Public Finance in the United States*. The Hague: W. P. Van Stockum, 1953.

BARTIZAL, JOHN R. *Budget Principle and Procedure*. Englewood Cliffs, N.J.: Prentice-Hall, 1942.

BEAUMONT, ENID. "The New York Case from a Public Administration Perspective," *The Bureaucrats*, 5, 1 (April 1976), 101–12.

BEKER, JEROME. "Measuring Cost Effectiveness in Human Services," *Canadian Welfare*, 51, 1 (January/February 1975), 5–6.

BENSON, GEORGE et al. (eds.). *The American Property Tax: Its History, Administration and Economic Impact*. Clairmont, Calif.: Institute for Studies in Federalism, Clairmont Men's College, 1965.

BLACK, GUY. "Externalities and Structure in PPB," *Public Administration Review*, 31, 6 (November/December 1971), 637–43.

BREAK, GEORGE F. *Agenda for Local Tax Reform*. Berkeley: Institute of Government Studies, University of California, 1970.

BRUNDAGE, PERCIVAL HACK. *The Bureau of the Budget*. New York: Holt, Rinehart & Winston, 1970.

BUCK, A. E. "Performance Budgeting for the Federal Government," *Tax Review* (July 1949).

GOOD, DAVID. "Envelope Budgeting: The Canadian Experience." Paper prepared for the 1983 Annual American Society for Public Administration National Conference, New York, April 17, 1983.

HARTMAN, ROBERT W. "Congress and Budget-Making," *Political Science Quarterly* 97, 3 (Fall 1982), 381–402.

LELOUP, LANCE T. "After the Blitz: Reagan and the Congressional Budget Process." Paper presented at the Southern Political Science Association Meeting, Memphis, Tenn., November 5–7, 1981.

RABIN, JACK and THOMAS D. LYNCH (eds.) *Handbook on Budgeting and Financial Management*, New York: Marcel Dekker, 1983.

WENZ, THOMAS W. and ANN P. NOLAN. "Budgeting for the Future: Target Base Budgeting," *Public Budgeting and Finance*, 2, 2 (Summer 1982), 88–91.

chapter 3

BUDGET BEHAVIOR

Public budgeting is done by human beings and one can understand a great deal about budgeting by examining the factors which influence human behavior within this special context. This chapter first examines how the key actors in the budget process interact. The next major topic is an in-depth examination of the agency budget office and the perspectives associated with the office. The final major topic is a careful examination of the strategies associated with the game of budgeting. This chapter examines:

1. the political influence patterns among the key actors in the budget process;
2. means commonly used to cultivate an active clientele;
3. the duties of an agency budget office;
4. the perspective of a budget officer and typical behavioral patterns;
5. four common philosophic attitudes of budget officers toward the budget process;
6. explanation of how confidence in the budget officer is developed;
7. the significance of program results in budgeting;
8. the preparation process for hearings;
9. the review setting;
10. spender's strategies;
11. cutter's strategies;
12. strategies to support new programs; and
13. some important cautions in public budgeting.

POLITICS AND PERSPECTIVE

Four Institutional Roles

Public budgeting can be understood in terms of four institutional roles. Each has a definable behavior. Exhibit 3-1 shows the interrelationship among the groups.

EXHIBIT 3-1   Interrelationships of Institutional Roles in Public Budgeting

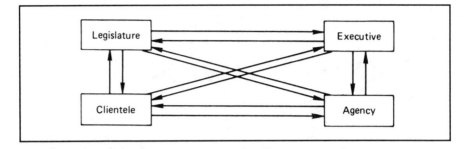

The four institutional roles are the agency, the executive, the legislature, and the clientele. Two other groups, the courts and the media, are significant, but are not discussed here because their influence patterns are unusual. Discussion of their influence is outside the scope of this text. The agency is the institution with the responsibility for managing the programs and preparing the initial budget. The executive is loosely defined here to mean the chief executive, his or her staff, and the central budget office. (The department, of which the agency is a part, plays an odd role, sometimes acting as an extension of the executive but often acting as superagency, depending on the stage of the budget process.) The legislature is the legislative branch of government, such as the Congress in the federal government. The clientele is a group affected by the agency's programs and it takes an active interest in the agency's policy.

The double lines in Exhibit 3-1 represent several two-way influence patterns. The agency influences the executive through its budget request and the executive's budget decision is one form of executive influence on the agency. The executive influences the legislature through its executive budget requests, and the passage of laws is one form of influence upon the executive. The agency's programs by definition affect its clientele. Clientele groups are well known for their lobbying (influencing) activity on legislators, but they also lobby and influence the chief executive and the agency. Less well known is that legislatures and executives can influence clientele groups directly. To make matters more complex, an influence pattern may involve more than two groups. For example, a clientele group influences Congress on appropriation legislation which ultimately becomes law and then the agency is influenced by the language of that appropriation legislation.

A case study involving the U.S. Maritime Administration illustrates the influence patterns. In the Nixon administration, there was a strong desire at the highest levels in the U.S. Office of Management and Budget to phase out the operating and ship-building subsidies at an accelerated rate. OMB required the Maritime Administration to launch an analytical study of exactly how this was to be accomplished. Somehow, Mrs. Sullivan, who headed the House Appropriation subcommittee, discovered the OMB study. She was extremely upset that OMB wished to change policy clearly established in the law and phoned OMB Director Mayo. The substance of that conversation was not recorded, but the director withdrew the request for the study. This series of events illustrates the influence of the central budget office on an agency as well as the strength of a single legislator on a central budget office.

Clientele influence on agencies is not fully appreciated. In *Policy Analysis for Public Policymaking*, this author presented several case studies involving the budget process in the U.S. Department of Transportation. In February 1970, the Office of Management and Budget called for a special analytical study by the Urban Mass Transportation Administration of that agency's policy guidance for capital grants reflected in the published *Information to Applicants*. In time, the study and a revised *Information to Applicants* was prepared. Before it became official, a letter was formally sent (as required by OMB Circular A-85) to inform state and local government associations of the proposed new guidelines. The Circular A-85 standard OMB guidance requires an agency-to-clientele interrelationship prior to the time that the final government policy becomes effective.

In this instance, representatives of the transit industry and the cities were taken by surprise. They took strong exception to the "unrealistic data demands and planning analyses" that would be imposed. They felt that DOT committed a breach of faith because there was no informal consultation prior to sending the official notification. They reacted by developing a counterstrategy—they met with agency officials and tried to soften the most undesirable aspects of the new selection criteria. The agency officials felt that they came close to the clientele's feeling while keeping within the strict OMB policy prescriptives. This case illustrates the infrequently documented influence of a clientele group on an agency.

Legislative groups and chief executives can directly influence clientele groups. The most noticed such influence is at the large conventions of these groups when high-ranking legislators or executives address the members. Less publicized meetings occur when legislative and executive officials request cooperation or seek lobbying support for key legislation.

End runs and finesses do occur in this complex four-way relationship. For example, an agency can influence its clientele group by pointing out the implications of existing proposed policy. The clientele group can then go to either the legislature or the executive to kill the proposed policy. A more complex situation would be when the agency has to proceed with some action (e.g., conserve energy) which its clientele group may find distasteful. The agency might be able to counter likely pressure by having the chief executive lobby the clientele group and the legislature. This would strengthen the chances of success for the agency by minimizing clientele resistance.

In the budget process, the agency-to-clientele-to-legislature triangular relationship is a common pattern. The more sophisticated clientele groups recognize that the size of the budget and the individual programs are significant. In many cases, an informal communication network exists between the agency and the clientele group. Any formal, publicly available information is monitored, analyzed, and communicated to clientele members. Sometimes active campaigns are launched to build a strong lobbying presence for particular budget issues of importance to the clientele. State and local patterns normally are not as complex as those found on the federal level. However, large state and local governments have patterns more similar to the federal level. The seriousness of lobbying and clientele groups not surprisingly relates to the money or potential money involved; thus large governments with large programs tend to have the active clientele groups. In medium and small governments, clientele groups can and do act less formally. Clientele interests are handled as nonpaid part-time activities via simple phone calls and meetings. Often, on-the-record views are expressed in public hearings, or possibly even a demonstration or media event might be organized. Highly emotional confrontations are rare on budget issues, but they do occur.

The agency, executive, legislature, and clientele each has a separate institutional role. Each perceives itself as a separate group although individual exceptions can be cited—for example, an agency political appointee may identify solely with the chief executive. Also, each group can be further subdivided, and subdivisions may come into conflict and threaten to harm the larger group. For example, the Maritime Administration is composed of maritime unions and operators. When they work together they are surprisingly powerful for their respective sizes, but the alliance can and does break down on specific issues. In the Congress, the substantive and appropriation committees sometimes are in conflict. In the executive, two staff agencies such as the White House staff and the Office of Management and Budget can also be in conflict on issues, but in the executive branch the chief executives can more easily arbitrate internal disputes than in the legislative branch.

Role Objectives and Enemies

The agency and its leadership almost always have pride or a sense that its programs are worthwhile. The career employee recognizes that his or her job and income are associated with the agency's objectives. In some instances, an almost missionary zeal and self-identification with the agency can exist among the top agency leadership. In other instances, the zeal may be only a belief that what the agency does is a worthwhile function. Rarely do top agency leaders disagree with the mission or the fundamental value of the agency and its programs.

Another factor to consider is the budget process itself. The agency is always placed in the position of requesting and defending. Reviewers are always doubting the agency and demanding facts and better arguments. Not surprisingly, agency executives often find themselves defending the agency when it comes under attack. President, governors, and mayors sometimes act surprised when their agency appointees argue the agency position. Given the dual elements of self-worth and role demands, chief executives should be more surprised if their appointees don't speak for their agencies.

Given those circumstances, issues are viewed from the perspective of the agency's mission and the people in the organization. Does a change further or detract from the agency's mission? Will the people in the organization benefit or lose from a change? Programs are justified with these questions well in mind.

The chief executive plays a different role. The executive wishes to economize, cut requests, and coordinate programs. There is an arm's length relationship between the executive and the agency leadership in spite of the fact that agency political appointees serve at the pleasure of the executive. The executive must maintain the option of saying "no" to an agency request. Requests must be reviewed carefully and cuts are necessary for purposes of economy and better allocation of resources around the executive branch. When the executive decision is reached, the chief executive expects that the agency will formally support the executive decision even though the agency may not perceive the decision to be in its own best interest. Discipline is maintained in several ways: formal statements are cleared by the executive's staff, budget requests must follow the executive's budget and allowance letter, the political influence of the chief executive is significant, and the agency head can be fired.

Another factor for state and local government agency heads to consider is that their chief executives can sometimes veto or reallocate items in line-item budgets. These powers vary greatly from one government to the next, but some chief executives can unilaterally reconstruct the council-approved budget using the line-item veto. The only limit on the power is the likely political resistance the chief executive would receive from the legislature or city council. When chief executives wield this type of power, agency officials would be hesitant to challenge or to try to circumvent them.

The legislature (sometimes called council, board, or commission) plays an entirely different role. It is the people's elected deliberative body, normally composed of well-intended, intelligent individuals. However, on budget matters the legislature is often confronted with confusing information and little time to make decisions. At the federal level and in some large state and local governments the legislatures may even dominate the policy-making process, but this is not often the situation. Normally, legislatures are not the initiators, but rather play a more reactive role. Attention is given more to pet projects and issues of local popular concern rather to than a unified, comprehensive approach to the budget.

The clientele members are interested in how an agency's program affects them. They meet and discuss in conferences the significance of existing legislation, the chief executive's attitudes toward programs, and the policies of the agency. Sometimes the clientele works as a whole, but often various subgroups act, with some coordination among the groups. Clientele groups vary, with success often depending on clientele leadership, the stakes involved, the organizational network, the dedication of the members to the issue, and the strategies and tactics employed.

The paths of clientele influence vary. Often a special agency-clientele relationship occurs because an unofficial policy of job rotation exists. For example, a former lobbyist or key member of a client group can be and often is appointed to a high level government position which is important to the client group. Sometimes clientele groups support the winning president or congressman. This also can lead to a cordial climate. Lobbying is the standard path of influence. Also formal and informal relationships can exist between the agency and the clientele, as illustrated in the UMTA and Maritime case examples cited earlier.

Agencies and clientele groups can have anticlientele groups. For example, consumer groups can oppose the manufacturing interests and government regulating bodies. In recent years, more groups from right-to-left political spectrum—Nader, environment, antinuclear, and so on—have become active. These groups are often significant.

Who the "good and bad guys" are depends on values, issues, and perspectives. For some agencies, there is a pattern in which various actors tend to be allies on most issues. This need not be the situation. From the agency's point of view, the executive may be the stumbling block on an issue and the essential ally on yet another issue. From the clientele's viewpoint, the agency may be an enemy causing useless red tape or a vital agency necessary for the survival of the clientele members. Each situation must be examined separately. Rarely does a uniform and consistent pattern exist over time, with one set of actors who are always friends and another set who are always enemies. The patterns evolve and change; thus the actors must adapt to a dynamic environment.

Cultivation of an Active Clientele

For most government agencies, there is no problem identifying a clientele group. Highway departments are well aware of their clientele. The Veterans' Administration hears from its clientele. However, some agencies cannot easily identify clientele groups. For example, the United States Information Agency does not serve people in this country. What group is its clientele? The U.S. Bureau of Prisons does not have an active clientele group. In such cases, the nature of the organization or its mission precludes a clientele group; thus the agency is handicapped in the pluralist style of American government.

The most obvious way to cultivate a clientele is to carry out the agency's programs, but some strategy is involved in building a supportive clientele. In the first place, the clientele members should understand and appreciate the full extent of the benefits they receive from the agency's programs. In the second place, most legislatures represent the whole population, so a breadth of clientele members across the nation, state, or city is best if the clientele wishes to lobby the legislature. Third, some clientele members may be in a better position to aid the agency, such as a group in the House Appropriation Committee chairperson's home district. Finally, mute clientele members are not that useful so they must be encouraged to be active politically.

Strategies of both expanding and concentrating the clientele are used. An agency can take care to provide grants or assistance across the country or build a balanced set of programs which appeal to several specific sectors of society. Agencies have their public information officers explain the pro-

grams, and attendance at clientele conferences is considered very important. Some clientele members can be acquired by changing or adding attrac-
tive services for that group. For example, in an area where senior citizens
are well organized, the parks department is wise to have programs for the
elderly. Often the intensity of support is important, so the program may be
altered to be sure to benefit a particularly influential group.

The clientele must be heard by the legislature and the executive. In
some instances, the clientele members are poorly organized or not adept in
dealing with American democratic institutions. Congressmen, senators, and
legislators often assume that if they do not hear from supporters, no one
cares. Given the need to cut, the tendency is to cut where no one cares
enough to complain. Legislators do consider themselves to be guardians of
the treasury, but they do not like the uncomfortable feeling they get when
cuts return to haunt them at the next election. Even saying "No" to an im-
passioned plea is not pleasant. An agency rarely advocates lobbying the
legislature, but its officers can explain the significance of lobbying and
stress that the small budget is a problem which can be corrected by the
legislature.

Sometimes agencies structure subunits to attract clientele. For example, the agency is broad-based but effective lobbying is done by narrow focus groups. The agency can appeal to those narrow groups. For example,
the National Institute of Health uses subunits focused upon specific dis-
eases which correspond to the active health clientele groups. The result is
a strong set of clientele groups. The hazard in this approach is that a glam-
orous subunit can lessen support for the other units.

Another approach is the creation of an advisory committee. Even the
most conservative group of advisors tends to advocate the desirability of the
agency's program. This can lead to increased and more effective clientele
support.

Agency Budget Office

The place for developing and orchestrating the budget process is the
agency budget office. The duties of such offices vary, as they sometimes
include the accounting function and an analytical/planning unit. There are
some common duties which describe what an agency budget office does.
The following is an excellent list of duties from one agency budget office—
the Budget Division of ACTION in the federal government:[1]

1. In conjunction with the appropriate operating officials, develops budget estimates for programs and offices, conducts budget reviews, and recommends
   budget allocations.
2. In conjunction with appropriate operating officials, develops, presents, and
   justifies ACTION's budget submission to the Office of Management and Budget and to the Congress, including financial and personnel exhibits, budget
   narrative material, and budget back-up data. Prepares Agency witnesses for
   hearings before the Office of Management and Budget and the Congress.

[1]Budget Execution Responsibilities, ACTION, 1975.

3. Recommends budget priorities as the result of Office of Management and Budget and Congressional budget guidance for use within the Agency.

4. Prepares apportionments, allotments, and maintains overall control of Agency financial resources and position allocations.

5. Issues operating budgets with position and average grade allocations to all offices, regions, and posts and insures budget execution with legislative authority and limitations.

6. Conducts budget reviews and analyses during the fiscal year and recommends reprogramming actions and other funding adjustments.

7. Recommends and implements budgetary procedures, budget controls, and reporting systems and makes recommendations regarding the financial aspects of the management information system to improve financial management within the Agency.

8. Works with appropriate operating officials to coordinate the budget with Agency plans, objectives, and programs.

9. Acts as the Agency's primary point of contact with other governmental agencies on budget matters.

Exhibits 3-2 and 3-3 illustrate the variety of activities of budget execution responsibilities and the complex interrelationships which commonly exist among people performing budget responsibilities.

Perspective of the Budget Officer

Much of the work of the budget officer is repetitive. Exhibits 3-2 and 3-3 point out the yearly routine. The budget process has an established pattern and after a few years the substantive issues of the agency also take on a familiar pattern. Budgeting is largely repetitive and the filling out of reports tends to make the work mechanical.

The budget officer sees the world in terms of dollars, accuracy, and legality. The agency and its activities must always be translated into money. Budget officers will discuss new and old ideas, but eventually they ask, "What does this mean in terms of money?" Accuracy is essential. As will be discussed later, having the confidence of others is quite useful to the budget officer and confidence is not increased by making mistakes, especially in simple math. Care must be taken to establish procedures which double-check tables, insure final typing is error free, and verify the accuracy of stated facts. Legality is also a concern. If money is spent for reasons not permitted by law, then the budget officer may go to jail. There are few agency level decisions which the budget officer does not know about and often the law fixes responsibility for agency action on the agency head and budget officer. Wisdom dictates that the budget officer must be sure of the legality of questionable matters in order to avoid later problems.

Deadlines are the guiding force for a budget officer. Sometimes they seem impossible and often they are crucial. A common situation is to see a budget officer working late at night or on the weekends in order to meet some deadline. If a deadline is missed, then someone—usually the agency head—will be upset. More significantly, the agency may have lost an important opportunity or handicapped itself in a decision-making situation.

Timeliness can mean even the survival of the agency's program. On the other hand, some deadlines are foolish and the wiser person will take the extra time to do a better job because timeliness is not significant. The decision to ignore a deadline should be based upon a knowledge of how and when the information will be utilized.

The budget can be used to minimize or surface disagreements. The budget officer is an artist who realizes that a budget can be presented in many ways in spite of the requirements of format. For political or internal management reasons, specific issues may best be hidden or minimized. This can be done by placing the issue within a larger, more dominant subject. In many situations, surfacing disagreement is a much better strategy. An issue can be surfaced by presenting it with some prominence in the budget document. This forces decision makers to deal with the problem and try to resolve it. In many instances, minimizing or surfacing a disagreement is mandated by outside forces, such as a major media story on the subject, which cannot be ignored. In some instances, these decisions are made by the budget officer; thus his or her political and management judgment is important.

Deadlines and other pressures force the budget officer to use the satisficing approach to many decision-making situations. When someone is demanding a budget submission, and the timeliness of that submission is important, then the budget officer may be pleased to find even a satisfactory answer. Budgeting is done under pressure and the budget officer must do the best that he or she can in the time available. Searching for ideal answers on all occasions is not compatible with budgeting.

Agency Budget Behavior

As explained earlier in this chapter, loyalty to an agency is a common behavioral phenomenon. This loyalty is similar to that found in professional athletes. When they work for a team, loyalty to the team is given. Budget officers believe in their agency's mission and feel that their role is important for the well-being of the agency. Blind loyalty does not exist because program weaknesses are well-known. A more balanced loyalty prevails which recognizes faults but believes the program is or can be essentially sound.

Individuals working in a public agency take pride in their work. This can lead to the desire to expand the projects and programs. Budget reviewers are often frustrated by agency desires to expand programs, but such expansion tendencies are positive indicators of the health of the program's management. Agencies should not be criticized for being enthusiastic. Reviewers should applaud positive attitudes while recognizing the reviewers' role may call for them to disapprove expansion.

Budgeting's political context often supersedes apparent rationality. What might appear to be the best solution is not necessarily the best position for the agency to take. Recall that agencies exist in a context of powerful interacting forces. When a person is sailing, the best sailing course may not be directly toward the ultimate objective. Sometimes tacking into the wind is necessary owing to the force of the opposing wind. In public admin-

EXHIBIT 3-2 Functions, Responsibilities, and Interrelationships of Budget Execution Personnel

FUNCTIONS	OFFICIALS: DIRECTOR/DEPUTY	ASSISTANT DIRECTOR FOR OPP	BUDGET DIRECTOR	ASSISTANT DIRECTOR FOR A&F	ALLOTMENT HOLDER	INTERMEDIATE BUDGET HOLDER (10 REGIONS; OFFICE)	OPERATING BUDGET MANAGER
Apportionment request	Responsibility delegated to OPP	Submits request to GMB	Prepares request from sum of allotments; monitors	Receive info copy of apportionment; monitor for pos. viol.			
Continuing resolution	Concur with GC interpretation		Coordinates activity; issues instructions				
Treasury warrant request			Prepares request	Request to Treasury			
Allotment issuance	Reviews, approves	Issues allotments	Prepares allotment from sum of operating budgets	Receive info. copy of allot.; monitor for pos. violation	Receive allotment; monitor		
Operating budget issuance			Directs; issues jointly; monitors		Review and approve budgets; jointly issue	Review and approve subordinate budget request	Recommend operating budget totals
Reapportionment	Request to the OMB	Concurs in request	Prepares request with backup				
Allotment reprogramming	Final approval in cases of question	Approves reprogramming	Recommends; prepares documents		Request reprogramming		
Operating budget reprogramming			Reviews requests; concurs in all decisions	Insures account reporting compatible with format	Review request; approve if operating group budgets change	Review; approve if operating group budget totals unchanged	Request reprogramming

Estimation of receipts/reimbursements	Concurs		Prepares; estimates; monitors				
Allotment management			Monitors		Manage within budget totals and restrict		Manage within budget totals and restrictions; Recommend change in operating budget; Recommend changes
Operating budget management			Monitors				
Quarterly review	Approves new budget allocations		Directs review; recommends new allocation		Prepare data; recommend new levels; Recommend changes	Recommend new levels for operating group; Recommend changes	
Year end review	Approves new budget allocation		Directs review; recommends changes	Complete review of open obligations			
Violation reports	Receive report; report to president and Congress			Instigate report to director with evidence			
Personnel and average grade ceiling	Reviews and approves allocation to 10 major offices	Develops/reviews allocation to 10 major offices	Recommends allocations to operating units		Recommend intermediate level totals	Recommend allocations to operating units within operating groups	
Review of past year performance			Analyzes; prepares report				
Preparation of status of funds report			Provides budget input to reports	Generate reports and distribute			

Source: Budget Execution Responsibilities, ACTION, 1975.

EXHIBIT 3-3 Flowchart of Budget Execution for Budget Division of ACTION.

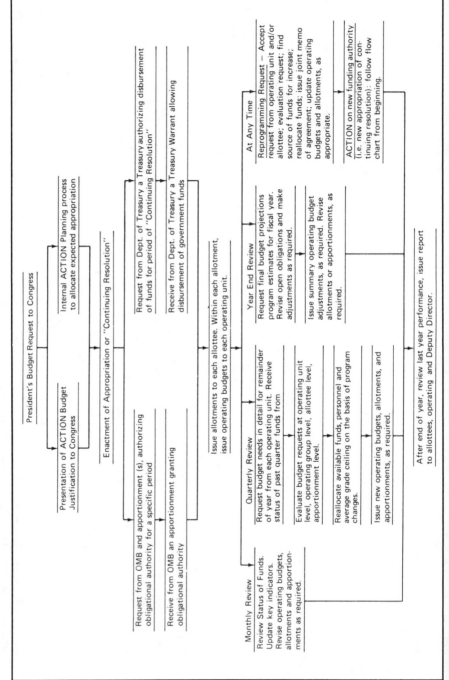

istration, the budget game strategy may not be to advocate or oppose a position directly but rather to wait for the clientele or legislature to react to circumstances. Judgment is essential.

There often is some flexibility in budgeting as a result of what some call gimmicks. How to employ those gimmicks is another important talent. For example, the timing of obligation and disbursements can be significant and this timing can be controlled by the budget officer. Another trick is that a given expense item can be assigned to one of two programs. This choice permits some often needed flexibility. Gimmicks exist because some discretion exists and a budget officer can use that discretion to ease the burden of managing the program. Skillful budget officers are aware of the available discretionary decisions and use them to ease the problems of public management.

Public budgeting requires decision makers. Even decisions not to act represent policy choices. If a budget reviewer delays a program or project for another year, that is a decision which often has important implications. Decisions may be based on sound reasoning, but they do affect people. Decision makers must be able to live with criticism because budget decisions often generate strong arguments. Also, decisions are often made on meager information, thus contributing to the possibility of self-doubt in the minds of public budget officers. If the budget officer cannot emotionally deal with criticism and doubt, then he or she should consider a different type of work. Doubt and criticism are a part of public budgeting.

Public budgeting requires the highest professional characteristics. Later in this chapter, the importance of confidence in the budget officer will be explained. Confidence is established through professionalism. Honesty and integrity are essential professional characteristics. This does not mean that the budget officer does not prepare the *strongest case possible* for a program, but it does mean that "possible" includes avoiding lies and misrepresentations. No one faults a budget officer for being sensitive to shifting political causes (e.g., environment, energy, inflation, unemployment) and framing budget justifications to take advantage of those shifting but temporarily persuasive rationales. This political sensitivity comes together with accuracy, legality, honesty, integrity, and other factors to constitute a professional.

One unfortunate characteristic of some budget officers is arrogance. This characteristic exists more in budget reviewers found in units like the department budget offices and the U.S. Office of Management and Budget (OMB). Lord Acton once stated that power corrupts and absolute power corrupts absolutely. Even budget officers and budget analysts possess some power because of the nature of their job; a few are corrupted but many more become intoxicated. They know they have power and they let others know it with their arrogance. For example, young OMB budget examiners may be mild-mannered before they start working for OMB, but once on the job they can visit the "field" and act in a cavalier, flippant, or even bossy manner to people with much higher civil service rank and longer experience. Such behavior is not professionally wise because it often leads to a needless lack of cooperation from the agency, thus making the examiner's job that much more difficult.

Budget officers are almost always career civil servants who work quite closely with politically appointed agency or department heads. This close rapport is sometimes influenced by the unusual position agency heads must face. Often they are expected to give their allegiance exclusively to the chief executive but the role of agency head strongly induces a loyalty to the agency. In some instances, these two loyalties are in conflict, thus presenting an agency head with an extremely difficult emotional dilemma. When such situations arise, the budget officer will become quite aware of the dilemma because the agency head's handling of that dilemma will influence the budget process. Understanding the dilemma is helpful, but there are no easy answers to this type of situation.

Public budgeting is an activity which requires responsible people. In the federal government, this responsibility is dramatized. If a budget officer over-obligates or permits to be spent an amount in excess of that apportioned by OMB, then a legal violation has occurred which can result in his or her being fired, fined, or sentenced to jail. Exhibit 3-4 is the quote from the Anti-deficiency Act which details the action required when violations occur. A fine or jail sentence results from willful violations. Such violations are rare.

One last important observation should be made about agency budget behavior. Good professionals love the game. They find it challenging and exciting. They love being important and having responsibility. They love the need to work under pressure and yet deliver quality work. They love knowing all the complexities of budgeting and being able to use their skills. They love the intrigue and excitement of both politics and public management.

EXHIBIT 3-4   Anti-deficiency Act (Section 3527 of Revised Statutes, as amended)

Actions required when violations occur.

1. *Administrative discipline; fines; or imprisonment.* In addition to any penalty of liability under other law, any officer or employee of the United States who shall violate subsections (a), (b), or (h) of this section shall be subjected to appropriate administrative discipline, including, when circumstances warrant, suspension from duty without pay or removal from office; and any officer or employee of the United States who shall knowingly and willfully violate subsections (a), (b), or (h) of this section shall, upon conviction, be fined not more than $5,000 or imprisoned for not more than two years, or both.

2. *Reports to President or Congress.* In the case of a violation of subsections (a), (b), or (h) of this section by an officer or employee of an agency, or of the District of Columbia, the head of the agency concerned or the Commissioner of the District of Columbia, shall immediately report to the President, through the Director of the Office of Management and Budget, and to the Congress all pertinent facts together with a statement of the action taken thereon.

Four Views

In chapter 1, decision-making models and their importance were explained. People working in budgeting are often influenced by these normative theories, and four ideal types can be used to describe typical reactions to those normative theories. The four ideal types are the true rational believer, the pure reactive person, the budget-wise person (the cynic), and the wise budget person.

The true rational believer. With the influence of PPB, there are people working in public budgeting who strongly believe that decision-making related to public budgeting should use the rational approach. If decisions don't follow that approach, then they consider the decision highly questionable and in error due to lack of professionalism or the unfortunate intrusion of politics into proper decision-making. They try to insure that as many decisions as possible, especially significant decisions, should follow the rational approach: (1) set goals and objectives, (2) define alternatives, (3) analyze alternatives, and (4) select the best decision or make the recommendation.

Such faith in the normative decision-making theory called the rational approach leads to unfortunate consequences in public budgeting. Many public organizations have vague multiple and sometimes mutually conflicting goals and objectives. Articulating specific goals and objectives may be impossible, but analysis may still be useful for decision-making. If analysis is limited to the rational approach, then analysis cannot be conducted. This is an unnecessary constraint applied to circumstances in which analysis could be useful. Thus the decision maker is unnecessarily handicapped. Another problem with the rational model is that it implies no limits exist to the defining of alternatives and the analysis of alternatives. As is pointed out in this author's book *Policy Analysis in Public Policymaking,* some individuals will proceed to spend large sums of money on analysis when the end results will be as useful as a much more limited analytical effort. Those individuals are motivated by the rational model to pursue the alternatives and exhaustively examine those alternatives. Another problem with the rational model is that its believers don't appreciate the importance of feedback in analysis; thus helpful feedback can be ignored.

A more subtle problem of the rational model is the inherent assumption that there is one overall perspective. Recall the earlier cited fable involving several blind men and an elephant. The storyteller stresses how each blind man examines a different segment of the elephant and proceeds to argue with the other blind men over the nature of the beast. The ironical thrust to the story is that all parties including the storyteller were inherently limited by their perspective. Any object or series of events can be described in an infinite number of ways and there is no one description, contrary to what the storyteller assumed. The rational model leads us to make the same mistake as the storyteller. One is wiser to recognize that there are only shared perceptions of felt needs which can be translated into formulations of problems and objectives. Unfortunately, the common use of the rational model does not encourage such sophistication.

The pure reactive person.   In contrast to the true rational believer is the pure reactive budget person. This type of person acts in a stimulus-response pattern. The budget calendar and the requests govern this type of person. Little thought is given to shaping events or somehow making a difference through the reactor's product. The job is merely a task to be done as defined in the job description or by the demands of the job. Decision-making models mean little to this type of person. However, the political-administrative dichotomy is used as the justification for his or her mechanical response. Such a person believes that political decisions should be left to the political appointee and that civil servants should merely respond to the wishes of the political appointees.

The hazard of this approach is that mindless or potentially foolish mistakes are not avoided. The budget person has a unique vantage point and can often understand both the political actors' viewpoints as well as the workings of government. By merely reacting, the government loses the important insight of the budget expert; thus more errors are likely to occur. An aggressive, outspoken budget staff can greatly improve government, but a reactive staff will permit policy makers to make unnecessary—often significant—errors. Most policy makers recognize the value of an aggressive and outspoken rather than a reactive budget staff.

The budget-wise person.   These people are aware of all the forms and tables, but discount them almost completely because the government's decisions are all political. They are often cynical about life in general and stress the public nature of "public administration." They can sometimes cite dramatic examples of gross politically inspired decision-making, sometimes involving corruption and often involving vote trading. Such decision-making often does preclude effective public management. This type of person stresses that such decision-making is inevitable and that all that a budget staff can do is react and watch events unfold. In some government settings, the cynic is right; but in many others, the political actors in the political process are influenced by well-prepared budget justifications, and professional budgeting does translate into effective public management. If a cynical view dominates where professional budgeting could make a difference, then a valuable opportunity for more effective government is lost.

The wise budget person.   People of this type recognize that politics is sometimes of overriding importance. They also believe that analysis has its limitations but can often greatly help in decision-making situations. Professional public budgeting can be extremely significant to the way government is managed. We hope that this text will help more people be wise budget persons.

Develop Confidence

Having the confidence of the budget reviewers, especially the appropriations committees, is extremely important to the budget officer. If confidence doesn't exist, any reviewer can ask hard questions and force the agency to justify every detail. If the appropriations committees lack confidence, they can write into the appropriation bill or committee report very specific special conditions, thus tying the hands of the agency and making program administration a nightmare. If confidence is established, the budget reviews are less difficult and greater administrative latitude is provided for public management discretion.

There is a natural tendency on the part of the reviewers to place confidence in budget officers because some facts and management judgment must be accepted on faith. The sheer complexity of the budget plus the lack of time to review budgets means that not everything can be reviewed in depth. Priorities of reviewers' efforts in examining are decided upon with the more questionable or politically sensitive topics receiving the greatest attention. Budget reviewers would like to trust the expertise of the best budget officer because valuable budget reviewer time can be saved. Thus, a budget officer is wise to establish a reputation as being highly professional.

The ideal model of a highly professional budget person is used by reviewers to "rate" budget officers. The criteria vary but a fairly accurate picture can be painted of the type of person most likely to be trusted. Such a person is

1. a master of detail;
2. hard working;
3. concise;
4. frank;
5. self-effacing and devoted to the work;
6. tight with the taxpayer's money;
7. capable of recognizing a political necessity when it is present; and
8. conscientious about keeping key reviewers (e.g., congressmen) informed of sensitive changes in policy or important developments.

Budget officers find that a reputation of playing it straight is wise. Lying, covering up, and being tricky are highly undesirable characteristics for the career civil servant. Memories can be long among top reviewing staffs. If reviewers, especially appropriations committees, feel that they have been misled, then strong punitive actions can be taken, such as tying the agency into administrative knots with special appropriation language. On the other hand, a positive reputation can even mean securing emergency or supplemental funds on the basis of skimpy hearings: that is, getting funds almost entirely on the integrity of the budget officer.

Reputations are enhanced with professional friendship. A close personal relationship with budget reviewers, such as the agency's Congressional subcommittee staff, can ease tensions. Years of outstanding service are even more significant than friendships because such experience often builds a sense of integrity and trust which constitutes "professional friendships." In many cases, these professional friendships are built upon shared work experiences and service together in professional associations.

One of the characteristics associated with building confidence is being capable of recognizing political "necessity." However, judgment can differ on the question of "necessity." Some accommodation to favors and pet projects does occur, but such practices can move from the unusual to the expected. When this occurs, effective public management cannot be carried out. Part of building confidence is being able to turn down political actors so that requests are not considered a "political necessity." Techniques for pleasant turn-downs include the following:

1. "My hands are tied"—other factors may exist, such as an executive mandate which precludes the favor.

2. "Maybe in the future"—the favor may be granted, but the timing is simply not wise then.

3. "But look at the other positive actions we have taken"—stress that other decisions were in their favor or to their liking and appeal to the notion that one should only expect to win a "fair share" of the time.

4. "It cannot be done"—economic, technical, or other reasons can be cited why the request is either impossible or extremely unwise to fulfill.

Other strategies can be employed to minimize granting favors. Action on the favor can be delayed. If they are truly serious, the political actors will pursue until they get action. Delay thus acts as a filter for the true "necessities." A parallel strategy is to give in on the most intensely sought favors and pet projects. Intensity can also be measured by means used to bring pressure upon the agency. Regardless of how intensity is shown, the strategy is to give in on the intense favors and resist on the less intense favors and pet projects.

Strategies and techniques can help, but in a few cases the consequences must be faced. Sometimes budget officers must face a no-win situation due to their professional or personal ethics or the need to support other persons in the bureaucracy such as the agency head. In some instances, the situation can be mitigated by allowing one political actor (e.g., a congressman) to do battle with another political actor (e.g., a political appointee or the media); but such a ploy can result in making two enemies and losing rather than gaining their confidence. In other situations, the budget officer may merely have to use time to heal relationships or hope that key actors don't blame the budget officer but blame the deed. The consequence may be severe, but sometimes one's professional integrity requires action which ironically can harm one's professional reputation.

There is no developed method for establishing confidence. All that can be done is to be aware of the techniques and strategies available, to observe successful budget officers, and to use careful judgment. No one approach is useful for all budget reviewers or all situations. Each set of circumstances must be considered separately before action is taken.

Results

Confidence in a government program often rests upon demonstrated results. Results are significant because the public and political leaders anticipate that some benefits will be evident from government programs.

There is an important distinction between an activity accomplishing its purpose and people feeling that they are being served. Politically, the latter is more significant. Often the distinction is only theoretical because accomplishment translates to people's realizing their lives have enhanced, but this need not be the case. The people—the agency's potential clientele—may be unaware of the importance of the program, may have come to take it for granted, or may not feel that the program is important. Earlier in this chapter, the significance of the clientele in the political process was noted. If the potential clientele members are not active supporters of the program, then the program may very well fail, given the normal political competition for funding support.

For an agency, serving an appreciative clientele is ideal. The best kind of result is one that provides services to a large and strategically placed appreciative clientele. The best type of clientele is one which brings its satisfaction to the attention of decision makers, such as the appropriation committees and the president. Not all agencies are blessed with such a happy harmony of circumstances, so attempts must be made to develop alternative means to build and maintain the essential support of key decision makers.

If an agency doesn't enjoy overwhelming public support, a persuasive case can be made with tangible accomplishments. In the budget justification process, emphasis is placed on the accomplishments of the program. The criteria used to judge success are sometimes the subject of debate and sometimes semantic confusion is used to rationalize odd criteria for success. In such circumstances, the merits of the accomplishments are less persuasive. Nevertheless, the citation of accomplishment is normally highly useful in any budget justification.

If the listing of results is not sufficiently impressive, the agency can extend an invitation to the decision makers or anyone likely to influence the decision makers (e.g., the media) to visit the agency. Budget reviewers and other influential people are shown the need (e.g., the poor being helped), the activity (e.g., the production of a missile), or heroic efforts by an overworked staff (e.g., emergency room care at a hospital). Often this technique is extremely useful. The U.S. space program used this approach quite successfully to maintain high public interest in its efforts. However, there are significant risks. The reviewers may not be impressed and this can translate into lower budgets rather than increased or sustained budget support.

A hazard of visits and other attempts to explain highly complex programs is the problem of explanation. Most political decision makers are not experts, so explanations and visits must be simplified to communicate the essential message without technical verbiage. If they are too simple, then the complex nature of the challenge is not understood and the level of funding seems unwarranted. If they are too complex, then the reviewer questions the clarity of the management direction and again the level of funding is reduced or the program is cut entirely. Selecting the exact visit format and explanation for complex programs can indeed be a challenge.

A hazard of demonstrating tangible accomplishment is that the program may be praised and then cut because the program objectives have been met. Government programs are designed to meet a problem and success may mean the problem ceases to exist. If that occurs, the program should cease to exist. The irony is that losing one's job seems like a punishment rather than a reward.

Some government programs are disadvantaged by not having tangible accomplishments which they can demonstrate. For example, unless the civil defense program is called on in an emergency, the civil defense agency cannot point to any tangible accomplishment. Another example is the International Communications Agency, which broadcasts propaganda overseas. How does one deal with such programs when tangible results cannot be shown? There are several ploys that can be used:

1. "Our program is priceless"—argue that results are not evident but what if the program did not exist? If we did not have civil defense, what cost would there be in human lives if disaster occurred?

2. "Results of our program cannot be measured"—argue that a demonstration of results is simply not possible given the nature of the program. This may be a truthful argument, but it will not be very persuasive.

3. "Results will be evident in the future"—argue that results are not evident now because the program is new or the program's results are only evident when an emergency occurs. This is a more appealing argument, but skeptics can say that an emergency is the wrong time to find out that the program does not work.

4. "Figures show"—argue facts and figures show results in spite of the fact that they really are not relevant. This is a foolish ploy, given the potential loss of confidence that could result.

5. "In this complex situation, the figures confirm"—argue by ignoring the questionable cause-effect relationships within a multiple causal situation. This is a reasonable ploy, but care must be taken in the wording so that the statements are positive but not false. Extreme claims which cannot be tested should be avoided.

6. "Please notice that we reviewed more than a thousand applicants"—argue by focusing not on results but on the procedures and process measures of the organization. The critical observant reviewer can always ask, "So what?" but making a display of facts and figures is better than saying nothing because the information does demonstrate some activity did take place.

7. "You must appreciate that we cannot prove the relationship of this education to later achievement, but we know such a relationship exists"—argue that faith establishes the relationship between the program and the desired benefits in society. If the subject is something that is taken for granted, then such an argument might be successful.

Preparing for Hearings

Hearings often are important in building confidence in a program and program officials. In some situations, hearings only serve to brief decision makers or to create a record to be used to convince others. However, hearings can and often do affect decision makers, given the competing pressures on their time and the inadequate preparation they give to the review of budget material. Hearings are particularly important in establishing con-

fidence. Program officials who cannot answer or who poorly answer questions create an impression that those running the organization don't really
understand what they are doing.

Rehearsals for budget hearings are essential. The number of hearings
vary by agency and government, but four hearings on the budget alone are
the minimum number in the federal government. As noted in an earlier
chapter, rehearsing, or holding mock hearings, is a standard practice.
Agency administrators play the role of key reviewers such as the appropriations committee chairperson. Tough questions are anticipated and answered before the hearing in order to avoid later difficulties. Mock hearings
are an excellent device to expose weak justifications, to build effective
agency coordination in handling questions, and to appreciate the perspective of the reviewer. Mock hearings also help the budget officer decide what
subjects should be discussed and stressed in the traditional opening statement.

The key to preparing for budgeting hearings is to do sufficient research to avoid or minimize surprises in the hearing. A surprise usually
makes the administrator appear to be ignorant and can rattle him or her
to the point of answering all the remaining questions poorly. A diligent
search of past hearings and statements often indicates what the reviewers
consider important. Also a review of the program itself and reactions to the
program are essential in framing the tough questions. Often the rapport of
the budget officer with others, such as people in the central budget office,
can be a vital resource for intelligence.

Briefing books for hearings are useful. Normally, they include only the
tough or standard questions and answers which are anticipated. They may
include a brief discussion on the perspectives of each reviewer, but such
information is often common knowledge. Also such descriptions can fall
into the wrong hands, leading to unnecessary embarrassment.

Questions in a hearing come from a variety of sources, including the
reviewer (e.g., senator), staff, clientele, and even the agency itself. Questions
are sometimes planted, with entire lists of questions supplied by the agency.
Sometimes the planted questions are the most difficult, so that the agency
can go on record on a subject in the best possible manner. Planted questions rarely occur at the department and OMB hearings, but they are common in the Congress, where friendly legislators wish to aid a program. In
some instances, the rapport between staffs is so close that the effect is the
same as planted questions.

Presentations at hearings tend to create a portrait of the agency leadership in the minds of the reviewers. Hearings are an opportunity to paint
a self-portrait of credibility and generate a favorable mood toward the
agency. The leadership can take on such mantles as protector-of-the-public-
safety, man-of-science, statesman, guardian-of-the-environment, and so on.
Effective hearing presentations tend to ward off unpleasant and time-
consuming probes of an agency.

The best way to make a positive impression at a hearing is to know
the budget. There is no adequate substitute for being knowledgeable, but
knowledge can be coupled with a good organized presentation. Normally,

presentations and answers which are brief and to the point but which offer an opportunity to go into more depth on follow-up questions are most effective. Care can be taken not to give the impression that important subjects are being slighted. An administrator can be forgiven for not knowing a detail and in fact such data are often supplied for the record after the hearing. Administrators are sometimes not forgiven for not knowing the answers to questions involving management direction. Questions—even on detail—often can be anticipated and answered or transmitted at the time of the hearing. Such action is extremely impressive and builds confidence.

Hearings are a game with certain taboos. Agency officials recognize that they have two masters—the legislature and the executive—but agency officials cannot challenge the chief executive's budget even though they may wish for more support, but everyone present can tell if the officials mean otherwise. This communication is achieved by:

1. exhibiting a marked lack of enthusiasm;
2. being too enthusiastic to be credible;
3. refusing to answer questions by protesting loyalty to the chief executive; and
4. yielding to sharp pointed questioning.

These taboos are significant. If the central budget office or the department feels the agency is not adhering to the established executive branch policy, then the agency head and other political appointees can be fired. "Speaking against the administration" can be taken extremely seriously; but in a few instances the central budget office or department may not wish the agency to resist legislative desires to increase the budget over executive branch requests as a political strategy. Each situation must be judged separately.

Another taboo is that the agency should not admit yielding to clientele pressure. The agency is accountable to all the people; thus yielding to one clientele is an admission of favoritism. It also admits that pressure can be successful. Instead, language is carefully phrased to indicate the agency wishes to receive advice from citizens and does act upon suggestions which have intrinsic value; the agency does respond to sound advice but the decision is made only on the merits of the advice. Pressure is not influential according to this taboo and should not be admitted to openly.

STRATEGIES

Reviewers versus Reviewed

The budget game requires advocates and reviewers. The agency is the advocate, but clientele groups and sometimes even legislators can also be called advocates. The reviewers are the department officials, the central budget office (e.g., OMB), the House appropriations subcommittee, and the Senate appropriations subcommittee. As the budget moves through the budget cycle, reviewers change roles and become advocates. For example, after the central budget office has reviewed the budget requests and final executive branch decisions are made, then that former reviewer is an advocate to the legislative appropriations subcommittees. The primary advocate, however, always is the agency. If the game is played well, there always exists an arm's length relationship between advocate and reviewer. Each plays the role with caution, care, and an awareness of the natural tendencies associated with each role. A requirement for a good game is that each party know the rules and strategy. Ideally the game should be played by professionals. An uneven game results in unreasonable cuts or unreasonably high budgets. Both results are undesirable.

One budget strategy failure illustrates the gamesmanship. Occasionally, an agency will resubmit the previous year's budget with the only change being the fiscal years mentioned in the text. When this occurs, the reviewers question the budget request because intervening variables since last year must cause some program changes. The possibility of an *identical* budget request approaches zero because administrative environments always change. A distinct likelihood exists that another reviewer may have ordered the agency to use the same budget level as the previous year's budget, but to use the *identical* budget request seems to imply lack of adaptability to changing conditions. Part of the game is to at least give the appearance of managing the program, and this is not done by using last year's budget.

Budget requests are rarely approved intact and reviewers normally reduce (cut) the request. There are several common rationales given for cutting budgets:

1. a climate of opinion existed which was against spending;
2. strong views by influential decision makers necessitated the cut;
3. spending on your program became a political football; and
4. there was an overriding need to balance the budget.

The reason cited may address the management capability or fundamental objectives of the agency's program. However, such statements are more difficult to rationalize against the superior expertise of the agency on those topics. The reasons cited above are less subject to dispute and appeal, thus they are more likely to be cited.

Some ironies can exist with budget cutting. An agency may wish to have a certain program cut or may even cut its own program. For example, maybe the agency leadership lost faith in a program, internal discipline called for cuts, or higher priorities in some programs meant cuts in other programs. Interestingly, cuts can stimulate mobilization of the agency clientele, thus eventually resulting in even higher budgets than would have occurred without those earlier cuts.

Another phenomenon which can occur is intra-legislative conflict. One obvious area of conflict is between the two chambers (House and Senate). Conference committees are intended to resolve such disputes, but strategies can be used so that one chamber's position dominates. For example, the Senate may raise the amount in order to achieve the desired amount through compromise. Another tactic is to have a chamber pass a resolution supporting its conferees, thus permitting them to cite the solidarity and intensity of feelings in their arguments. Conference committees are often unpredictable and most agencies would prefer to avoid this uncertainty unless one chamber cuts their requests significantly. A less obvious area of conflict is between the substantive committee and the appropriations committee. In some instances, the agency can be the innocent victim of such disputes.

Spenders' Strategies

There are game strategies that an agency can apply in seeking to get its budget requests approved. This section explains the various strategies which are commonly used, but does not attempt to comment in depth upon how, when, and in what way the strategies should be applied to maximize their effectiveness. Such matters require judgment based upon each separate budget situation.

There are some fairly common safety strategies which are employed. Budget requests are often padded because the agency wishes to be able to meet unanticipated contingencies and to compensate for the fact that reviewers often almost automatically cut requests. Obvious or nondefensible "padding" can lead to an important loss of confidence, but "extras" can normally be easily defended. A related strategy is always to ask for more. This demonstrates an aggressive agency which has a strong belief in its mission. The increase may not be merited, but the reviewers are forced to address the increase and may forget to argue the possibility of a program level decrease. In connection with this strategy, the agency is careful to spend or obligate all the current year's funds. If there is any surplus, the reviewer may argue that the agency's current funding is more than adequate and there is no need for additional money. Another safe strategy is to alter the written or oral budget presentations as much as possible to highlight the best aspects of the agency's program and minimize the worst aspects.

Budgeting is a complex activity. "Sleight-of-hand" tricks do exist and they can be part of a budget strategy. For example, numbers in budgets are rounded often to the nearest hundred thousand or even million. For some small but politically important budget items, the practice of rounding can be an advantage. Another "trick" is to recast the budget into different categories than those used in the previous year. The redone categories can be utilized to focus attention upon or away from programs, depending upon the budget's strategic purposes. Also, redone categories inhibit longitudinal analysis and this may be an advantage to the agency. In addition, there are a variety of back-door spending devices; one of them is no-year funds. One sleight-of-hand technique is to use unobligated appropriations or disobligated appropriations (i.e., funds previously obligated but for which obligation was subsequently withdrawn, often because of nonuse by grantees) to finance projects beyond the apparent level of budget year appropriations. For example, let us say that an agency has $15 million left over from last year's budget and also has $20 million disobligated from previous years.

This $35 million technically should be deducted from the budget request, but normally the subtraction is not cited or is poorly cited by the agency.

Another sleight-of-hand trick is the fund transfer. An agency can often transfer money from one account to another. By using several transfers among several funds, illusions can be created about the money that was obligated. This unprofessional trick can be used also to defraud the government or mislead reviewing groups such as prospective bond buyers. Careful accounting can uncover such abuses, but such work is detailed and time consuming.

Most spender strategies are direct and simple. The agency merely points out that the tasks it performs have expanded and more money is needed to fund the program. Another strategy is to point out the backlog of requests or tasks. The argument is then made that an increase is needed to eliminate the backlog and that a cut would increase the size of the backlog. A third strategy or argument is to appeal to a national standard by showing that the agency can meet the standard with a given level of budget support. This strategy is used often by highly professional groups (e.g., medical and educational).

Sometimes the strategy is to argue with economic concepts. A program activity may involve a fee, such as an entrance fee or license. The agency argues that a given budget level would attract more people to the activity, thus increasing the revenue from the activity. The increased revenue might be larger than the expenses in the budget. A more complex argument is that an increased budget for a program like a subsidy would increase the operation and payroll size. The argument is made that because of the multiplier effect of the subsidy the government would recover more in additional taxes (e.g., income tax) than was paid out for the subsidy. Another argument is that an increased budget would permit greater productivity owing to a better cost average per unit or the use of the extra money to purchase labor-saving devices.

Other arguments are predicated more on emotion. The agency argues that the revenue of the government has grown and that the agency should receive a fair share of the growth. A bolder strategy is to argue that a high-level commitment exists on the project and there is no option but to fund the program. A less bold but equally emotional strategy is to plead that the program is "squeezed to the bone" and a certain funding level is essential for meaningful program operation.

In many situations, the agency wishes to start a new program but the newness must be masked. Once funded, a "foot-in-the-door wedge" or "camel's nose under the tent" has been established. This precedent greatly helps the agency convince reviewers because the standard for new programs tends to be harsher than the standard for existing programs. The agency will often argue that the money does not represent a new initiative but rather a continuation of old programs. This may be quite true literally, but the new dimension may constitute an entire new major emphasis which logically should be considered a new program. However, such treatment would bias the reviewers against the effort.

Spenders' strategies can constitute a high political risk for the agency and agency officials. One strategy is to react to a request for cuts by suggesting cuts be taken first on projects which enjoy strong political support. By cutting the "sacred cows" or popular programs, the cutter is placed in a politically difficult position and may withdraw the request to cut the program. The risk for the agency head is that the chief executive may be offended by the use of this strategy and fire the political appointee. A second strategy is to shift the blame. The agency points out that if the full requested amount is not funded, then certain specific activities will not be undertaken. The agency makes it clear to the reviewer that the responsibility for not funding the activity will be placed on the reviewer. In some situations, reviewers are sobered by such responsibility and the related political implications; thus they act favorably on the budget request. A third strategy is to argue that a cut is irresponsible and that the project must be funded at the requested level or not funded at all. This is a sound argument for many projects because there is a lower limit at which the project cannot be sustained as viable. The risk in such an argument is that the reviewer may indeed decide to cut the whole project.

Another high-risk strategy is to spend fast to be short. The agency deliberately spends the money at a fast rate and then goes back to the reviewers for supplemental appropriations. This strategy is employed infrequently but does occur, especially when the agency is asked to absorb large cuts. This is an extremely high-risk strategy because of the likelihood that the top agency officials will be considered to be irresponsible and poor managers. Firing of top officials is often a result of the use of such strategies.

Cutters' Strategies

Just as there are game strategies for an agency, there are strategies for the reviewing groups. Some strategies are safe and are fairly standard. Other strategies are essentially counterstrategies to be used against spenders' arguments and ploys. The discussion here, like the previous spenders' section, is addressed to explaining the strategies and not to an in-depth treatment of their application in a variety of contingencies.

The safe approaches include reducing increases, questioning hidden "revenues," cutting less visible items, and employing delay. The political support for existing programs can be quite strong and the pressure for increases may be strong also. However, the exact size of the increase is almost always open to discussion and cuts in the increases are easier to sustain. Another safe approach is to investigate and try to isolate "hidden" revenue, such as the use of the previous fiscal year's appropriations or the use of existing government property rather than the purchase of new property. Normally, some savings can be found with this approach and few can fault the results. Another approach is to cut the less visible or less politically supported items. This approach should be employed with some discretion because such "saving" may be false economy. For example, the replacement program for a city water pipe system can be deferred but the wiser policy is probably a yearly systematic program. Delay is a particularly easily applied strategy. Whenever another study is conducted or delays are caused for other reasons, the result is that the item is not included in the budget. This is one of the most successful cutter's strategies because all that need be done to justify a delaying study is to raise a question.

Several fairly standard arguments and ploys exist. One is always to cut something. If no cuts are made, the credible power of the reviewer is questioned. Also, the reviewers are aware that the spenders have a natural tendency to include items that they could do without. Thus cuts will eliminate those "frills." A second approach is to argue that initial allocations are unnecessary. If nothing starts, then budget expansion is diminished. A third approach is to defer or record projects on the grounds that initial dollars cannot be spent correctly by the end of the fiscal year. New programs normally experience difficulty in staffing themselves; thus they rarely can do a decent job in the first year. By arguing that a program will not do a decent job in the first year, the cutter can each year prevent the program from coming into existence. A fourth approach is never to allow a precedent to be established. Precedents lead to continued budget requests. An effective ploy is to argue that there is only so much money and that some is available for program increases. The question is then asked: Whose turn is it? This focuses the debate away from the amount and gets the various units to argue against each other. A sophisticated ploy to be used in a few circumstances is to eliminate interagency competition, which tends to.be more expensive due to the expansive nature of competition itself in the public sector.

The cutter need not accept or live with strategies employed by the spender. Counterstrategies do exist. If the agency says the increase is "so small," the counter is to argue that no item is too small to eliminate or to suggest that such small items can be absorbed without a budget increase. If the agency argues that they should have a fair share of the growth, the cutter can ask what is "fair" and never accept any definition. Another counterstrategy is to challenge work load data. Often such data are collected poorly and can be easily challenged on methodological grounds. The cutter can normally argue that productivity increases—for a number of reasons, such as a worker's becoming more experienced at a new job (i.e., learning curve)—should mean that increases or even decreases are appropriate in a given program.

One spender's strategy is to place the blame on the cutter for the cuts, but that blame need not be accepted. The cutter can force the agency officials to say what they believe should be cut first. If the spender is likely to put forth political "sacred cows" for cutting, the cutter can anticipate and neutralize the strategy by insisting that the agency must suggest items to be cut but stipulating which items cannot be considered as candidates for cutting.

Cutters normally have the advantage because they need only question and the spender has the burden of proof. The strongest asset the spender has is expertise, and care must be taken to maintain the expert's credibility. Spenders can employ strategies but most of them must be executed with an aura of expertise.

New Programs

The previous strategies are for normal day-to-day budget situations. New programs require extraordinary efforts on the part of the spenders. Often new programs are established in reaction to a crisis or what some consider to be a crisis. Such crises rarely are manufactured, but groups do take advantage of crises to establish new programs or radically increase existing programs. The political climate in a crisis is such that political forces concur that the need is obvious and the debate centers on the "solutions." But even that debate is different in that the political climate calls for a solution, and delay is an unacceptable condition. Standards are lowered and the key is effectiveness. Efficiency becomes a less significant topic. In such an environment, agencies have a much greater opportunity to get viable ideas accepted and new or radical increases in programs do occur.

Agency or clientele advertising and salesmanship can sometimes result in the creation of new programs. Dramatic names or labels such as *Mission 66* or *Headstart* can be significant in capturing enough popular attention. Good presentations are necessary. A well-organized effort can start new programs, but the presence of anticlientele groups (even small groups) can be fatal to such efforts. Rarely are advertising and salesmanship adequate by themselves. Normally they must be linked to a cause of the day (e.g., environment, pollution, national defense, inflation, unemployment). Ironically, overselling sometimes can be dysfunctional because the new program can become so popular that the agency's other programs suffer. Advertising and salesmanship should not be underrated, but the times and places are more significant in the beginning of most new programs.

Cautions

Unlike a parlor game, the budget game has serious consequences. Spenders' and cutters' strategies are used and sometimes one side or the other plays the game poorly. This is unfortunate because the budget process is usually best served when both sides play the game well. One particularly serious game fault is when the agency leadership forgets that the agency is a *public* agency designed to serve *all* the people. True, the clientele is only part of the public and most of the agency's dealings need only concern the clientele, but circumstances do exist where the public nature of an agency prohibits continuous harmonious relations with the clientele group (e.g., a coal company dealing with the Interior Department on a strip mining question). Public agencies can be captured by their clientele.

The mood of the times often is much more important than given strategies of spenders or cutters. Such moods change and they create a significant climate which favors, disfavors, or is neutral to specific programs. Government officials are sensitive to current events and recognize that those events are much like the weather for the farmer. The weather is very important and the farmer can do some things to mitigate the bad effects of weather, but it is still a largely uncontrolled governing force. Some political storms must be accepted as either a favorable or unfavorable reality by government officials.

One last caution is noted. If the mood of the times becomes favorable to a program and the reviewers become converts to the mission of an agency, the agency will discover that its new role expectation according to the reviewers is to think and act very big. The meaning of "big" depends on the size of the government and the dimensions of the problem. If the agency doesn't think in expansive terms, then criticisms, such as being overly concerned about "petty economies," are likely to occur. Such role expectations are sometimes difficult to comprehend given the normal budget process, but the agency must accommodate to the role expectation or be subject to remarkably unpleasant political pressure.

REVIEW QUESTIONS

1. What political influence patterns exist in the federal government in terms of budgeting? Why are they important to understand?
2. Why is it important for an agency to cultivate a clientele? How is that done? What problems and cautions are important to understand?
3. What are the typical duties of an agency budget officer? What views and behaviors should be anticipated?
4. What is the agency budget officer's perspective? Contrast that to the executive and legislative perspective.
5. Why are confidence, results, and hearings important? Explain how confidence can be enhanced. How can one prepare for hearings?
6. What strategies can be used by advocates of spending and by reviewers critical of spending?

REFERENCES

ANTHONY, ROBERT. "Closing the Loop Between Planning and Performance," *Public Administration Review* (May/June 1971).

ANTON, THOMAS J. *The Politics of State Expenditure in Illinois.* Urbana: University of Illinois Press, 1966.

AXELROD, DONALD. "Post-Burkhead: The State of the Art or Science of Budgeting," *Public Administration Review* (November/December 1973).

PARKER, STEVE. "Budgeting as an Expression of Power" in Jack Rabin and Thomas D. Lynch (eds.), *Handbook on Public Budgeting and Financial Management.* New York: Marcel Dekker, 1983.

WILDAVSKY, AARON. *The Politics of the Budgeting Process.* Boston: Little, Brown, 1964.

chapter 4

BUDGET FORMATS AND PREPARATION

This chapter addresses the topics of budget formats, building the budget, budget reviews, and legislative adoption. It covers:

1. why budget formats are significant;
2. the various budget formats and how they apply to general policy, budget balancing, and the improvement of government management;
3. the role and work of the central budget office in initiating the process of building the budget;
4. the central role and tasks of the agency in preparing the budget;
5. the importance of the steps associated with executive and legislative reviews of the budget;
6. the use of executive budget hearings in the review process;
7. the ingredients and preparation of the executive budget document;
8. the Congressional budget timetable;
9. the legislature's deliberative process on the budget; and
10. the formats used in legislative adoptions of budgets.

BUDGET FORMAT

The Important Means

Formats are important and procedures are not neutral. The *means* of budgeting affect the *ends* of budgeting. How? Decision makers tend to think about what is put in front of them. Thus, budget classifications tend to define reality for budget makers and reviewers by channeling their attention and thought to specific areas. To illustrate this point, Edward A. Lehan in *Simplified Governmental Budgeting* asked his readers to examine two exhibits

EXHIBIT 4-1   A Line-Item Format

CODE ENFORCEMENT	BUDGET
Personal Service	$60,238
Contractual Service	7,863
Supplies	1,376
Total	$69,477

similar to Exhibit 4-1 and Exhibit 4-2 and to prepare simple follow-up questions.

The line-item format focuses thinking and discussion on things to be bought and tempts officials to alter expenditure patterns in ways largely unrelated to policy issues on service levels.

A third format—performance budgeting—is illustrated in Exhibit 4-3. Note how the reader's mind tends to be directed toward questions of efficiency.

Which budget format (line-item, program, performance, PPB, ZBB, TBB) is the best? Given that the format does influence the decision-making focus, then the selection of a format depends on the desired decision-making environment. What mind-set do you wish to create? The three major concerns of a budget officer are (1) to raise the level of debate, (2) to insure that policy control is maintained, and (3) to improve the quality of management in the government. Given these objectives, the choice of format can still vary substantially, depending on the political and managerial context.

Fortunately, the three objectives of a budget office can be met not only by the recommended budget but also by the operating budget, the capital budget, other budget office documents, and meetings. Thus, some flexibility exists in the means to accomplish the objectives. However, in this chapter, only the format of the recommended budget will be addressed. In an excellent book, *Effective Budgetary Presentations: The Cutting Edge* compiled by Girard Miller, the Government Finance Officers Association presented examples of the common components of local government budgets. These components are the budget cover, table of contents, organization charts, transmittal letter, financial summaries, goals and objectives, divider pages,

EXHIBIT 4-2   A Program Format

CODE ENFORCEMENT	BUDGET
Plan examination	$12,331
Inspection	40,339
Education	15,529
Total	$68,199

EXHIBIT 4-3   A Performance Budget Format

CODE ENFORCEMENT	ITEMS	BUDGET	UNIT COST
Plan examinations	744	$12,331	$16.57
Inspections	19,371	40,339	2.08
Education (graduates or trainees)	12,333	15,526	1.26
Total		$68,196	

Typical questions:
1. Are there any inefficiencies?
2. Can we lower unit cost? How?
3. Why is the unit cost of plan examination so high?

revenues, departmental and activity budgets, program budget summaries, performance measurements, enterprise and internal service funds, capital outlay, special analyses, accompanying documents, reader's guides, budgetary procedures, budget preparation instructions, and legislative adoption. Students are encouraged to review this unique collection of samples to understand some of the format possibilities available to a budget office.

In summary, each format channels thought differently. Line-item budgeting tends to take decision makers away from policy issues and focus attention on expenditure savings. Program budgeting tends to focus attention on policy differences and on choices among policy options. Performance budgeting places the focus on questions of efficiency rather than of effectiveness.

Distinguished Budgets

In 1984, the Government Finance Officers' Association (GFOA) established an annual Awards for Distinguished Budget Presentations. The procedures followed in the awards program are similar to those in the GFOA Certificate of Conformance in Financial Reporting program. Interested local governments send their last annual budget, supporting material, and an entry fee to GFOA. Each budget is reviewed by at least three GFOA member reviewers, using evaluation criteria that stress the budget as a policy document, an operations guide, a financial plan, and a communication device.

GFOA recognizes the budget as a policy-setting instrument and wishes to make sure that policy-making is explicit. The criteria call for general government and specific unit statements of policy, which can be in the form of goals and objectives, mission statements, or strategies. Any change in policy since the last annual budget should be explained in the budget document. Ideally, the rationale for the policy as well as the policy implementation and monitoring process should be explained. In addition, the criteria demand that the budget development process, including its later amendments, should be explained in the budget document itself.

GFOA realizes that the budget is also an important operational guide during the current year to all the units in government. Thus, clarity of purpose in terms useful to bureaucratic units is imperative. Budget programs and line-items must be tied to the government's organizational units. The criteria call for stating the work force of each unit in terms of the organization chart and presenting the information for both the current and budget years. The criteria also expect the capital spending decisions to be explained in terms of their effects on daily operations and operating expenditures. In addition, specific objectives, performance targets, and important deadlines of department heads should also be included in the budget. The budget must provide a means to measure and permit accountability for performance or lack of performance in government.

GFOA recognizes that the technical relationship of financial structure to the operations of government must be defined in the budget. Thus, the following technical topics must be explained in the budget, but in a manner understandable to the lay reader:

1. the major revenue sources;
2. the bases for forecasting, including predictions of events or factors that will influence forecasts;
3. the organization of funds used by the government;
4. the end of the year projections of financial conditions;
5. a capital financing element (a separate capital budget is possible for larger governments);
6. a consolidated picture of operations and financial activity;
7. the debt management issues; and
8. the accountability basis used by the government.

To GFOA, communication to the public is extremely important. The image of government is often not positive. Part of the problem is the public does not understand what government does for them. Given that the budget is normally the single best comprehensive presentation on what a government is going to do with its tax resources, GFOA believes care must be taken to communicate those policies in a manner in which the general public can understand government's programs, policies, and financial needs. To accomplish the goal of better communication, the GFOA criteria call for the following:

1. Availability to the public of the draft budget prior to its adoption by the government decision makers.
2. Clear summary information on the budget, covering topics of interest so that the media and the public can understand key points such as the size of programs, the revenue sources, and the policy changes of concern to the public.
3. Normal communication devices, which aid in understanding large complex sets of information. Those devices include a budget message, a table of contents, a glossary of terms, an identification of the basic units in the budget, charts and graphs with narrative explanations, key assumptions used in preparing the budget, a cross-index, and supplemental information, including statistical tables.

The evaluation criteria define "a good budget document" and largely implies what is a good budget process. The criteria are not predicated on any particular approach, such as ZBB, but they do encourage the use of program categories and performance measures. The criteria do reflect some definite normative guidance on what GFOA considers important in a budget document.

The award program for Distinguished Budget Presentations is taken quite seriously by GFOA and local governments. Of the first 81 governments submitting their budgets for review, 51 (63 percent) received the award. Given that governments are not required to participate and few truly unprofessional governments would participate, the rate of failure is significant. The first city to receive an "especially notable" award was Dayton, Ohio. Those governments that have received a budget award from GFOA are justifiably proud of their professional achievement. Not only is the budget award program defining "good budgeting," it also serves as an important stimulant for improving the quality of local government budgeting in general.

Ends Defining Means

From a format design perspective, the desired ends should influence what format or formats should be used. A tendency of budget presenters is to use a standard approach for all programs, and this is desirable because it permits comparisons. Nevertheless, various programs do deserve individual presentations in order to highlight the most useful information for decision-making purposes. Format designers should decide first on the general format and then on extra information useful for specific programs.

Three common concerns should be weighed when deciding on format:

1. How to help decision makers deal with *general policy* matters?
2. How should the *budget* be *balanced?*
3. How can decisions of policy makers be used to *improve* the *quality* of *government management?*

Four common difficulties associated with helping elected decision makers formulate policy are (1) trying to get elected officials to focus upon the major policy issues rather than insignificant and time-consuming issues which make relatively little difference to the future of the community, (2) fostering a decision-making environment in which counterproductive political tensions are reduced so that important and timely policy can be made, (3) sensitizing decision makers to the future year implications of their decisions, and (4) achieving an awareness that budget decisions do relate to specific government actions which affect individuals and society. The first difficulty is commonly handled with program budgeting and formalized budget approaches like PPB and ZBB. The latter is especially useful as a means to inform novice political executives of the policy implications of budget decisions. The second difficulty, according to one noted author, Aaron Wildavsky, can be handled well by line-item budgeting, which permits more face-saving because it focuses attention on relatively unemotional subjects such as salaries, travel, and supplies. The third difficulty is handled by requiring revenue and expenditure forecasts to be made possibly five or more years beyond the BY. Requiring a financial program schedule is also an appropriate procedural way to meet this concern. The fourth difficulty is resolved by having program budgets include performance measures which show the products or services produced by government programs as well as their impact on individuals and society.

Dealing with the challenge of balanced budgets commonly requires (1) getting both policy makers and government agencies to accept the existence of resource constraints, (2) helping policy makers justify to the public the need for more government resources (i.e., higher property taxes), and (3) shifting political pressure from the more controversial revenue sources to the more acceptable revenue sources. The first type of situation is best suited for a TBB approach, which assumes a given revenue level and works from that assumption. Ideally, with TBB, budget decisions beyond the arbitrarily established limit simply should not be considered. The limitation of such an approach is that government problems are not limited by arbitrarily established revenue limits. The second situation occurs when policy makers decide that more taxes are needed, but the public is not yet supportive of that policy position. Budgets can be constructed to stress the need, how government action can resolve that need, and the necessity for more money if that need is to be resolved. Program budgeting is particularly useful if it is combined with appropriate measures of program services and social needs. The third situation is more complex. Governments receive their revenues from various sources, of which some are more politically sensitive at various times than others. One way to help deal with that political reality is to minimize pressure on the politically sensitive revenue sources by shifting as much cost as possible to less sensitive revenue sources. For example, if property tax is a hot political issue, then user fee revenues can be increased as much as possible to cover expenses. The budget format can show, for each expense item, the source of revenue. This would permit the probing inquiry which would seek to shift the burden to the least politically sensitive revenue source.

Striving to improve government management usually includes (1) stressing efficiency and productivity in government management, (2) establishing top level control procedures in order to ensure that policy is carried out and that fraud and abuse are minimized, (3) establishing proper review practices to minimize overhead costs, (4) stopping unnecessary end-of-the-year purchases, and (5) improving management through better use of new technology and development of professionals and other employees. The first concern is normally addressed with performance budgeting or, more commonly, separate ad hoc productivity studies, internal audits, and the hiring of more program reviewers. Edward A. Lehan advocates a format (see chapter 5) which includes marginal analysis and allows decision makers to consider the optimum funding level which will result in the greatest productivity. Exhibit 4-4 is an example of a performance budget developed by Edward A. Lehan for the government of Jamaica. The second concern can be addressed in the operating budget by using a line-item format which

EXHIBIT 4-4 Jamaica Budget/1986-87

Problem Definition and Goal. The estimated 1986–87 workload totals 5,100 analyses. This projection embraces 2,000 pharmaceutical investigations, 1,800 toxicological reports, 300 analyses of food and 1,340 investigations related to customs and excise duties.

Although the workload increased by 23% in 1985–86, and is expected to rise again in 1986–87, the potential demand for analyses is estimated to be far higher, perhaps as high as 12,000 annually. Indeed, in 1974–75, when the Lab was able to respond more promptly to requests, it produced over 12,000 analyses. As will be pointed out, more intensive use of the Lab can significantly reduce unit costs.

In addition to accuracy, Lab effectiveness and efficiency depends on *speed.* Progressively declining over the years, the Lab's responsiveness, measured by proportion of analyses done "on-time", is estimated at 30% for 1986–87 given existing staffing and equipment.

In 1986–87, recognizing the constraints of existing equipment, but assuming full staffing, the Lab aims to deliver 1,530 analyses on-time, or 30% of its total project workload.

Target Population. Lab services are used by hospitals and health clinics (625,000 patient contacts), the Courts Custom and Excise Revenue Officers, 8 pharmaceutical manufacturers and private individuals, labs and food processors.

ANALYTICAL WORKLOAD	1984–85	1985–86	1986–87
Backlog April 1	59	84	100
Requested Analyses	4,000	4,500	5,020
Tests Completed "On-time"	3,975	4,484	} 1,530
Tests Completed "Over-due"			3,570
Backlog March 31	84	100	20

MINISTRY OF HEALTH GOVERNMENT CHEMIST

EXPENDITURES (000's)	1986–87 BUDGET	1985–86 REVISED	1985–86 APPROVED	1984–85 ACTUAL
Analytical Services	874	502	722	429
FINANCING PLAN				
Service Charges	127	3	NA	3
Taxation Revenue	747	499	722	426
	874	502	722	429
PERFORMANCE DATA				
Analyses	5,100	4,884	NA	3,975
Paid Hours	74,880		NA	
Hours/Analysis	14.7		NA	
Cost/Analysis*	$ 144		NA	
On-time Delivery Ratio	30%			

*Reflects a $734,000 operating budget

Performance Criteria. The Lab assists in the enforcement of the Public Health Act, Dangerous Drugs Act, Excise Duty Act, Coroner's Act.

Analyses are performed in accordance with the methods of the AOAC, and the standards and methods of the Codex Alimentarius, British Pharacopoeia and Codex, US Pharmacopoeia and National Formulary.

Recommended time limits for completion of analyses:

Toxicology emergencies	- 6 staff hours per sample
Pharmaceutical Samples	- 8 staff hours per component
Coroner's cases	- 10 staff hours per specimen
Customs and Excise	- 2 staff hours per component
Veterinary samples	- 10 staff hours per specimen
Food sample analyses	- 6 staff hours per component

Preferred Solution: Impacts and Benefits. Based on the 1986–87 approved budget, supporting an allotment of 23,400 technical staff workhours, the Lab's workplan calls for an estimated production of 1275 investigations each quarter, or 5,100 for the year.

Based on an operating budget of $734,000, reflecting an adjustment of $140,000 for an investment in equipment which should be amortized in future budgets, the Lab's unit cost for 1986–87 is projected at $144.

The plan assumes 36 posts. If fully staffed, the Lab team should be able to increase the percentage of "on-time" deliveries to 30%, up from the ratio of 1985–86.

This 30% ratio is unacceptable, as Lab reporting delays result in needless livestock losses, and longer-than-needed hospital stays.

By making a one-time $1.2 million investment in state-of-the-art equipment, amortized over five years, assuming an upgraded staff, the productivity of the Lab could soar to 12,000 investigations per year, at a unit cost of $109. With new equipment, "on-time" deliveries could reach 100%, resulting in significant net benefits as outlined below:

ESTIMATED ANNUAL COST

Operating Budget (1986–87 Budget Adjusted)	1,000,000
Equipment Investment amortized at 20% annually (1)	312,000
	1,312,000

ESTIMATED ANNUAL BENEFITS

Increased Customs and Excise Revenue (2)	5,000,000
Reduced Livestock Losses (2)	3,000,000
Reduced Hospital Stays	+ but ?
	8,000,000

NET ANNUAL BENEFIT

1. $1.2 million loan repaid in five years at 10% interest, $360,000, resulting in a total investment of $1,560,000.
2. Conservative estimates provided by responsible officials.

(continued)

EXHIBIT 4-4 (continued)

EXPENDITURE ANALYSIS	CODE	INPUT FACTOR	INPUT UNITS	UNIT PRICE	1986-87 BUDGET	1985-86 REVISED	1985-86 APPROVED	1984-85 ACTUAL
Personal Emoluments	01	Staff Hours	74,880	7.28	545	382	417	333
Travel Expenses	02	Vehicles	4	4,500	22	12	20	13
Supplies and Materials	03	Various factors	NA	NA	45	9	40	21
Public Utilities	06	Various factors	NA	NA	53	64	50	53
Operating & Maintenance	07	Various factors	NA	NA	5	10	5	9
Subscriptions	08	Reference Documents	18	3,555	64	25	40	—
Equipment	14	Units	2	70,000	140	—	150	—
					874	502	722	429

Source: Adapted from the 1986–87 Jamacia Budget.

assigns dollars to specific units. Another strategy often employed is to increase audit and inspector general staffs. The third concern is associated with a greater organizational sophistication. Formats which include overhead comparative and longitudinal cost data focus attention on that concern and are helpful. The fourth concern can be addressed by good accounting practices. Accounting data illustrating the problem can be included in the budget or in a special analysis accompanying the budget. The fifth concern can be spotlighted in the budget by a narrative which discusses plans for the use of new technology and how staff will be developed. First-priority use of new funds can be singled out for upgrading technology, which should result in productivity improvements. Professional development (i.e., training) can be included as one of the fringe benefits of employment and made less vulnerable to normal line-item budget cuts.

In summary, one can choose among budget formats in order to better highlight particular concerns. Such highlighting will not necessarily guarantee specific decisions, but it will channel thought.

BUILDING THE BUDGET

Program Financial Schedule

On a quarterly basis, each department and agency can be required to transmit a program financial schedule to the central budget office. This now fairly common budget requirement provides useful information to the budget office. On a quarterly basis, the central budget office can better forecast expenditure needs. The schedule categorizes the program by activity, method of finance, and fiscal year. Schedules commonly forecast five years beyond the budget year and include output measures associated with the desirable appropriation levels. The schedules are also divided into obligations and expenditures, thus providing useful information to economists and analysts concerned with the government's cash flow. Thus, the data can be used to estimate likely expenditure demands. This is useful data in preparing the budget call and issuing executive guidance on budget preparation.

These forecasts should not be viewed as extremely accurate, but merely as an indication of likely financial patterns given existing policy. In each quarter, policy can change and other factors can evolve, making periodic updating essential. The program financial schedule is particularly significant prior to the development of the central budget office's budget call. The total of the schedules equals a reasonably high estimate of what all the departments and agencies will request. This intelligence is useful in framing budget office guidance for building the budget.

Budget Call

Budget coordination.   Exhibit 4-5 presents a slightly modified budget calendar used by the city of Los Angeles. The calendar is important to the building of the budget because it establishes essential deadlines. Preparing

EXHIBIT 4-5   Budget Calendar, Los Angeles

DATE	ACTION TO BE COMPLETED
January 2	Mayor's Budget Policy letter requesting Department heads to submit proposed work programs and budget estimates for ensuing fiscal year. Necessary forms and revisions to budget manual are transmitted with that letter.
February 1	City Administrative Officer approves staff budget assignments which are thereafter distributed to the staff.
February 15	Current level work programs and budget estimates received from department heads.
March 1	Service betterment budget estimates, if any, received from department heads.
April 10	City Administrative Officer reviews tentative Capital Improvement Expenditure Program and, upon approval, transmits it to the Public Works Priority Committee by April 10.
April 10	City Administrative Officer submits annual salary recommendations to City Council by April 10.
April 10–30	Hearings conducted by the Public Works Priority Committee to determine final priority of capital projects to be included in Capital Improvement Expenditure Program for ensuing year.
April 10–17	Preliminary budget hearings held by City Administrative Officer and Budget Coordinator with the Assistant Budget Coordinator and staff analyst for each department.
April 18–28	City Administrative Officer assisted by Budget Coordinator conducts departmental budget hearings with each department head at which time the staff analysts' recommendations for that department budget are presented and department head is given an opportunity to express his viewpoint.
May 1[1]	Final date for submission by City Controller of the official estimates of revenue from all sources (other than general property taxes).
May 1[1]	City Administrative Officer submits his official estimate of revenue from general property taxes.
May 1–5	Mayor, assisted by City Administrative officer, conducts budget conferences with each department head. Attended by Council members, press and taxpayer groups.
May 5–12	Final budget decisions made by Mayor assisted by City Administrative Officer.
May 12–31	Budget printed under supervision of City Administrative Officer.
June 1[1]	Mayor submits proposed budget to City Council.
June 1–20	Council considers Mayor's veto of any item and may override Mayor's veto by two-thirds vote.
June 20–25[1]	Mayor considers any modifications made by City Council and may veto such changes.
June 25–28[1]	Council considers Mayor's veto of any item and may override Mayor's veto by two-thirds vote.
July 1[1]	Beginning of fiscal year—Budget takes effect.

[1]Charter requirement.

a budget is a complex undertaking involving the whole government. Coordination is achieved by first deciding who must do what when. This is decided in the calendar. The budget calendar milestones of a local government include:

1. distribution of instructions and forms;
2. preparation of revenue estimates;
3. return of completed budget request forms;
4. completion of review and preliminary preparation work assigned to the central budget agency;
5. completion of executive review and executive determination of final budget content;
6. submission of the budget to the legislative body;
7. completion of budget hearings;
8. preliminary legislative determination of the content of the appropriation ordinance or budget to be approved;
9. final action by the legislative body;
10. executive approval or veto of the adopted budget and legislative action;
11. completion of administrative actions, if any, needed to finalize budget appropriations; and
12. beginning of fiscal year.

Once the preliminary estimates of expenditures and budget calendar have been prepared, the central budget office can proceed with preparing for the budget call. The call gives guidance to all the departments and agencies on how to go about preparing the budget. In many governments, including the federal government, much of the guidance is standardized and established in official bulletins and circulars such as OMB Circular A-11. Agency budget officials need only refer to the established procedures and report forms. In addition to the standard operating procedures, each year special guidance is issued in the form of a "policy" letter, "allowance" letter, an executive policy message, or a statement on the budget. The "policy" letter is used in the federal government to convey executive guidance and budget ceilings. The "allowance" letter comes later to inform federal agencies and departments of presidential or OMB decisions after the executive review process.

Budget guidance. The executive policy message or statement on the budget at the state and local level requests budget information and establishes guidance. For example, the policy may be one of "hold-the-line," retrenchment, or expansion. Also, programs and activities to be emphasized or deemphasized are announced. Common subjects discussed in municipal statements include:

1. mandated increases, such as pension payments, salary increments, and debt service;
2. raise or change in taxes;

3. request to hold the line or identify inadequate services requiring expanded effort;
4. plea for economy;
5. explanation of local economic trends influencing the budget; and
6. explanation of who must provide what information and when it is due (the budget calendar).

The detailed explanation call may be in the form of a budget instructions booklet which provides guidance to the agencies and departments. The booklet contains:

1. the preliminary statement of executive budget policy;
2. the table of contents, including listing of forms;
3. the budget calendar;
4. general instructions; and
5. specific instructions for each form, including a sample form.

Budget office follow-through is essential. The instructions must be sent to the chief departmental officials. Each level of government will repackage the instructions and reissue them to lower levels. Eventually, the program managers receive the information requests. Meetings are useful at all levels to clarify and avoid possible confusion. Special care should be taken to explain any changes in the procedures. Every official involved should understand the current financial status and likely trends, including personnel pay trends. Emphasis must always be given to the need for accurate, prompt, uniform replies. The types of forms required are explained in Municipal Finance Officers Association publications cited in this chapter's references.

The budget call always asks for a statement of government functions, activities, and work programs, or some narrative explaining what services are to be received for the tax dollar. The general instructions asking for this budget explanation normally stress the desirability of brevity, clarity, and comprehensiveness. The explanation should reflect any program changes and even emphasize those changes. Each level in the executive branch uses the information, with the central budget and department levels focusing upon having a complete inventory of government activities keyed to specific units assigned to functions and activities. The descriptive detail is greater at the unit and agency level.

Agency call.   Exhibit 4-6 is a sample agency call for estimates used in past federal budget training manuals. The call draws attention to the executive policy and the required forms to be used in the agency. The call points out that the agency is still operating under a continuing resolution for the current year. Reference is made to instructions which are particularly sensitive. The call states who should prepare the information (i.e., assistant directors and division heads) and when the information is due (e.g., August 20). Note that only 20 days are allowed to compile the information. Tight dead-

EXHIBIT 4-6   Agency Call for Estimates (Sample)

August 1, 19PY

MEMORANDUM TO ASSIST DIRECTORS AND DIVISION HEADS

Subject: *Instructions for Preparation of the Budget Estimates for FY 19BY*

The 19BY budget submission to the Office of Management and Budget (OMB) will conform generally to the program and activity structure used for the 19CY budget estimate. The overall budget estimate will be prepared to reflect policy and program decisions which resulted from budget meetings held by the Director on the 19BY budget.

For purposes of the presentation to OMB, descriptive materials for the various programs should be brief statements covering the points outlined in the following format. It is expected that the submission to the Congress will be a more detailed budget.

Since no appropriation has been approved for the Agency for 19CY, the program estimates for that fiscal year will be the same as in the 19CY Budget to the Congress. Under item "C." of the instructions, supplementary data is being requested for the preparation of staff salary estimates and travel and other administrative expenses that are spread among the activities shown in the Salaries and Expenses appropriation.

Estimates and drafts of the justification material must be received by the Budget Office by August 20.

Comptroller

Source: Resource Conservation Agency, Washington, D.C. 20550.

lines do occur in budgeting. If zero base budgeting were used, the instructions would require alternative decision packages and priority rankings.

Preparing a budget at the agency level is a difficult task. The material must be assembled from the units and the budget figures in particular must conform to agency policy set down by the agency head. Personnel statistics and cost information is normally calculated by the budget office to compute the salaries and expense portion of the budget. If the agency has field units, the process is more complex because more groups are involved. Extreme accuracy and consistency are important because their absence denotes sloppy preparation and poor management.

The format of the agency budget requests varies greatly depending upon which budget reform happens to be in vogue. The format can be a detailed line-item presentation that permits greater control over the bureaucracy, a program budget that stresses policy issues and their budget implications, a performance budget that relates input to program accomplishments, a zero base budget that focuses on marginal value and prioritization, or an incremental budget that stresses changes from past policy decisions. The format selected is important, but a more important factor is the quality of professionalism devoted to preparing and reviewing the budget. Good professionalism calls for in-depth understanding of the agency and the related budget implications. How this is done is explained in chapter 6. Too often the format is established by some budget reform movement instead of being tailored to the type of programs administered by the agency as well as to the needs of the central budget office.

BUDGET REVIEWS

Once the agency prepares the budget, the review process begins in the executive and legislative branches. The agency first meets with the department officials. They conduct a complete examination of the budget request, often including budget hearings. Departmental budget decisions are made and the agency budget request is revised based on department level decisions. Normally, the department recommends cuts but is a more friendly reviewer than the central budget office. The latter unit next reviews the agency or compiled departmental budget. Recommendations are made by the central budget office to the chief executive and sometimes departmental officials make direct last-minute appeals to the chief executive. Finally, the chief executive's budget is released.

Executive Budget Hearings

Normally, the agency submits its budget to the reviewing party, who carefully analyzes the submission. Chapter 5 describes how program and budget analyses can be conducted. After the initial analysis of the submission and any other available material, the reviewing party, such as the department budget office, is prepared to seek additional information. Often this is done by formal written questions to the agency on specific inquiries and sometimes more informal inquiries are made. The reviewers—budget examiners—prepare an analysis of the material and prepare background material for a hearing. Hearings need not be held but they enable the budget officer and the executive to obtain a better understanding of an agency's request and reasons supporting that request.

Agencies also prepare for hearings. The depth of preparation varies but the agency is wise to prepare carefully. Anticipated questions from the reviewers can be developed, and responses can be written and studied by the agency's representatives. A plan of action or strategy can be prepared, keeping in mind the factors discussed in the chapter on budget behavior.

The hearing itself is semi-formal, with testimony rarely transcribed. The chief executive of the department should chair the meeting to ask questions and understand the budget request. The principal budget officer is present and plays an active role. Often questions are prepared for the chief executive to facilitate the process. The agency presents a statement and questions follow or the review is handled entirely with questions and answers. Regardless of the style used, the agency should explain its program, especially any program changes. The questioners should probe for elaborations on vague points as well as potential political or management problems. The hearing is only for information purposes and this forum is inappropriate for tentative or final decisions because more deliberation is necessary.

After the hearing is completed, the budget analysts carefully review their notes and reconsider the submission and other material. Guidance from the departmental chief executive is also reviewed. Often the reviewers may ask some additional questions by phone or in writing. The departmental budget office then prepares its final analysis and recommendations.

The departmental chief executive is then briefed on the budget. The briefing depends upon the management style of the chief executives. Some delegate the entire responsibility to the budget office and others review the requests in detail. Normally, the pressure of time on the chief executive prevents long, detailed reviews of requests. A set of briefing information usually includes:

1. summary of agency requests;
2. recommendations of budget office;
3. summary of the past year's chief executive's ideas relative to the budget;
4. added suggestions by the budget office;
5. preliminary budget (balanced for state and local government); and
6. summary of policy issues.

A similar process exists at the gubernatorial or presidential level of government. This review takes place after the departmental reviews.

Executive Budget Document

Budget message.   Budgets sent to legislatures and city councils are almost always accompanied by a budget message. The contents vary depending upon the political situation. Normally, the message includes a discussion of the financial condition of the government and a commentary on the current year operating budget, such as "the current budget is and will continue to be balanced." Revenue highlights are mentioned, including revenue estimates, new revenue sources, and prospects on increased or new taxes. The government is usually put into perspective by citing major trends in finance, population changes, income level shifts, and so on. The principal elements of the proposed expenditures are explained, including the rationale for any major program changes. Sensitive topics like "mandatory" increases as well as pay and fringe benefit policy are mentioned. Problem areas not addressed by the proposed budget are cited, often with an explanation for that omission. At the local level, the message could also explain the relationship between the operating and capital budgeting. The message summarizes the highlights of the budget and blunts political criticism if possible.

Budget summary.   A summary of the budget is essential. It should present consolidated summaries of revenues and appropriations. At the federal level, various economics-related information is presented. At the local level, the comparative statement of resources includes:

1. cash surplus at the end of the first prior year;
2. estimated receipts for the current year;
3. anticipated expenditures during the current year;
4. estimated cash surplus at the end of the current year;
5. anticipated income during the budget year;
6. proposed expenditures during the budget year; and
7. projected cash surplus at the end of the budget year.

Additional information can be included in the local budget summary. A statement on the tax rate and the assessed valuation of the property, including amount of land, improvements, and exemptions, is often included. A statement on other revenue sources is useful. The statement of appropriations by organization unit can be included. Finally, a summary of appropriation to various activities can be mentioned.

Budget detail.   After the summary material, the detailed revenue and expenditure estimates are presented. The revenue estimates are grouped by funds and presented by comparing the budget year estimates with the prior year and current year. Appropriate footnotes are added to explain tax rates, tax base, and nonrecurring humps or valleys in the estimates. All assumptions used in preparing the revenue estimates are explained. The detailed expenditure estimates often include:

1. a narrative explanation of the functions of each department, suborganization unit, and activity, as well as a separate section for comments on the major changes proposed in each activity;
2. a listing by department and suborganization unit of the objects of expenditure and by activity with an identification of proposed resource changes;
3. a listing by position title for each unit and activity as well as any proposed changes; and
4. an identification of the work load volume being undertaken in conjunction with each activity.

The executive budget document is often considered to be the budget even though the legislature may make some changes. In some jurisdictions, the budget is the final document passed and approved by the legislature. Regardless of the stress given the executive budget document, it is extremely influential in the decision-making process. The document is the chief executive's plan. Any modification must be done with the awareness that any changes cannot be simply additions or deletions. Even in the federal government, additions to the budget raise the question of either "Where is the extra money going to come from?" or "What programs are going to be cut?"

If deletions are suggested, the easier but still difficult question raised is either "Where is the extra money going to be spent?" or "What taxes should be cut?" These are not simple questions and the executive budget becomes the point of departure for legislative consideration of the budget.

Congressional Budget Timetable

Budget milestones.   In the earlier discussion of the budget calendar there are target dates set for legislative action on the budget. For many governments, the executive may be considered presumptuous to state target dates for the legislatures because of the separation of powers concept. In spite of that attitude, most budget people can estimate fairly accurately what the target dates are in the legislative budget process. Often the legislative body will state its own targets in its rules. The one forcing deadline is the beginning of the new fiscal year, by which, everyone agrees, the budget should be adopted. The other deadlines fall between the time when the legislature receives the chief executive's budget and the beginning of the fiscal year.

In the federal government, the Congressional deadlines were set by the 1974 Budget Act. These critical targets, coupled with serious prodding by the budget committees, encourage the Congress to pass timely appropriation legislation, avoiding the pre-1974 practice of passing appropriation legislation three to six months into the current year. Both the targets and the active pushing of the budget committees are essential. The targets set a standard. Budget committees use social and political pressure to achieve responsible Congressional action.

The seriousness of not passing timely appropriations is often overlooked. If no appropriation legislation is passed, then the government cannot pay its employees or anyone else. Government operations cease to exist because no one has the authority to spend money. If a decision has not been reached on appropriations prior to the beginning of the new fiscal year, then a legislative body passes a continuing resolution which normally says that the government can continue to obligate and spend at last year's budget levels. The wording of the continuing resolution could also say the government can proceed at the lower of either last year's budget or the approved version of the House or Senate bill. The wording is normally framed to permit spending at the lowest amount the legislature is likely to pass. Managing a program under a continuing resolution is no significant problem unless the final legislation provides the manager with significantly less or more money than the continuing resolution. If less money is provided, the entire program may have to stop. If more money is provided, the program may have to obligate money recklessly in order to use it during the remainder of the fiscal year. Either situation is bad public management which can be compounded by repeated yearly use of the continuing resolution, as happened with Congress.

Congressional budget timetable.   The Congressional budget deliberative process starts with the presidential submission of the Current Services

Budget. This budget alerts the Congress, especially the Congressional Budget Office, the budget committees, and the appropriation committees, that they should be anticipating specific revenue, expenditure, and debt levels unless current policy is changed. The Current Services Budget also provides a baseline of comparison to the later presidential budget.

The presidential budget, with the Current Services Budget, is sent to the Congress 15 days after Congress convenes in the new calendar year (e.g., January 20). The budget normally follows the State of the Union Address to Congress by about one week. Presidents usually address Congress with a specific budget message which is more detailed and specific than the earlier State of the Union speech. The budget messages vary in content with a president's style, but the earlier discussion follows a common pattern, with the exception that more emphasis is often placed on the national economy.

By February 1, the Congressional Budget Office must send its annual report to the budget committees. This report analyzes the economy, the Current Services Budget, and the president's budget. Alternative levels of spending are suggested. Interestingly, the original legislation called for an April 1 submission, but the CBO realized this did not give the budget committees sufficient time to digest the CBO report so the date was changed by mutual consent.

By March 15, the various committees, like appropriation, must submit their respective reports to the budget committees. This is a tentative financial guess by the committees on revenue, expenditure, and debt. The committees use the CBO report, the president's budget, and the detailed backup information supplied by the agencies to help them arrive at reasonable budget estimates.

One month later, on April 15, each budget committee reports its recommended budget resolution. This resolution represents the difficult compromise on the entire budget: the revenues, expenditures, and debt, as well as targets for each committee important to the budget process. One month later, on May 15, each chamber votes on its own resolution. An inability to reach a decision would destroy the process. Opposition can come from the conservatives for spending too much money and from the liberals for spending too little money. The resolutions need not be the same in each chamber. May 15 is also the deadline for reporting all authorization bills. The Congress doesn't want unanticipated expenses resulting from authorization legislation, so this deadline is essential.

Seven days after Labor Day in September final action on appropriation bills is required. This gives the appropriation committees several months to hold their hearings and make their difficult decisions.

By September 15, final action on the second budget resolution is required. This permits last-minute changes possibly due to intervening circumstances since the first resolution was passed. Often, there may be no difference between the first and second resolution, but an opportunity for flexibility has been provided. By September 25, all final actions on budget reconciliation should be passed, thus providing a uniform consolidated Congressional budget in each chamber.

The remaining days in September are used to resolve differences between chambers, pass the legislation, permit a presidential veto, and reconcile or override the veto. All this can be done if there is perfect cooperation among the chambers and the president. If not, then delays will result and a continuing resolution may be necessary because the federal fiscal year begins on October 1.

Legislative Considerations

At all levels of government, legislative bodies consider budgets and budget supporting material. This information is the key to proper legislative understanding of government operations. The considerations and the subsequent legislation permit the legislative oversight activity to exist. The purse strings are important. If weaknesses are identified, legislators can retailor policy often with their redrafted budget. The budget consideration in legislatures is a much more open process than the executive review. Thus legislative budget hearings serve as a forum for better community understanding of government as well as a device to permit citizens to express their views on budget matters.

The time needed for legislative consideration of the budget varies with the size of government. Committees must have time to study the budget and related information, conduct hearings with public officials and possibly with interested citizens, discuss policy internally, and finally enact the legislation. Normally, 60 days is a reasonable time for smaller local governments.

Legislative organization to deal with the budgets also depends largely on the size of government. Larger governments should have standing committees with highly competent professional staff support. Committees and staffs can be organized on a partisan or a nonpartisan basis. Given the complexity of government and budgeting, more of the smaller states and local governments should hire professionally trained and experienced public administrators. Exhibit 4-7 presents an illustrative page from a legislative analyst's review of a budget request. The reader will notice how a good analyst can focus attention upon the items which should concern the legislator.

The hearing is the standard method used to gather information and focus upon potential problems of concern to the legislature. Often these problems are isolated through careful staff program and budget analysis. The legislative hearing is conducted differently from the executive hearing. With legislative hearings, a transcript is often maintained and there are more co-equal questioners of the agency personnel. Some legislators are friendly and others are hostile. Just as in the executive hearings, the agency is wise to prepare for the hearings with briefing books, to plan strategies and tactics, and to have rehearsals. The hearings are usually scheduled more at the convenience of the legislative committee than of the agency. Follow-up questions are common, as in executive hearings. Decisions are not made at hearings, but rather at closed door "mark-up" sessions.

If public participation is part of the hearing, then the committee normally takes care to give due notice of the time and place of the meeting.

EXHIBIT 4-7   Legislative Analyst's Review Sheet, Department of Hospitals and Institutions, 1963 Budget Request

NEWARK CITY HOSPITAL

The 1963 Budget request of $6,469,185.00 for the Newark City Hospital shows an increase of $229,131.67 over 1962 Operations as follows:

1963 Budget Appropriations	$6,453,424.00	1963 Request	$6,469,185.00
1962 Emergencies	115,149.96		
	$6,568,573.96		
Less Cancellations	328,520.63		
Net 1962 Operations	$6,240,053.33	1962 Operations	$6,240,053.33
		Increase	$ 229,131.67

The request for 1,270 employees is 25 less than the 1,295 in 1962.

PAGE NO.	LINE NO.	
4		There were 29,669 less patient days in 1962 than in 1961 resulting from a drop in admissions from 18,760 in 1961 to 15,460 in 1962, a net drop of 3,300.
5		The average day's stay per patient dropped from 9.5 to 9.1. The average daily admissions dropped from 60.9 in 1961 to 56.4 in 1962, a net drop of 4.5 admissions. The average daily census of patients in the hospital dropped from 575.6 in 1961 to 549.9 in 1962, a drop of 25.7 in 1962.
6	1 & 2	What is the status of the Medical Director and the Assistant Medical Director?
6	3	Will the Comptroller's position be filled? Is the present incumbent Joseph Rubino to remain on the hospital payroll?
10	12A	Has this position been filled?
19	37	Is this position going to remain in the hospital?
25		New employee, Director of Surgery. In accordance with policy followed in similar cases the appropriation for this employee will be deleted because there is no valid ordinance supporting it. The appropriation will be made after adoption of the ordinance and before final adoption of the budget by amending the approved budget.
41	103A	Bernice Lippe replaced the Director of Nurses on January 14, 1963 at the minimum salary of $7,500.00. Her salary as Assistant Director of Nursing Education on Page 112 was $6,460. One pay should be deleted from the Director of Nurses' appropriation and one pay remaining in the Assistant Director of Nursing Education's line on Page 112.

Failure to give due notice or to notify all the likely interested "publics" can result in heated public criticism.

The legislatures normally have the power to modify the executive's budget, but that is not always the case in local government. Even if the power exists, modifications are difficult because all components of the budget are interdependent. If one figure is adjusted upward, another figure must be cut if the budget is to balance. Exhibit 4-8 illustrates one city council's modifications.

The adoption of the budget can vary in terms of detail. Appropriations should be itemized by department in order to fix responsibility. Some argue that they should be itemized by major object classification and others by program or activity. There is no one correct way. Object classification is good for greater control, especially when there is a low threshold of trust afforded the government's middle and lower level managers. Program classifications are good for situations which need management flexibility to operate effectively and efficiently. Detailed line-item budgets are extremely inflexible. Necessary taxes and a formal resolution on the final official revenue estimate accompany or are passed at the same time as the budget.

**EXHIBIT 4-8   Schedule Setting Forth Changes Made by City Council
in City Manager's Original Estimate of 1990–91 Budget**

	MANAGER'S ESTIMATE	REVISED AMOUNT
Office of City Manager	$146,135	$138,246
Reason for Change—Reduced cost of annual report, reduction of .5 man year administrative analyst. Add cost of salary increase.		
Secretary-Treasurer	166,844	169,484
Reason for change—Add cost of salary increase.		
Accounting	77,686	74,751
Reason for change—Delete one accountant position. Add cost of salary increase.		
Data Processing	179,470	181,303
Reason for change—Add cost of salary increase.		
Purchasing	30,867	31,539
Reason for change—Add cost of salary increase.		
Tax	400,390	408,861
Reason for change—Add cost of salary increase.		
Legal	99,472	101,636
Reason for change—Add cost of salary increase.		
Retirement Administrator	22,731	23,043
Reason for change—Add cost of salary increase.		
Personnel and Civil Service	29,703	50,349
Reason for change—Add cost of salary increase. Add cost of salary and wage survey.		

LEGISLATIVE ADOPTION[1]

The ultimate budget is the legislative adoption version, which can be several appropriation laws (the federal government's approach), one massive, complex appropriation law (used by many states), or a relatively brief text (used by some local governments). Sometimes the budget submitted to the legislative body includes the recommended act or ordinance.

Often budget ordinances are complex because of state legal requirements. In some jurisdictions, the resolution includes tax rates, purchasing authority, personnel action authorizations, and transfer procedures. Some use broad legislative grants of authority and others have extensive line-item detail for each government unit.

The ordinance:

1. acknowledges receipt of an executive budget from the county manager;
2. recounts earlier publication and a public hearing;
3. summarizes appropriation by fund and category;
4. estimates revenue;
5. levies property taxes;
6. authorizes administrative transfers of appropriations within a fund; and
7. approves and reapproves funds for ongoing capital improvements.

REVIEW QUESTIONS

1. Explain how budget formats channel thought. Explain how formats can direct thought to and highlight general policy matters, budget balancing issues, and improvement of the quality of government management.
2. Why are the program financial schedule and budget calendar important preliminary steps to the budget call?
3. What budget instructions are important in building a budget? Why?
4. Contrast executive and legislative hearings.
5. Why is the central budget office "powerful"?
6. What information should be in an executive budget? Why?
7. Explain the significance of the Congressional budget timetable.
8. Contrast the virtues of a simple versus a comprehensive budget ordinance or law.

REFERENCES

ARONSON, J. RICHARD and ELI SCHWARTZ (eds.). *Management Policies in Local Government Finance*. Washington, D.C.: International City Management Association, 1975.

[1]Much of the material in this section comes from Girard Miller (compiler), *Effective Budgetary Presentations: The Cutting Edge* (Chicago: Government Officers Finance Association, 1982).

BURKHEAD, JESSE. *Government Budgeting.* New York: John Wiley, 1956.
FISHER, LOUIS. *Presidential Spending Power.* Princeton, N.J.: Princeton University Press, 1975.
JASPER, HERERT N. "A Congressional Budget: Will It Work This Time?," *The Bureaucrat,* 3, 4 (January 1975), 429–43.
LEHAN, EDWARD A. *Simplified Governmental Budgeting.* Chicago: Municipal Finance Officers Association, 1982.
MILLER, GIRARD (compiler). *Effective Budgetary Presentations: The Cutting Edge.* Chicago: Municipal Finance Officers Association, 1982.
MOAK, LENNOX L. and KATHRYN W. KILLIAN. *Operating Budget Manual.* Chicago: Municipal Finance Officers Association, 1963.
MUNICIPAL PERFORMANCE REPORT, 1, 4 (August 1974).
SMITH, LINDA L. "The Congressional Budget Process—Why It Worked This Time," *The Bureaucrat,* 6, 1 (1977), 88–111.
U.S. Civil Service Commission, Bureau of Training, The Management Science Training Center. *Budget Formulation,* 1976.

chapter 5

ANALYSIS APPLIED
TO BUDGETING

Budgeting requires analysis, and this chapter introduces a wide variety of analytical techniques useful in public budgeting. It is not a how-to-do-it chapter, rather it shows how significant types of analysis relate to budgeting. The first section focuses on the theoretical foundation on which analysis can be applied in the public sector. The following sections describe the difficulties associated with applying the theory, describe useful elementary analysis, explain the important analytical tool called *crosswalk*, focus on revenue and expenditure forecasting, explain productivity analysis, and explain benefit-cost analysis. At the completion of this chapter, the reader should know:

1. a theoretically useful model that is consistent with the context of a democratic society;
2. application difficulties associated with the model;
3. simple analytical techniques that help us understand key relationships;
4. the three common approaches to revenue forecasting as well as the basics of econometrics;
5. expenditure forecasting approaches including bargaining, unit cost, and time series methods;
6. how an econometric model can be useful in expenditure forecasting and simulation;
7. the basics of productivity analysis, underlying productivity through regression analysis, and how to strengthen budget requests;
8. the difference between benefit-cost and cost-effectiveness analysis;
9. the fundamental concepts associated with benefit-cost analysis; and
10. the analytical limitations to the benefit-cost technique.

THEORETICAL FOUNDATION

A Budget System Approach and Accountability

The Budget System Approach (Exhibit 5-1) is based on the assumed desirability of accountability in the public sector as well as an assumed chain of cause and effect within the system. The cause and effect chain runs from input (e.g., money, expertise, policy direction), to process (i.e., the performance of administrative activities), to outputs (i.e., the products and services produced by the unit), and finally to outcomes (i.e., the impacts on individuals and society). Between the beginning of the chain and the end— and especially between outputs and outcomes—intervening variables from the political, economic, and social environment are likely to exist. Nevertheless, this theory assumes that the input eventually and necessarily causes the outcomes, even though that cause may not be sufficient to produce the effect itself.

Accountability is theoretically made possible by recognizing that the chain of cause and effect can be monitored through three feedback mechanisms—control, productivity and progress reporting, and program effectiveness—as well as reactions from the intervening variables, including lobbying from clientele groups and media news stories about the impact of the program on the public. The more formal feedback mechanisms permit policy makers and management to know what process as well as program outputs and outcomes actually exist, so they can be compared to intended process, outputs and outcomes. Thus, policy makers and managers can be expected to be aware of and be accountable for the results of their decisions and their performance.

The Budget System Approach can be used in a democratic or authoritarian society. In a democratic society, policy differences among various leaders and peoples are a primary and institutionally accepted aspect of policy making. Social values compete in an ongoing (and, one hopes, nonvi-

EXHIBIT 5-1   Budget System Approach

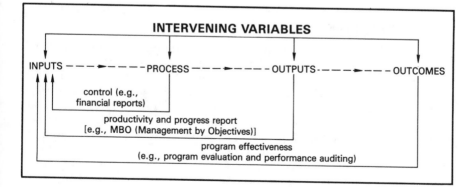

olent) conflict over the nation's policy. The theory does not assume there is one correct government solution or best set of values. It *does* assume that the conflict in political values does not necessarily give consistent and clear guidance to government program managers and that logically consistent government policy will not necessarily be selected. Given that democratic reality, the theory expects that normally the persons supplying information will communicate salient data, which permits policy makers to confront and deal intelligently with their multiple-valued electorate. To be useful in this theory, program output measures, in particular, should be understood and defined in the political context of the government and the larger society it serves.

Public budgeting is a phenomenon that exists at the nexus of policy making and management. The chain of cause and effect within the system links policy and management. In government, the assumption is made that its programs do and even should influence individuals and society. In addition, increases and decreases in government programs will make an important impact on individuals and society. Budgeting, in part, is the allocation of resources based upon decisions, but implicit in each such decision is a process to carry out that allocation. Management cannot be separated totally from policy because the means to carry out the policy does influence eventual outcomes. This theory assumes that there is a chain of cause and effect, or at least policy makers believe such a chain exists.

The Budget System Approach helps decision makers and budget analysts who are preparing information in support of decision makers. Two important concerns of budget analysis are program effectiveness and efficiency. Insight on the first is achieved by looking at program outcomes and the ratio of input to outcome. Insight on the latter is achieved by examining process and the ratio of input to output, with consideration given to providing the same or similar level of work with fewer resources. The role of the budget analyst in the budget office is not to make policy but to raise the level of debate among the policy makers so that they can focus upon the truly significant policy and related management questions. Thus, the budget office should facilitate accountability and encourage more intelligent decisions about the allocation of government resources.

Program Impact Theory

The focus in budget examination is upon understanding existing and planned management strategy as well as upon program effectiveness. Regardless of the approach (e.g., PPB, ZBB, or TBB) to budget preparation, a common theoretical framework exists, which assumes a cause-and-effect interrelation between the program's inputs and its ultimate impacts on the society or environment. The examiner (also called the budget analyst) assumes that such a relationship can and should exist, and then attempts to discover if the actual or intended approach to managing the program can and is likely to lead to the intended program outputs and outcomes. Also, the examiner wants those results accomplished with the greatest program effectiveness consistent with the political values of the policy makers.

Almost all government programs are intended to affect society or individuals in some way or the necessary legislation would not have been passed. Often, the desired impacts on society are vague and even internally contradictory, but there almost always is some purpose behind each law and government program. There is an assumed cause-and-effect relationship: The government program is intended to produce an effect on society. This assumption is central to much of the analysis useful in budgeting. Often budget analysts try to determine if a resource request and even the program itself is worthwhile given the results of that program.

The burden of proving the worth of a program and a specific resource request is placed on the agency. The agency must justify the budget to the department, the executive, and the legislative body. Often those involved act as if absolute proof exists that a given program is worthwhile. Unfortunately, those holding such a view are not sensitive to the philosopher Descartes, who held that absolute proof for any subject other than one's own existence (*Cogito, ergo sum.*) is not possible; therefore, we must use other criteria in evaluating it.

In public administration, the criterion of "necessary but not sufficient cause" is normally the best. For example, if the ultimate desired effect is to reduce the crime rate, holding the police force responsible for that effect may seem reasonable until one realizes that poor police work is not the only reason for the existence of crime. Good police work may be necessary, but it alone is not sufficient to reach a low crime rate. Too often analysts and decision makers apply the harsher "necessary and sufficient" criterion in judging the worth of government programs. This unfortunate conceptual mistake merely leads to false expectations and frustrated administrators and citizens.

Conceptually, an analyst should be able to develop a program impact theory. Given a set of resources and the conditions in society, a government program can produce outputs which in turn will lead to outcomes. The resources, in part, are reflected in the budget request. The outputs are the achieved objectives of management. Those objectives provide guidance to the lower officials and administrators in the bureaucracy. The outcomes are the achieved objectives one cites in program evaluations. Those impacts or outcomes are what higher level decision makers should view in judging the government program.

The program impact theory is the heart of any good budget justification. The person justifying the budget should be arguing that the agency will achieve the legally stated desired effects (i.e., the law's purpose) on society or individuals if the agency is given the requested resources. The program impact theory should be the conceptual means to relate the resource requests to the stated end results caused in society.

If the desired end results do not occur, then two types of failure are possible: (1) the agency did not do its job correctly or (2) the theory was incorrect. If the agency conceptually separated outputs and outcomes correctly and gathered the necessary data, then the type of failure can be determined. If the objectives of management were met, then one type of failure can be eliminated. This permits proper focus upon theoretical failure, which is the responsibility of the highest level decision makers for using poor theory or the academic community for not developing adequate theories. Once the failure is identified, then attention can be focused upon discarding faulty theories and developing more useful theoretical understandings. This identification of failure is particularly significant and helps us understand the relationship of social science research and the needs of higher level administrators.

Data measures are critical because the assumption is made that each key portion of the model (e.g., input, process, output, and outcome) can be accurately described. Data measures for input tend to be easy to define because line-item budget detail or aggregate numbers representing money and positions almost always exist. Data measures for process normally are not difficult to acquire and not critically needed for most budget analyses. Output data measures are obtained by asking what the unit produces in terms of products or services. For most units and programs, isolating data measures is not difficult, but the information may not be collected on a routine basis. Outcome data measures are often very difficult to obtain, as government units normally do not routinely record the individual and societal impacts of their programs.

Deciding what data measures to use is not an easy task. Normally, the best process to follow is to reason backward while focusing upon a specific unit and program. The question "What impact does this particular program have upon the organization (if the program is administered by a service unit to an organization) or upon society (if the program directly affects society)?" should be asked. Then the analyst should seek specific means to measure that impact. Next, the analyst should identify the program outputs by seeking to understand exactly what the unit does or produces which causes those previously identified program outcomes. Data measures of output should give an accurate picture of what takes place. Outputs are defined and are relevant only in the context of program outcomes. The process stage can be omitted, but it does permit a more in-depth analysis which helps postulate recommended efficiency improvements. The last stage in reasoning backwards is the input. What input contributes to and affects the process, output, and outcome? Input which does not contribute to output and outcome, is not needed.

APPLICATION DIFFICULTIES

The application of a theoretical model in public administration can be difficult, but the difficulties can be anticipated. Commonly, analysts and line officials using the model will (1) mix-up outputs, outcomes, and process data measures, (2) confuse the types of appropriate output measures, (3) not understand how to apply the concept to staff and service units, and (4) not fully appreciate that an inability to determine outcome and output measures may indicate program nonperformance.

Mix-Up

The most common mistake, when applying this model, is to mix-up the model elements and measures. For example, an agency may insist upon using descriptive measures which explain its administrative process. Those measures often indicate work effort (e.g., ten hours to write the report) or ratio of staff to clients (e.g., student/teacher ratio of 30 to 1). There is nothing wrong with such measures *per se,* but program output and outcome measures must also be determined, and each measure should be correctly defined. Questions addressed to program effectiveness cannot be answered with process data alone.

Another mix-up is confusing outcomes and outputs. In fact, the two are often used interchangeably. This is an unfortunate mistake as it leads to improper use of analysis. Proper identification of model components makes it possible to determine program effectiveness and efficiency. The best approach to avoiding such confusion is to address program outcome first and reason backward to program outputs.

Types of Output Measures

Public administrators are sometimes unaware that program outputs, especially services, consist of two types which should be treated differently. The first type is the result of a project with a defined end product or service. Constructing a building or writing a report are examples of that output type. The second type reflects a desire to provide ongoing services or products within some defined limits of acceptability. As long as the service is done correctly within those limits, then the output is judged satisfactory. Failure or less than satisfactory service is defined by the number of occasions that the level of service falls outside the ideal limits.

A common mistake is to be unaware of how best to define the second type of output. Administrators will judge a license bureau by the number of licenses issued rather than the percent of licenses issued within an acceptable waiting time. The quality of output is not considered, and important managerial considerations are ignored. End products or services are counted, but the program output quality is overlooked.

Staff and Service Units

When first introduced to the model, individuals tend to focus upon units which are the primary service producers within the government. As they start to apply the model, they discover staff units (e.g., budget offices) and service units even within line departments (e.g., bus maintenance). They become confused about how to apply the concept in situations in which staff and service units do not have a direct impact upon citizens and society.

The best approach is to work backward from outcomes. If the analyst or manager is focusing upon a bus maintenance unit in public transit, the first point to understand is that the overall unit outcome is to improve the movement of people along traffic routes and permit the mobility of the transportation disadvantage. How does the maintenance unit contribute to that overall transit outcome? The answer is the unit's outcome—for example, keeping a percentage of the bus fleet in operation at all times. Since public transit program output is measured in terms of ridership, the next question should focus upon how the actual work or work products of the bus maintenance unit contribute to ridership. For example, the unit preventatively maintains 10 buses each week. That would be one of the unit's program outputs.

For many professionals, the question of how to handle a staff unit like a budget office is confusing. The first point to understand is that the role of a staff unit is to service the government so that it can work effectively. For example, a budget unit should (1) help raise the level of debate for policy makers so that they are more likely to make better decisions, (2) monitor budget execution so that the policy of the duly constituted decision makers is followed unless a conscious decision is made not to follow that policy, and (3) promote and foster better public management within the government. Specific data measures can be developed for each program output and outcome. The second point is that outcomes should be understood as a function of the program outputs. For example, program outputs such as the annual budget document and various reports are not sufficient program outcome measures *per se*. The outputs should be judged in terms of their contribution to program outcome, such as raising the level of policy debate. The budget execution system should be judged in terms of its success in getting government units to follow policy. Various *ad hoc* reports and studies should be judged in terms of their impact on improving public management or raising the level of policy debate. Thus, budget office output must be understood in terms of its positive contribution to the office's outcomes.

Nonperformance Option

Sometimes program outputs and outcomes are unsuccessfully defined. The potential reasons for failure include the professional inadequacy of the budget analyst and insufficient cooperation from an agency which refuses to define necessary data measures. Perfect measures are often inappropriate for use, owing to the time it takes to collect those measures or to high costs in collecting the data. Therefore, trading off the quality of the measure against the effort to collect it is a common professional challenge. An unacceptable situation occurs when top agency personnel fail to make a reasonable attempt to resolve trade-off problems. In such cases, budget office leadership must be apprised of the situation and must decide whether to attempt to force the agency to develop the desired output and outcome measures. Not all such battles can be won; the budget office must decide if that particular battle should be fought and when it should be fought. Normally, government executive leadership is willing to support the budget office leadership on such matters, as it is in the best interest of executive leadership to have such information.

A possible reason why program outcomes and outputs cannot be defined is that the agency may not be performing any useful service. Often when an agency is particularly uncooperative in defining outcomes and outputs the behavior is simply a defensive attempt to cover up poor management. That possibility must always be appreciated by the budget office and top management. Care must be taken that other explanations are eliminated because charges of agency cover-up are likely to evoke attacks upon the professional competency of the budget analyst by the program manager. If problems of this type are possible, budget office leadership should involve top management assistance as soon as possible so that an intelligent approach can be taken to deal with this type of defensive behavior.

DATA MEASURE CONSTRAINTS

The application of this model is always dependent upon the constraints associated with the use of data measures. To use this model properly, an understanding of quantitative techniques and research methods is necessary. For example, some measures used will apply only to an ordinal data scale, and the uninformed will misapply analytical techniques meant to be used for only ratio data scales. For the most sophisticated use of analysis, the best scale is ratio, but that is often impractical or impossible given the character of the problem and data.

The best measures to use are uniform in nature and contain a high number of units of output for which one assumes the same level of quality in each unit of output. For example, the water and sewer systems measure their output in gallons of water or sewerage processed at an acceptable level of quality. Measures of this type permit the use of the most powerful analytical techniques. Unfortunately, not all program outputs are susceptible to this ideal type of measure. For example, a planning unit's outputs are not useful for budget analytical purposes if these outputs are merely considered to be updated comprehensive plans. The usefulness of those plans must be judged using some type of ordinal or even interval scale.

A common ploy by agency officials is to use measures which are ratios between ideal and actual performance. For example, animal control agencies might compare the number of strays to actual captured dogs. Normally, the ratio shows that the program is doing reasonably well, but the impression is given that more resources (input) would improve the ratio. The problem with such ratios is that the ideal is often a highly questionable figure, and the ratio may not be measuring the true outcomes and outputs. If the stray dog problem is defined as the existence of stray dogs, then the measure of dogs captured may be quite correct. If the dog problem is more accurately described as strays in inappropriate areas, then outcomes should be defined differently. Maybe the dog problem is capturing strays within a given time after a complaint has been registered. If so, again the animal control unit outputs should be restated to indicate how many dogs are not captured within acceptable time constraints. Notice that occasionally the outcome and output can be identical or almost identical for operational purposes.

Although perfect program outcomes and outputs may be found, there is the problem of selecting one or more data measures. In some circumstances, the data measures selected could be more expensive to acquire than the cost of the programs they are to measure. Obviously, practical trade-offs must be made in deciding if added clarity in the budget decision-making process is worth the added cost of the data measure.

Another problem with data measures is that they can react with and influence negatively the workings of a program. For example, the knowledge that data is used by decision makers can encourage some managers to distort the data or engage in defensive behavior which avoids facing up to and resolving managerial problems. The negative energy which can be created by data measures must be understood and countered to the extent possible.

One tactic is to use nonreactive measures. For example, worn tile in front of a museum exhibit indicates popularity. Normally, nonreactive measures are easily available and often inexpensive to acquire. Another advantage is that their apparent lack of connection with key program events means that monitoring them will not affect the measurement instrument itself. The problems with nonreactive measures are that they can be isolated only by a creative imagination and that their positive relationship with program outcomes and outputs is not often perfect. Nevertheless, good nonreactive measures should be used when practical.

ELEMENTARY ANALYSIS

Defining Relationships

Most analysis used in budgeting is not complex. Trend charts, scatter diagrams, and simple regression analysis, marginal cost analysis, discounting to present value, and Kraemer's Chi Square are all relatively simple analytical techniques. Often relationships involving budget requests, final budgets, year-end estimates of current expenses, and actual performance are important. If relationships can be established, then the budget analyst's job is made easier. Normally, relationships are best described using a conventional scale, but sometimes a logarithmic scale or index numbers can be employed to better highlight the significance of the data. One common relationship is to show a given variable as it changes over time. If a trend is apparent, then long-term forecasting is made easier and future consequences become more predictable.

In many situations the relationship between two variables is more difficult to determine. One approach is to place the two variables on two axes, as illustrated in Exhibit 5-2. The analyst then places dots representing each simultaneous occurrence of the two variables. The result is a scatter diagram which may indicate a relationship between the two variables. Exhibit 5-2

EXHIBIT 5-2   Illustration of Statistical Analysis

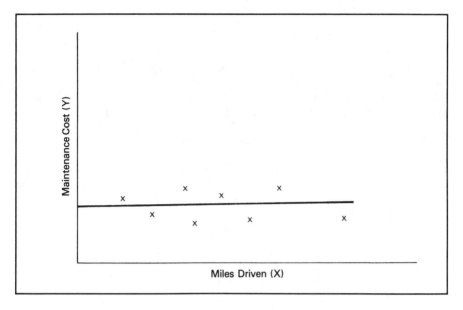

shows such a relationship for a car between maintenance cost and miles driven. The line is a simple regression analysis defining that relationship.

Marginal Cost and Discounting

Another useful technique is marginal cost. The initial cost of a government program is often expensive, while further effort leads to lower unit costs. This means that in many circumstances the analyst should understand that marginal costs are lower. This might prove to be highly significant. For example, if an agency is asking for a proportionate increase in funding, the analyst might question this request because marginal costs should not increase proportionately.

In order to perform marginal cost analysis, the data must be separated into one-time fixed costs and recurring costs. Common one-time fixed costs include research, project planning, engineering, tests, evaluations, land purchases, facility construction, equipment, and initial training. Common recurring costs include personnel expenses, employee benefits, maintenance, direct contributions to people, payments for services, and overall and replacement training. The fixed costs remain the same, but the recurring costs increase with added units. Thus, as the units increase the unit cost decreases. These data can be plotted on a simple chart or described in simple statistical expressions.

Another technique is discounting to present value. A dollar received or spent in the future is not equivalent to a dollar received or spent today.

Therefore, adjustments should be made if comparisons are to be made. The technique is similar to the statistical concept used to compute compound interest at the bank. This technique is useful when comparisons must be made, but the two subjects must not occur during the same time period or involve different financing methods.

Fred A. Kramer has cited a simple but common situation to illustrate the use of this analytical technique.[1] A city must choose between contracting with a private garbage collector for $65,000 per year or having city employees do it. The latter option would require a $40,000 truck and a $55,000 yearly operating expense. Without discounting, the best option is apparently to let the city employees collect the garbage. With them, the cost is $315,000 over the five years of the truck's life. With a private contractor, the cost is $325,000. Thus, using city workers would apparently save the city $10,000 over the five year period. With discounting, the best option is the private contractor. The following shows the important arithmetic:

SAVINGS IN THE YEAR	× 8% DISCOUNT FACTOR	= PRESENT VALUE
1	$10,000	.926	$ 9,260
2	10,000	.857	8,570
3	10,000	.794	7,940
4	10,000	.735	7,350
5	10,000	.681	6,810
	Total Present Value of Annual Savings =	$39,930

In the example, the private contract is the best buy because the total present value of annual savings is less than the $40,000 capital investment. If city employees were used, the city would pay $40,000 for a truck but save a total of $50,000 over five years. The application of discounting to the yearly savings lets us realize that the true savings are not $50,000, but $39,930, because the value of money over time must be considered. Thus, discounting shows us that the options are nearly equal, but the contracting option saves the city $70.

Caution must be stressed in using the discount technique. Numbers have a way of seeming so final and clear. Realistically, the ingredients in the question should be carefully weighed in terms of their sensitive character. An output of a program is sensitive when the results can be altered by minor changes in a variable. If the analysis is highly sensitive, then any recommendations made on the basis of the analysis should be questioned because the technique does not warrant the implied certitude. This technique can be abused by changing the annual returns or savings, the life of the asset, the amount of the investment, the discount rate, or the annual returns in the earlier years. This does not mean the technique should not be used, but it should be used with a complete understanding of the possible distortions.

[1]Fred A. Kramer, "The Discounting to Present Value Technique as a Decision Tool" in *Special Bulletin* 1976E (Chicago: Municipal Finance Officers Association, November 24, 1976).

CROSSWALKS

Conceptual Bridge

One of the most useful analytical tools for the budget examiner is the crosswalk. It is a simple matrix table relating different categories. It serves as a conceptual bridge between two organizational means to describe and control agency activities. By constructing several bridges, the examiner can explore various organizational perspectives on what should be done and what is done as well as check important interrelations. Some of the more common categories which can be crosswalked are:

1. programs, projects, activities, tasks;
2. uniform object classifications;
3. appropriation structure;
4. major organizational units;
5. objectives used in connection with management-by-objectives or program evaluations; and
6. funds (including grants-in-aid) used in government accounting.

A very useful crosswalk is between the program and the uniform object classification (also called line-item). In many sophisticated budget offices, both program and line-item categories are used. In order to maintain consistency, the crosswalk is a valuable tool because it shows the interrelationship of the two ways of looking at the budget. In addition, a careful examination of the crosswalk helps to isolate potential problems, such as inadequate resources for some line-items in some programs.

Another useful crosswalk is between fund and line-item. Often an agency can draw upon several funds in its daily operations. Thus, a given line-item expense may be associated with two or more funds. The crosswalk is a display of information that can help the manager decide which fund to charge for a given line-item. By looking at a cumulative crosswalk of expenses in an organization, a budget analyst can see if the funds were used together in a meaningful way and more intelligently judge the budget request in a given fund for the next year.

The appropriation to unit crosswalk is also useful. Sometimes a legislature provides funds which are used by several organizational units. A tool to keep track of which unit is responsible for each portion of the money is the crosswalk. Without such a tool, lower management responsibility is unclear and judging management performance becomes more difficult.

At the federal level, the program and authorization crosswalk is very useful at the agency level. In the executive branch, budgets are prepared using the concept of program. In the legislative branch, budgets are justified and discussed in terms of legal authorization language. Thus, the agency budget official must use both the concept of program and legal authorization in justifying and defending requests for funds. As a means to more easily translate and insure a consistency between executive and legislative information, the crosswalk is a valuable tool.

An unused but potentially significant crosswalk is between the MBO objectives and the program structure or appropriation structure. MBO can be an extremely useful public management technique, but often it is applied without reference to the budget. This is foolish because how can one reasonably expect objectives to be met without also establishing that necessary resources are available to conduct the program? The two should not be treated in isolation, but they are by many agencies. If they are treated separately this strongly indicates a lack of coordination of management direction within the agency because both MBO and the budget are tools to achieve management direction.

If the agency has activities which fulfill more than one objective at a time, then a program evaluation objective—program structure crosswalk—is treated somewhat differently from the other crosswalks. Normally, each matrix square states dollar amounts representing mutually exclusive activities. This permits the crosswalk to be validated for internal consistency by merely checking if the horizontal and vertical summary columns are equal. In the case of evaluation objectives, dollar amounts can be counted more than once if they fulfill more than one purpose. For example, a given activity may increase safety and reduce energy consumption (e.g., enforcing the 55-mile-per-hour speed limit). Thus, the crosswalk matrix squares would show the dollar amount (maybe even the name of the activity) under two different vertical categories. This type of double counting can also exist with a crosswalk using MBO objectives.

Determining Consistency

The budget examiner can ask to see various crosswalks for the reasons suggested above. Essentially, crosswalks help the examiner determine if the agency has internally consistent management direction and control capability to insure the integrity of that direction. If the agency does not act with one management direction, the crosswalks expose that problem. If the agency cannot provide crosswalks, this suggests poor management. It is possible for the agency to manage its affairs well without using crosswalks, but it should be able to construct them if there is a consistent management direction. If crosswalks cannot be constructed or if the ones provided show inconsistent management policy, then the budget examiner can probe further to isolate the exact nature and reasons for the internal management inconsistency.

Crosswalks can also be used to check for external consistency of management direction with past publicly announced positions and orders of higher authorities. A set of crosswalks is among the best evidence of the exact management policies of an agency. Those policies may not be consistent with the agency's past policies or positions articulated to the public or policy directives from higher authorities. If the budget examiner happens to have the crosswalks from past budgets, then they can be compared with the most recent crosswalks. In this manner, policy shifts can be isolated. Budget examiners can also determine if the policy direction from the crosswalks matches public positions and policy established by higher authorities.

If there is inconsistency, then further probing may be warranted to determine the reason for the inconsistency.

REVENUE FORECASTING

Three Approaches

Revenue forecasting calls for a separate treatment of each revenue source. The standard approach is, first, to determine the patterns associated with each revenue source. Next, the base must be determined and then the forecast is made based on assumptions and the determined pattern. Forecasting is merely a sophisticated form of guessing which depends on good data and good judgment, often refined through experience. The techniques of forecasting range from the simple to the complex, but all should be used with the principle of conservatism (i.e., underestimating revenue and overestimating expenditures) in mind.

Notwithstanding this accepted advice, governments do not always use that principle. In a study by William Earle Klay and Gloria A. Grizzle of state government forecasts of sales tax receipts, they discovered a slight tendency on the average to overstate revenue.

Information is important to revenue forecasting, and certain background information should be retained. This includes copies of legislation, legal history, administration factors concerning the tax, or any change in the tax; charts showing changes in the tax rate over time and the monthly yield, with an explanation of any abnormal change in the trend line; and data on any significant variables which affect the revenue yield.

The three revenue forecasting approaches are qualitative, time series, and causal analysis. Qualitative (also called judgmental) approaches are, in essence, based solely or primarily upon human judgment, but math can be involved. William Earle Klay of Florida State University surveyed the revenue forecasting practices of all fifty states and found that thirty used panels, interagency work committees, or conferences in their revenue forecasts. Normally, economists constituted these "expert" groups of forecasters, but occasionally politicians were included. Expert judgment is best used when key revenue elements are highly variable, no history exists, or revenues are strongly influenced by political considerations (e.g., intergovernmental transfers).

Time series (e.g., trend analysis) is based upon data which has been collected over time and can be shown chronologically on graphs. One such approach involves using the last completed year as a basis for the revenue estimate (in France, this method is called "rule of penultimate year"), assuming that there is growth in the economy and related revenue sources. Another simple technique—the method of averages—is to average the revenue generated over the last three to five years. Again, the assumption is made that there is a growth trend in the tax source, rather than a decline or an uneven tax yield. A more sophisticated method involves using moving averages and attributing greater weight to more recent revenue yields. A still more sophisticated method is the Box-Jenkins method, which will be described later in the expenditure estimates section. Normally, the trends are shown on arithmetic graphs, but some analysts prefer semilogarithmic graphs because they reveal rates of change in tax yields more clearly.

When using time series techniques, the forecaster is especially interested in the nature of seasonal fluctuations which occur within a year, the nature of multiyear cycles, and the nature of any possible long-run trends which might underlie the seasonal and cyclical fluctuations. The major weakness of this approach is that economic turning points are not easily identified. Trend analysis should be used to forecast revenue items which are not highly variable and which (1) amount to minor percentages of the budget or (2) are not dependent upon economic or political considerations.

Causal methods deal, not with the history of a single variable, but with the historical interrelationship between two or more variables. One or more predictor variables forecast tax yield directly or indirectly by first forecasting the future tax base. For example, multiplying the estimate of the average tax to be collected per taxpayer by an estimate of the number of taxpayers results in a forecast of income tax revenue. Various survey techniques can be used to determine these two predictor variable estimates. Some communities use a payroll tax. To forecast the revenue, they estimate the area payroll and tax rate and multiply them. A variation is to calculate the tax rate by occupational groups. A third method is first to determine the interrelationship between personal income and leading economic indicators and then to use the leading indicators to determine personal income. The tax yield is determined from the personal income. For sales taxes, the area or state sales are forecasted, and the tax yield is calculated from that level of sales.

These causal forecasting methods are predicated upon selecting the correct predictor variables, defining their interrelationship to tax yield correctly and, finally, collecting accurate data. An added advantage to these methods is that they can help policy makers reflect upon various "what if" options for taxes and other policies so that they can better gauge the implications of their policy choices. Drawbacks to these methods include the need to collect extensive accurate data, the cost of developing causal models, and high computer costs. Fortunately, computer costs are decreasing. If revenues are strongly influenced by changing economic conditions, causal models (e.g., econometrics) are especially useful.

Accuracy in revenue forecasting is important, especially when the forecast predicts more money than is actually received by a government which must have a balanced budget. The results are painful government midyear adjustments which result in frozen positions, elimination of travel and other easily cut costs and, finally, payless "paydays." If forecasts embarrassingly result in unpredicted surpluses, then the government faces the politically difficult task of explaining tax rates which appear to be unnecessarily high. In the study by William Earle Klay and Gloria A. Gizzle of state sales tax forecast accuracy, they discovered one state underestimated by 31.6 percent and another overestimated by 40.6 percent. Thus, major errors in forecasting do occur. Measuring historic accuracy of revenue forecasts within a jurisdiction is simply a matter of contrasting forecasts with actual receipts. Once these comparisons are made, it is possible to determine where forecasting improvements are needed. Normally, large inaccuracy in small revenue items is not significant because often such inaccuracies tend to cancel each other out in the aggregate. Serious problems occur when there are modest errors in large revenue items because they can mean significant revenue shortfalls. Normally, the further away the forecast from the forecasted event, the more likely it is that there will be forecasting errors; thus, forecasters prefer late forecasts whenever possible.

Econometric Forecasts

Econometric forecasts are complex causal analyses which have many causal variables and are often computer-dependent. The age of econometrics began in the 1930s with Jan Tinbergen, a Dutch economist. He developed a number of equations to represent the workings of his nation's economy. In America, the use of econometrics by state governments has mostly occurred since 1978, with few local governments using the technique today (some exceptions are New Orleans, Dallas, Winston-Salem, and Mobile). The basic equation is $Y = f(X)$, with Y, the dependent variable, affected by the independent, explanatory, predictor variable X. The statement merely says that Y is somehow dependent on (is a function of) the value of X. To develop a revenue forecasting model, the following are essential:

- to develop a data history or time series for all variables;
- to develop a set of mathematical expressions which best explains the past relationships among the variables; and
- to devise a means of identifying the future values which one or more of the explanatory variables will assume.

Causal models may consist of a single regression equation or several regression equations. Semoon Chang used a single regression equation for his econometric model for Mobile's sales tax receipts. At the other extreme, Florida's state estimates make use of 123 regression equations. Many analysts rely upon popular national econometric models such as those provided by Chase Econometrics, Data Resources, Inc., and Wharton Econometric Forecasting Associates. Worthy of note is an observation by John Peterson of the Government Finance Officers Association: "As a general rule, sophisticated models have been ignored by practitioners in the past. After their construction and initial operation by consultants, they have sometimes ended up gathering dust on the shelf."[2] This method involves statistics, and unless staff can explain statistical concepts so that officials can understand them, informed official judgment may be impossible. To use this technique, the following statistical concepts should be understood:

[2]J. E. Peterson, "State and Local Fiscal Forecasting" in *Resources in Review* (Chicago: Government Finance Officers Association, 1979), p. 16.

1. R squared coefficient of determination, which shows the proportion of variation in the dependent variable attributable to variation in the independent variables;
2. the T test of relationship with a particular independent variable;
3. the F test concerning the significance of the equation as a whole;
4. the Durbin-Watson statistic, which is an indicator of whether serial correlation exists, thereby suggesting that important information has been omitted;
5. the standard error of estimate; and
6. the mean absolute percentage of error.

EXPENDITURE FORECASTING

Bargaining and Unit Cost Approaches

The burden for estimating expenditures normally rests upon the agency, but the techniques are often similar to those of revenue forecasting. In some situations, a bargaining approach is used in which the agency's estimate of its optimum program is tempered by the economic and political climate, including budget call instructions. (Agency estimates can be based upon detailed work plans involving months of preparation or upon quick judgments involving a few minutes.) The central budget office reviews the request, refining, cutting, and adding to the judgment of the agency, with the possible participation of political executive and legislative officials. The final adopted expenditures represent the collective judgment of dozens of officials and staff.

Another set of expenditure forecasting techniques is based on accounting information which uses unit cost data. This method is similar to "fiscal impact analysis," which calculates the municipal costs of proposed local real estate developments by using per capita cost multipliers, the average cost of providing a certain level or standard of service, and other simple calculations. The three major steps in the unit cost approach are: (1) choosing a level of analysis, (2) analyzing units and unit costs, and (3) making necessary assumptions and calculations.

In selecting the level of analysis, budget analysts will often use the object code level, but subcode or function levels can be used. An example of subcode level use is found in Arlington County, Virginia, which records each employee's anniversary date, wage rate, grade, longevity increase (if any), fringe benefit costs, and other data. Using this information, the computer does an annual projection of the wages and fringe costs for each employee, and aggregates these costs into the desired object codes, divisional units, departments, and funds. An example of function-department level use is found in Syracuse, New York, where expenditures by department are broken down into labor, nonlabor, fringe, and miscellaneous expenditures. These relatively gross aggregates are aggregated for a jurisdiction forecast.

The second step of analysis of units and unit costs is done by examining past and current units and unit costs, such as the gallons of heating fuel charged to object code 306 of the Building Management Department. A more sophisticated version would be to multiply the unit cost by the price index when one is calculating specific future year forecasts.

The third step is to include assumptions for future years and then simply to multiply. For example, in the heating fuel situation, assume that 50,000 gallons are to be consumed in the BY at a cost of $2 per gallon; 50,000 multiplied by $2 equals $100,000, to be budgeted in object code 306 of the Building Management Department. The result is an annual or multi-year forecast for a particular expenditure which can be aggregated to arrive at a total expenditure forecast.

Time Series Methods

Many agencies use an incremental or trend line approach in expenditure forecasting. Historical data defines the trend line, which shows the expenditure pattern over time. The slope of the line is the rate of change. The formula for a line is $Y = a + bX$ where Y is the dependent variable, X is the independent variable, and b is the slope of the line. The trend line establishes a historical pattern, and the forecaster need only take the next time period (e.g., BY) and read up to the trend line and over to the expenditure level. In Exhibit 5-3, this approach shows that the expenditure forecast for the BY is $50,000. Judgment is used to determine any appropriate deviation from the trend based upon factors likely to cause unusual change.

Two other time series methods are moving averages and exponential smoothing. In moving averages, one adds up the expenditures in past time periods and averages them. The assumption is that averaging the values will

EXHIBIT 5-3   Trend Line Forecast

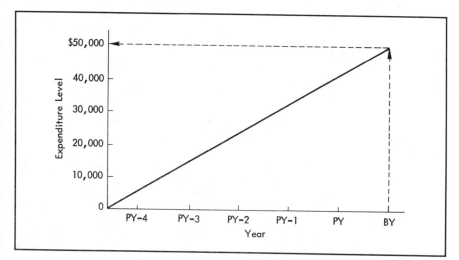

minimize data randomness and seasonality. Thus, the more data points used, the smoother the forecast. The limitations of the method are as follows: (1) it depends on sufficient data observations, thus it is not useful for new programs; (2) it is only useful for short-term forecasts involving one to three time periods; and (3) it is unable to forecast a change in the basic trend. In exponential smoothing, one uses the last forecast value and the estimated "alpha factor weight" of any value between 0 to 1 (e.g., 0.1, 0.5, 0.9) and takes the difference between the forecast value for the most recent time period and the actual value-realized. For example, $5000 was spent in the CY and $4500 in PY. To calculate the BY with a 0.3 alpha factor, we calculate $5000 + 0.3($4500 − $5000), which yields a BY forecast of $4850. If the forecaster expects little data randomness, then a small alpha factor would be used; conversely, much data randomness would make a high alpha factor appropriate. The major value of this technique over moving averages is that fewer data points are needed and recent rapid trend changes are better reflected. The inherent disadvantage of the technique is the necessity for arbitrary assignment of an alpha factor.

A third time series technique is adaptive filtering. The four steps of the technique are as follows: (1) a forecast is developed by taking a weighted average of the previous observations, (2) the forecast and actual value realized are compared and errors calculated, (3) the weights in the weighted average are adjusted to minimize calculated error, and (4) the new set of weights is applied to forecast the subsequent period. The process is repeated as new actual data become known. This technique requires many calculations and is normally done with a computer. The technique is particularly useful when a great deal of historical data is available and those data exhibit considerable randomness.

A fourth, emerging technique is autoregressive moving averages (ARMA), of which there are two types: autoregressive models and moving average models. Autoregressive models (AR) assume that future values are linear combinations of past values. Moving average models (MA) assume that future values are linear combinations of past errors. Autoregressive models use past data on the dependent variable at various time intervals to develop the forecast. Moving average models seek to eliminate the randomness of data by dropping a past observation as a new one becomes available. Box-Jenkins techniques are used to select and test ARMA models. ARMA techniques tend to produce very good one- to three-year forecasts. The techniques are very complex, but advances in computer software have eliminated many time and cost problems.

The Box-Jenkins method is a systematic elimination procedure to identify the most appropriate ARMA model and determine the appropriate forecasting model. First, the model is identified by means of various statistical tests and judgmental evaluations. Second, a trial-and-error approach using statistical estimation techniques is employed to determine the data array with the smallest mean square error. Third, after an adequate model is constructed, a forecasting equation is derived which reflects the data through the current period. A bonus of this technique is that it not only forecasts, but it does so with delineated limits of reliability.

Expenditure Econometric Model

Various expenditures are largely predicated on factors which lend themselves to econometric models. For example, at the state level, social service expenditures are directly related to the state economy, and education and criminal justice expenditures are related to state demographics and economic factors. Models can be used which not only predict likely expenditures but also help policy makers understand the most sensitive factors which influence each functional activity.

One such example is the Massachusetts Welfare Model developed by Data Resources, Inc. That model is used for short-term forecasts and sensitivity analyses of eligibles, case load, and expenditures in various welfare assistance categories. The model contains: (1) earnings distribution of the state and individuals; (2) an estimation routine for calculating Aid to Families with Dependent Children (AFDC) and General Relief (GR) eligibles from a combination of welfare policy standards and state demographic parameters applied to the earnings distributions for families and unrelated individuals; (3) econometric equations explaining eligibles' rate of participation in AFDC and GR, by sex and family status; (4) econometric equations explaining average expenditures per case in AFDC and GR; (5) identities deriving AFDC and GR case loads by a combination of items 2 and 3; and (6) identities deriving AFDC and GR total expenditures by a combination of items 4 and 5. The model uses 77 variables, including economic, welfare policy, and endogenous variables, as well as welfare eligibles definitions, rates of participation, miscellaneous inputs, and numerous simultaneous econometric equations.

The model is used both for forecasting and simulation ("what if" analysis). It forecasts welfare eligibles, case load, and expenditures by program. It forecasts the earnings distributions of families and individuals. It simulates the impact on eligibles, case load, and expenditures of alternative U.S. and state economic scenarios. It simulates the impact on welfare case load of changes in the unemployment compensation program. And finally, it simulates the impact on eligibles, case load, and expenditures of alternative welfare policies such as (1) cost-of-living increases, (2) a change in the income deduction for work-related expenses, (3) a change in the assistance tables reflecting new budget levels by family size and living arrangements, and (4) a change in federal statutes.

In forecasting, the model works in several steps. First, the U.S. and state economic data are used to derive family earnings distributions and to determine persons eligible for welfare. Next, welfare participation rates are calculated, using such factors as work availability and wage opportunities (normally, if the economy has worsened, welfare benefits and participation are higher). Welfare case load and total projected welfare expenditures are calculated. Finally, administrative costs are determined.

In simulations, the model works with "what if" scenarios. For example, "What if 5 percent federal eligibility regulations are changed to exclude persons with any income?" The model calculates the changes and predicts the mean monthly case load and other factors.

PRODUCTIVITY ANALYSIS

Productivity

Productivity is a measure of efficiency usually expressed as the ratio of the quantity of output to the quantity of input used in the production of that output. Commonly, productivity focuses upon output per man hour of change or changes in cost per unit of output. It does not measure the work completed versus the work needed to be completed.

The concept of productivity is often misunderstood. It is falsely tied to harder physical work, when it is in fact tied to doing the work with less effort but still increasing output. This is normally done by better work procedures, better use of machines, or better worker attitude toward the job. In quantifying productivity, the mistake is made of using outcomes (benefits to individuals and society) instead of outputs (products of the program). There are normally too many intervening variables between outcomes and outputs to permit a meaningful usage of outcomes. Another conceptual confusion is that an increase in productivity may reflect a cost reduction, but a cost reduction is not always a result of an increase in productivity. Other reasons for cost reduction can exist, such as a simple budget cut. However, too often we do equate productivity with cost reduction.

A study on productivity in the federal government was conducted in the mid-1970s, and its findings on the reasons for increases in productivity are enlightening. A commonly cited reason for a productivity increase was an increase in the work load, thus allowing the agency to lower its unit cost. Fixed and variable costs explain how productive advantages can result from increased work loads. In other cases, productivity increased because of improved training, increased and better use of job evaluations, greater upward mobility, or the use of a career ladder to develop the work force. In some instances, greater productivity was due to automation and the use of new labor-saving equipment.

Although productivity is a simple concept, there are not simple uniform answers for increasing productivity. Each situation must be examined separately. The federal study illustrates this point by saying the greater productivity resulted from (1) improved morale resulting from job redesign and enrichment, and (2) reorganization and work simplification. The study seems to say that making a job more complex and making a job simpler both result in greater productivity. This apparent contradiction can be resolved by understanding the human factor related to the job situation. For some people, the job is too complex and beyond their abilities. The answer is work simplification. For some people, the job is too simple and their boredom leads to poor work habits. The answer is job enrichment, such as rotation or a larger range of responsibilities. Sound increased productivity recommendations must be based on a knowledge of management science as well as human behavior. Exhibit 5-4 is a useful checklist developed by the National Center for Productivity and Quality of Work Life.

The same federal study also cited some common reasons for declines in productivity. Increased product complexity cannot always be factored

EXHIBIT 5-4 What Do You Know About Your Productivity?

The following set of questions can be used as a self-audit to determine what your organization is doing and what your organization may need to do to make programs more productive.

1. **IS THE EFFICIENCY OF STAFF PERSONNEL MEASURED?**
   Are critical outputs identified for each program?
   Are work counts and time utilization records maintained for these critical outputs?
   Are unit times developed for the outputs?
   Are trend data available for the unit times?
   Is unit cost information available?
   Are efficiency data reported periodically to management?
   Are unit times compared among regions? Are they compared with other organizations doing similar work in or out of government?

2. **ARE PERFORMANCE STANDARDS SET FOR CRITICAL PROGRAM OUTPUTS?**
   Are time standards used?
   What percentage of the work is covered by standards?
   Are performance reports regularly prepared and distributed to persons responsible for performance?
   Are standards used by supervisors of day-to-day operations to plan and schedule work?
   Are the standards used in planning and budgeting?

3. **IS PROGRAM EFFECTIVENESS MEASURED?**
   Are performance indicators available that address program effectiveness?
   Do performance indicators include the target population, the level of service, and the desired impact?
   Are measurable goals tied to indicators of program effectiveness?

4. **IS THE QUALITY OF WORK PROPERLY CONTROLLED?**
   Are error and timeliness data maintained and reported on a regular basis?
   Are quality standards used?
   Is quality of performance measured and reported on a regular basis?

5. **IS OVERALL PRODUCTIVITY PERFORMANCE MEASURED?**
   Are measures used that combine effectiveness and efficiency by relating to results?
   Are cost-effectiveness measures used?
   Are the major cost elements identified for each program and are costs determined?

6. **ARE METHODS AND PROCEDURES ANALYZED FREQUENTLY?**
   Are your managers currently aware of what others are doing in operations similar to yours?
   Are mechanization and new technology continually reviewed for possible application to your operation?
   Are staff specialists asked to make improvement studies?
   Do supervisors and employees make suggestions on improving operational details?

7. **ARE EMPLOYEES MOTIVATED TO PERFORM AT A SATISFACTORY LEVEL?**
   Are employees told how well they perform?
   Are merit increases and awards tied to performance?
   Are "quality of working life" motivational techniques used?

Source: Improving Productivity: A Self Audit and Guide, National Center for Productivity and Quality of Work Life, Washington, D.C., Fall 1978, pp. 10–11, 13.

out of the measurements, and that complexity can mean less productivity. For example, increased environmental, safety, and legal requirements mean added work steps, equipment, or additional features. This may be in the public interest, but one of the disadvantages is increased production costs, thus a loss in productivity. Another reason for loss is a steady and sharp decline in work load which is not matched by staff reductions. Either human compassion or labor agreements can mean lower productivity, but again other practical reasons supersede the desire for efficiency. A third common reason for a decline is, ironically, the installation of a new or automated system. For a period of time during the installation, both the automated and old system must be operated, thus decreasing productivity until the old system is phased out. These reasons are significant and suggest the complex issues which prevent us from always achieving increased productivity.

Simple Regression Analysis

The basic assumption of regression analysis is that change in the dependent variable Y is related to change in the independent variable X, either positively or negatively. In regression analysis the independent variable need not necessarily cause the dependent variable, but a relationship does exist which may be causal in nature. Simple regression analysis uses a straight line $Y = a + bX$ to describe the relationship. The slope b is the regression coefficient and measures the change in Y given one unit of change in X. The constant a represents the distance between the point where the regression line intercepts the Y axis and the origin. In order to draw the regression line, the method of least squares is used. This type of analysis assumes a normal probability distribution for the observations and assumes that the error values are independent of each other (i.e., no autocorrelation exists).

Exhibit 5-5, Exhibit 5-6, and Exhibit 5-7 are used in a simple linear regression for neighborhood libraries in an urban county. The independent variable X is the full-time-equivalent circulation staff working at each library unit. There is an assumed relationship between circulation staff size and actual books in circulation during the CY. Exhibit 5-6 and Exhibit 5-7 states the input and output data and show how the least square method is used to determine the line on Exhibit 5-5. Note that the line fits or explains the various actual data observations which are coded library names.

How does this type of analysis assist in the budget process? Essentially, the regression line is the CY average productivity curve for the library system. Libraries to the left and above the line are more productive; hence an examination can be undertaken to see what they are doing right. Of course, an examination can also be addressed to the least productive units. Another useful feature of this analysis is that any requested additional FTE circulation staff of a unit should generate, ideally, the normal productivity output. Budget analysts can query, "Will the library indeed generate the desired circulation or will productivity be lowered if that additional staff is added?"

EXHIBIT 5-5   Book Circulation

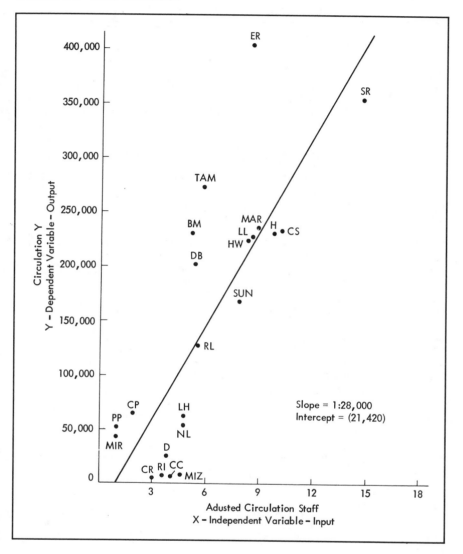

Regression analysis can be useful in determining and fostering greater productivity.

Multiple regression is considered more useful than simple regression analysis because more independent variables can be used. Thus, it should yield a more accurate fit when compared to actual data. Normally, however, the number of variables should be kept to a minimum (e.g., four).

EXHIBITS 5-6 and 5-7   Productivity for Libraries—Circulation Staff (Input): Circulation (Output)

LIBRARY OUTLETS	INPUT	OUTPUT	$(x-\bar{x})$	$(y-\bar{y})$	$(x-\bar{x})(y-\bar{y})$	$(x-\bar{x})^2$
BM	4.5	233170	−1.54	85750.68	−132134.01	2.37
CP	2	62222	−4.04	−85197.32	344274.62	16.33
CR	3	2939	−3.04	−144480.32	439351.51	9.25
CC	4	4929	−2.04	−142490.32	290809.79	4.17
CS	10.7	238127	4.66	90707.68	422615.34	21.71
D	3.6	25615	−2.44	−121804.32	297313.27	5.96
D/CC	0	0	0.00	0.00	0.00	0.00
DR	5.6	203404	−0.44	55984.68	−24684.16	0.19
ER	8.3	406135	2.26	258715.68	584462.24	5.10
H	9.7	236389	3.66	88969.68	325548.15	13.39
HW	8.6	2048727	2.56	57307.68	146655.57	6.55
LL	8.7	227368	2.66	79948.68	212590.81	7.07
LH	4.8	63214	−1.24	−84205.32	104491.14	1.54
M	8.8	234892	2.76	87472.68	241345.08	7.61
MR	1	45184	−5.04	−102235.32	515358.94	25.41
MZ	4.5	7449	−1.54	−139970.32	215681.54	2.37
NL	4.7	55722	−1.34	−91697.32	122957.77	1.80
PP	1	50406	−5.04	−97013.32	489035.32	25.41
RL	5.7	137722	−0.34	−9697.32	3305.90	0.12
RI	5.5	5129	−0.54	−142290.32	76966.13	0.29
SR	14.7	355862	8.66	208442.68	1804924.13	74.98
SI	7.8	165386	1.76	17966.68	31605.03	3.09
TM	5.7	277234	−0.34	129814.68	−44255.01	0.12
Total	132.9	3243225	0.00	0.00	6468219.11	234.83
Averages	6.04	147419.32				
Slope	27543.89					
Intercept	−18970.81					

$$b = \frac{\Sigma(x-\bar{x})(y-\bar{y})}{\Sigma(x-\bar{y})^2}$$

$$b = \frac{6468219.11}{234.85} = 27,543.89 \text{ slope}$$

$y = bx + c$
$c = y - bx$
$c = 147419.32 - ((27543.89)(6.04))$
$c = -18970.81 \text{ intercept at y}$

NOTE: Due to computer rounding, this number is 25.04 higher than these summary numbers indicate.

Productivity and Budgeting

Agencies can strengthen their budget requests by citing productivity measures. Reviewing authorities normally more readily accept cost estimates based upon data involving productivity. Those requests are more impressive and help establish agency credibility. Exhibit 5-8 is extracted from the 1975 U.S. Budget Appendix. It illustrates how hard facts strengthen the agency's justification of its budget even in an agency such as the Mediation

EXHIBIT 5-8   Selected Illustration of a Presentation of Output Data in the 1975 Budget Appendix *Federal Mediation and Conciliation Service Salaries and Expenses*

The Service, under title II of the Labor Management Relations Act of 1947, assists labor and management in mediation and prevention of disputes affecting industries engaged in interstate commerce and defense production, other than rail and air transportation, whenever in its judgment such disputes threaten to cause a substantial interruption of commerce. Under the authority of Executive Order 11491 of October 29, 1969, as amended by Executive Order 11616, dated August 26, 1971, the Service also makes its mediation and conciliation facilities available to Federal agencies and organizations representing Federal employees in the resolution of negotiation disputes.

1. *Mediation Service.* During 1973, dispute notices and other notifications affecting 117,884 employers were received by the Service. Cases totaling 21,745 were assigned for mediation, and 21,032 mediation assignments were closed during the year. About 89% of the mediation assignments closed which required the services of mediators were settled without work stoppages. A total of 26,973 mediation conferences were conducted by mediators during 1973. The workload shown above includes assignments closed in both the private and public sectors. Cases in process at the end of 1973 totaled 5,449; this is the normal carryover of open cases from month to month, with seasonal fluctuations. The following chart shows a 5-year comparison of workload data:

DISPUTE WORKLOAD DATA

	1969	1970	1971	1972	1973
Cases in process at the beginning of the year	5,260	5,113	5,020	4,889	4,736
Mediation assignments	21,839	19,769	21,727	19,308	21,745
Mediation assignments closed	21,986	19,862	21,858	19,461	21,032
Cases in process at end of year	5,113	5,020	4,889	4,736	5,449
Mediation conferences conducted	31,605	30,334	32,293	29,223	26,973

Source: Extracted from p. 878 of the 1975 Budget Appendix

**EXHIBIT 5-9   Illustration of Selected Agency Productivity Trends;
The Defense Supply Agency**

Since the activation of DSA, constant management attention to the basic goal of maximum efficiency has produced significant operating economies. In the early years of DSA, 1962-1966, increased productivity was realized through manpower reductions as numerous organizational and procedural improvements were effected. However, it was not until FY 1967 that a formal output and productivity evaluation system was installed. Since that time, overall output per man-year has increased almost 30 percent.

Chart 1 depicts the composite productivity trend for the agency from FY 1967 through FY 1973. The index shown was derived from the basic data which constituted DSA's input to the Government-wide productivity project. Improvement has averaged about 5 percent per year for the past six years. DSA currently employs about 52,000 military and civilian personnel in performing its assigned mission. Had the increase in productivity reflected on this chart not been realized, today's job would require about 10,000 more personnel than are currently employed.

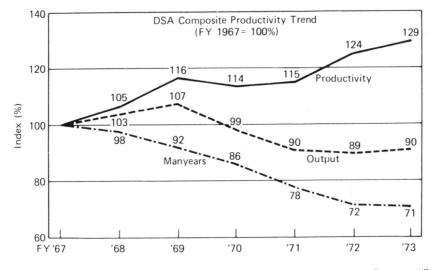

Source: Adapted from pp. 35–36 of the Joint Financial Management Improvement Program, "Report on Federal Productivity, Volume II: Productivity Case Studies," June 1974.

---

and Conciliation Service. Exhibit 5-9 illustrates how productivity measures can be melded into a budget justification document. The most helpful data and measures are the following:

1. productivity indices which relate end products produced to manpower or cost measures;

2. unit cost ratios which relate work performed to all or a part of the cost of performing the work;

3. work measuring ratios which relate work performed to manpower needs in carrying out the work;
4. program or work load data which show trends in the program work; and
5. statistical data, such as regression analysis, which relate experience data to manpower.

THE BENEFIT-COST CONCEPT

Concept: What and Why

Benefit-cost analysis is based on the rather simple belief that projects should be judged on the basis of project cost versus project benefits. At best, benefit-cost analysis is a guide for investment decision. It can help decision makers decide if specific expenditures should be undertaken, if the scale of the project is appropriate, and what the optimum project size should be. Some treat benefit-cost as a framework for a general theory of government investment.

Cost-effectiveness is sometimes confused with benefit-cost analysis, but there are advantages to maintaining the distinction. Cost-effectiveness assumes benefits and does not compare them with cost as in benefit-cost analysis. In cost-effectiveness analysis, the analyst wishes to determine the least costly means to achieve the objective. Frequently, all methods of analysis using inputs, alternatives, and outputs mean cost-effectiveness analysis including benefit-cost. However, cost-effectiveness can often be the more effective analytical technique, and blurring the distinction between the techniques tends to blind practitioners to the comparative advantages of the two techniques. Both have their advantages, but often cost-effectiveness can be used where benefit-cost is a meaningless technique.

The sophisticated benefit-cost analysis is useful. It can establish a framework for reasonably consistent and uniform project evaluations at the staff level. This can lead to added discipline in the political process because weak projects will appear inferior, thus making their funding difficult in an open political setting. The technique is most useful when the choice set is narrow and the decision involves economic alternative investments. The technique draws increasing criticism when intangibles and complex social values are present in the analysis. Value perspectives such as reallocation of wealth are not addressed well with benefit-cost analysis.

Benefit-cost analysis involves defining a choice set, analytical constraints, measurements, and a choice model. Analysis must be made manageable so that the work can be done within a reasonable time frame. Thus, parameters or range of projects must be established. Analytical constraints (e.g., legal, political, distributional, financial, and physical) must be understood, stated, and either treated as side considerations of the analysis or included in the analytical objective functions. Benefit-cost analysis involves measurements; therefore, all the challenges and analytical limitations of data apply to benefit-cost analysis. Those challenges and limitations must be understood or serious analytical mistakes will be made and decision makers will be given misleading advice. A full treatment of this topic is beyond the scope of this text, but is covered in books concerning research methods. The choice model is the means used to relate the estimated costs and benefits. It is the formula. The model (formula) is used to decide how the measures will be incorporated into the overall analysis.

Procedures

The procedures of benefit-cost analysis involve defining the objective functions, benefits, and costs as well as calculating present value. The objective functions specify without weighing the ultimate values used in the analysis. Examples include increasing national income, aggregate consumption, supply of foreign exchange, and employment. The functions must be quantifiable, or they cannot be treated in the analysis. Benefits are defined normally as present value of the contributions in relationship to the objective function. Costs are sometimes defined in terms of reducing the objective function. They are also the present value of the resources that are employed and are valued as opportunity costs as a consequence of implementing the project.

The calculations in benefit-cost analysis are complex owing to several factors. Both benefits and costs must be measured over time in order to permit a broad view of project impacts, especially economic consequences. Benefits are measured by the market price of the project outputs or the price consumers are willing to pay. Costs are measured by the monetary outlays necessary to undertake the investment. Both occur over time. Unlike the private sector, externalities (i.e., project effects on others which occur because of the project's existence—such as down-stream pollution from a plant) are calculated into public sector benefit-cost analysis. Also, opportunity costs are valued because full employment and scarce resources are assumed to exist. This means that some worthwhile choices are forgone once the decision is made to undertake the project, and this is a project cost. If the assumption is incorrect (e.g., if full employment does not exist, then costs should be revised downward).

Alternative Choice Models

The decision on projects is often made by ranking alternative projects. The ranking depends on the choice model (formula) used. The various models do not give the analyst the same results. The four models are the following:

Benefit-cost	Based on discounted present value
Benefit/cost	Ratio of present value of benefits and costs
Rate of return or marginal investment efficiency	Discount rate which puts the benefits and costs at equilibrium
Payout period	Number of years of benefit needed so that the benefit equals the cost

Each model has its inherent bias. The benefit-cost model biases the decision in favor of large projects because of the manner in which the figures are calculated. Any deductions from benefits rather than adding to costs would affect ratios and thus would affect the benefit/cost model. If benefits or costs do not occur evenly over time, this may not be properly computed in mathematical models unless special provisions permit this unevenness.

Virtually all practitioners prefer the benefit-cost (discounted present value) model. It focuses on explicit treatment of budgetary and other constraints as well as project indivisibility and interdependencies. This model forces the separate treatment of those matters without confusing them with the determination of the proper discount rate. Also, calculation of present value is not a behind-the-scenes adjustment because it must be treated openly in the analysis.

Benefit-Cost Ingredients

A purpose of this chapter is not to explain how benefit-cost analysis is done but rather to stress the sophisticated analytical nature of the technique as well as the inherent limitations of the technique. Too many professionals advocate and even use the technique without understanding its true analytical sophistication. It is a worthwhile technique, and it should be studied by those interested in public budgeting. However, the first step is to recognize the complex nature of this type of analysis and to be especially sensitive to its limitations.

The remainder of this section examines key factors associated with benefit-cost analysis. Stress is placed on the limitations and cautions which should be associated with this technique. This stress is meant to sensitize the reader to the analytical problems associated with the technique. A full explanation of how to apply the technique is beyond the scope of this text, and readers are encouraged to learn more about this and other analytical techniques in further study.

Benefits and Estimation

Benefits are classified as primary, secondary, and intangible. Primary benefits are the values of goods or services resulting from project conditions. They are included in the analysis. Common examples are additional crops due to land irrigation and annual savings in flood damages. Associated costs (e.g., seed for irrigated land) are subtracted from primary benefits. Secondary benefits either stem from or are induced by the project, but do not directly result from the project. Their inclusion as benefits is subject to controversy. Intangibles are nondollar-value benefits (e.g., aesthetic quality of the landscape) which by definition cannot be included in the benefit-cost calculations.

What gets counted as "benefits" is important. Therefore, if the major benefits are intangibles, then the analysis often loses much of its worth.

Also, if the major benefits are secondary, the inclusion of them is controversial and the resulting analytical conclusions would be subject to a complex debate involving the technique more than the project. The purpose of analysis is to aid decision makers, and the result of using controversial techniques is to confuse further the decision-making process.

Benefit-cost analysis is almost always used prior to the project's existence; therefore, costs and benefits are estimated over the projected life of the project. Cost estimates include construction engineering, relocation of households, erosion, and third-party effects. Benefits are harder to estimate, especially if they do not occur evenly over time. Decisions must be made on when to stop counting, what not to count, how to count, and how to aggregate benefits. These decisions may greatly affect the analysis; therefore, controversial decisions may lead to controversial analytical conclusions.

One commonly voiced concern is how to handle costs which have already been made (i.e., sunk costs). This is not a controversial subject because they are almost uniformly treated as not relevant to the project cost and are not calculated. Sunk costs may be of significant political concern, but they are not added into the project cost.

Discount Rate

The most controversial ingredient of benefit-cost analysis is the discount rate. The controversy centers not on its proper role in the analysis, but on how it should be determined. It is significant because a higher rate means that fewer projects will be justified, especially if they have costs accumulating over a long period of time. The rationale for a discount rate is that the resources used in a particular project could have been invested elsewhere to yield future resources larger than the amount invested; therefore, this should be taken into consideration in the analysis.

Several approaches to determining discount rates are advocated. One says that a discount rate should have a bias toward present goods over future goods, whereas another argues for giving higher value to future goods. Others argue opportunity cost should be based upon equivalent private investments, whereas still others say external effects should be added and subtracted from those private opportunity costs. The debate is endless and most analysts end up by using an arbitrary interest cost of federal funds in a certain period to select a rate.

If the projects analyzed are similar in size and duration, then the rate used is not significant as long as the same approach is used for all projects. If not, then the analytical results become controversial.

Externalities, Risk, and Other Considerations

Externalities are included in benefit-cost analysis, but they are difficult to determine. Technological externalities involve the physical input-output relationship of other producing units. Pecuniary externalities involve the influences of the project on the prices of other producing units. For example, a public recreation facility may affect demand on, and thus the price of, nearby private facilities. Measurement of externalities is treacherous. Ideally, only "important externalities" are included in the analysis. Interestingly, the influence on the local wage rate is normally not included as "important." Controversy can easily exist on the inclusion of externalities as well as the measurement of them.

Often benefits and costs involve risk and uncertainty. Risk can be described by a probability function normally based on experience. Uncertainty, in its purest meaning, is not subject to probability determination. This means that risk can be included in the analysis, but uncertainty cannot be included. Methods of calculating risk and uncertainty vary. Some methods establish a higher permissible rate than 1.0. Some use a higher rate of discount, and some rationalize the arbitrary benefit stream cutoff by referring to risk and uncertainty. An analyst can deal with risk by including a probability function in an already complex formula, but uncertainty by definition must be treated arbitrarily. Such treatment leads to controversy over the analytical results.

Two other considerations illustrate the complexity of this technique. As was pointed out, sometimes private opportunity costs are used to determine public project opportunity costs. The danger is that private market costs are higher owing to the different tax statuses and costs of financing. Another consideration is that user charges may not be independent of the benefit measures. User charges will restrict use, thus benefits will be reduced. Benefit-cost analysis requires a great deal of thought and care. If that professional treatment is not afforded, then embarrassing controversy can develop over the quality of the analysis.

Benefit-cost analysis is biased toward values associated with money. It does not work well with projects concerning social equality, and the poor tend to be discriminated against with this technique. For example, the value of life is often computed in terms of earning power, thus an airplane passenger is treated as worth more than a bus rider. Values such as equality of opportunity cannot be treated well with this technique. If the project involves such values, then the use of the benefit-cost technique itself will be controversial.

REVIEW QUESTIONS

1. Explain the budget system model, its consistency with democratic theory, and the importance of data measures.
2. Explain the various application difficulties associated with using the budget system model.
3. Compare and contrast a scatter diagram, marginal costs, and discounting. In what ways is each a useful analytical technique in budgeting?

4. Explain the significance of a crosswalk as an analytical tool. What would be crosswalked and why?

5. Compare and contrast qualitative, time series, and causal analysis approaches to revenue forecasting. Explain why good forecasting is important to government.

6. Compare and contrast the various approaches to expenditure forecasting.

7. Misunderstanding the productivity concept can lead to what types of difficulties? What are some of the most common reasons for government not to increase productivity? Why are there no simple uniform answers to the question of how to increase productivity?

8. Explain how regression analysis can help one achieve greater productivity.

9. Compare and contrast benefit-cost and cost-effectiveness analyses.

10. Explain why benefit-cost is a sophisticated and difficult technique to apply. Explain how benefit-cost analysis can be abused as a technique. How can benefit-cost analysis be counterproductive to decision-making?

REFERENCES

BURKHEAD, JESSE and JERRY MINER. *Public Expenditure.* Chicago: Aldine, 1971.
Committee for Economic Development. *Improving Productivity in State and Local Government.* New York: Committee for Economic Development, March 1976.
DAVIES, THOMAS R. and JAMES A. ZINGALE. "Advanced Software for Revenue Forecasting: What to Consider Before Investing in Technology." Paper prepared for the 1983 American Society for Public Administration National Conference, New York, April 17, 1983.
HATRY, HARRY P. "Overview of Modern Program Analysis Characteristics and Techniques: Modern Program Analysis—Hero or Villain?" Washington, D.C.: Urban Institute, 1969.
———, LOUIS BLAIR, DONALD FISK, and WAYNE KIMMEL. *Program Analysis for State and Local Governments.* Washington, D.C.: Urban Institute, 1976.
ISAAC, STEPHEN, in collaboration with William B. Michael. *Handbook in Research and Evaluation.* San Diego, Calif.: Edits Publishers, 1971.
KLAY, WILLIAM EARLE. "Revenue Forecasting: An Administrative Perspective" in Jack Rabin and Thomas D. Lynch (eds.), *Handbook on Public Budgeting and Financial Management.* New York: Marcel Dekker, 1983.
KLAY, WILLIAM EARLE and GLORIA A. GRIZZLE. "Revenue Forecasting in the States: New Dimensions of Budgetary Forecasting." Paper delivered to the American Society for Public Administration at Anaheim, Calif., April 14, 1986.
KRAMER, FRED A. "The Discounting to Present Value Technique as a Decision Tool," *Special Bulletin* 1976E (November 24, 1976).
MOAK, LENNOX L. and KATHRYN W. KILLIAN. *Operating Budget Manual.* Chicago: Municipal Finance Officers Association, 1963.
ROSS, JOHN P. and JESSE BURKHEAD. *Productivity in the Local Government Sector.* Lexington, Mass.: Heath, 1974.

TOULMIN, LLEWELLYN M. and GLENDAL E. WRIGHT. "Expenditure Forecasting" in Jack Rabin and Thomas D. Lynch (eds.), *Handbook on Public Budgeting and Financial Management*. New York: Marcel Dekker, 1983.

U.S. Joint Financial Management Improvement Program. *Productivity Programs in the Federal Government*. Washington, D.C.: U.S. Joint Financial Management Improvement Program, July 1976.

Urban Institute and International City Management Association. *Measuring the Effectiveness of Basic Municipal Services*. Washington, D.C.: International City Management Association, February 1974.

WRIGHT, CHESTER and MICHAEL D. TATE. *Economics and Systems Analysis: Introduction for Public Managers*. Reading, Mass.: Addison-Wesley, 1973.

chapter 6

ANALYTICAL PROCESSES

In public budgeting, there are five analytical processes which are designed to help professionals deal more intelligently with their policy and administrative challenges. Each one—program analysis, budget examination, process analysis, program evaluation, and auditing—is briefly described here, but greater attention is given to budget examination and process analysis due to their central importance to public budgeting. The reports produced from each process should be viewed as normally useful input to better budgets. Program analysis looks *de novo* at the policy implications of major programmatic budget decisions. Budget examination is the primary analytical process which actually produces the budget. Process analysis is a careful focus upon the management process itself so that improvements can be identified. Program evaluation looks backward and helps the budget examiner decide if the program was effective or sufficiently effective to justify the requested money in the BY. Auditing is also reflective in character and helps the budget examiner focus on questions of both effectiveness and efficiency. The chapter will explain:

1. the approach essential for useful program analysis;
2. how budget examination can be undertaken using the various concepts and techniques explained in the text;
3. a useful approach to look closely at the process and identify process improvements;
4. the basics of program evaluation; and
5. the essentials of auditing, especially the types of information which can be forthcoming from a "good" program audit.

PROGRAM ANALYSIS

In program analysis—sometimes called policy analysis—the focus is on considering the new policy options which are implicit in the budget. Such analyses are often highly quantitative in character, but that need not be true. There are elements common to all program analyses, regardless of their character. A frequent complaint of high level executive officials is that they really could not get the agencies to provide the information necessary to judge budget requests. Often this is more an admission of professional incompetency than a commentary on the budget process. If a reasonable effort, as explained here, is put into budget examining by competent professionals, then the central review staff will be in a position to make reasoned judgments based upon agency requests and alternative policy options. Good program analysis should isolate sensitive policy questions and identify the likely implications of the various viable policy options within the limitations of the data and the analytical technique used.

Selecting Issues

Selection of potential issues can proceed systematically. What are the unsettled influential issues which determine program direction and emphasis? What issues are being raised by key influential people in the legislature, executive, clientele, media, and judicial settings? What are the apparent policy dilemmas facing the agency? The analysts can use these questions to develop a reasonable list of potential issues for analysis. Normally program issues are abundant. The usual problem is not to find issues but to select the best issues for program review purposes. The Urban Institute has developed the following criteria for selecting issues for analysis.

Importance of an Issue

1. Is there a decision to be made by the government? Can the analysis significantly influence the adoption of various alternatives?
2. Does the issue involve large costs or major consequences for services?
3. Is there substantial room for improving program performance?

Feasibility of Analysis

4. Can the problem be handled by program analysis?
5. Is there time for the analysis to be done before the key decisions must be made?
6. Are personnel and funds available to do the analysis?
7. Do sufficient data exist to undertake the analysis, and can needed data be gathered within the time available?

The first consideration is the importance of the issue. As suggested by the previous criteria, the potential significance of an analysis of the issue, the consequence, and the potential for improvement should be considered.

If no one will use an analysis of an issue, then proceeding with the analysis is certainly foolish. Given a lack of time to perform analysis, the analyst is normally wise to concentrate on the big issue, especially if notable improvements are possible.

The next consideration is the feasibility of analysis. Many problems do not lend themselves to program analysis or the time available is so brief that useful analysis cannot be conducted prior to the time the key decisions are made. Personnel, fund, or data limitations may exist which preclude analysis. Each of these factors must honestly be assessed before work on program analysis begins or the effort may be worthless.

Exhibit 6-1 presents some illustrations of the issues which might be subject to program analysis.

Issue Assessment

Once the issues have been defined, then a preliminary assessment can be made before an in-depth analysis is conducted. In most situations, an agency suggests issues and the central budget office decides which issues to investigate. Those issues may or may not be the ones suggested by the agency. The involvement of the central budget office is wise as it helps to insure the significance of the report once it is written, but the lack of a preliminary assessment of the issues is not wise. In far too many analytical situations, reports have been commissioned without a proper appreciation of what was requested. The instructions requesting the study may have been too vague or misleading. Another possibility is that further thought will reveal that there is no real need for an analysis, thus saving thousands or even millions of dollars. Preliminary assessments are extremely useful.

The issue assessment is a written presentation which identifies and describes the major features of a significant issue facing the government. The assessment is only a few pages long, but it clearly sets out the ingredients which would be considered in a major issue study. According to Harry P. Hatry of the Urban Institute, the outline or major subjects in an issue assessment are as follows:

1. *The Problem.* What is the problem and its causes? Identify specific groups (e.g., the poor) affected. How are they affected? Identify characteristics of the group. How large and significant is the problem now? What are the likely future dimensions of the problem?

2. *Objectives and Evaluation Criteria.* Define the fundamental purposes and benefits of the program. Identify the evaluation criteria by which progress toward the program objectives should be judged.

3. *Current Activities and Agencies Involved.* Identify all relevant groups involved in attempting to deal with the problem. Identify what each group is doing, including costs and impacts. Activities, costs, and benefits should be projected into the future.

4. *Other Significant Factors.* Cite the other major factors, including political realities, that affect the problem. Identify unusual resources, timing limitations, or other factors of significance.

EXHIBIT 6-1   Illustrative Issues for Program Analysis

LAW ENFORCEMENT

1. What is the most effective way of distributing limited police forces—by time of day, day of week, and geographical location?
2. What types of police units (foot patrolmen, one- or two-man police cars, special task forces, canine corps units, or others) should be used and in what mix?
3. What types of equipment (considering both current and new technologies) should be used for weaponry, for communications, and for transportation?
4. How can the judicial process be improved to provide more expeditious service, keep potentially dangerous persons from running loose, and at the same time protect the rights of the innocent?
5. How can criminal detention institutions be improved to maximize the probability of rehabilitation, while remaining a deterrent to further crime?

FIRE PROTECTION

1. Where should fire stations be located, and how many are needed?
2. How should firefighting units be deployed, and how large should units be?
3. What types of equipment should be used for communications, transportation, and firefighting?
4. Are there fire prevention activities, such as inspection of potential fire hazards or school educational programs, that can be used effectively?

HEALTH AND SOCIAL SERVICES

1. What mix of treatment programs should do the most to meet the needs of the expected mix of clients?
2. What prevention programs are desirable for the groups that seem most likely to suffer particular ailments?

HOUSING

1. To what extent can housing code enforcement programs be used to decrease the number of families living in substandard housing? Will such programs have an adverse effect on the overall supply of low-income housing in the community?
2. What is the appropriate mix of code enforcement with other housing programs to make housing in the community adequate?
3. What is the best mix of housing rehabilitation, housing maintenance, and new construction to improve the quantity and quality of housing?

EMPLOYMENT

1. What relative support should be given to training and employment programs which serve different client groups?
2. What should be the mix among outreach programs, training programs, job-finding and matching programs, antidiscrimination programs, and post-employment follow-up programs?

(continued)

EXHIBIT 6-1   **(continued)**

WASTE

1. How should waste be collected and disposed of, given alternative visual, air, water, and pollution standards?
2. What specific equipment and routings should be used?

RECREATION AND LEISURE

1. What type, location, and size of recreation facilities should be provided for those desiring them?
2. How should recreation facilities be divided among summer and winter, daytime and night-time, and indoor and outdoor activities?
3. What, and how many, special summer programs should be made available for out-of-school youths?
4. What charges, if any, should be made to users, considering such factors as differential usage and ability to pay?

Source: Harry Hatry, Louis Blair, Donald Fisk and Wayne Kimmel, Program Analysis for State and Local Government. The Urban Institute, 1976 p. 11.

5. *Alternatives.* Describe alternative programs designed to meet the problem and the major characteristics of each.
6. *Recommendations for Follow-up.* Making choices among alternatives is inappropriate because, by definition, this work is only an assessment. Recommendations can be made on the next administrative step (e.g., full-scale analysis). What is the best timing for and scope of the needed follow-up analysis? Should the analysis be a quick response or an in-depth study? Frank descriptions of analytical difficulties should be cited. What major data problems exist? How should they be dealt with under the circumstances?

The assessment serves as the basis for deciding to request a special analytical study and for framing instructions for the study.

Commentary on Analysis

The conduct of analysis largely depends upon the subject to be analyzed, the context of the study, and the techniques used. Each of these subjects is outside the scope of this chapter and can properly be studied under the heading of microeconomics, operations research, systems analysis, and statistics. Chapter 6 discusses some elementary analytical concepts useful in budgeting as well as in explaining benefit-cost analysis.

There are ten factors—five technical and five bureaucratic—which particularly influence the results of analysis. Those factors are the following:

1. study size;
2. study timing;
3. methodological adequacy;
4. consideration of implementation;
5. nature of problem studied;
6. decision maker interest;
7. implementor's participation;
8. single-agency issue;
9. proposed changes in funding; and
10. immediate decision needed.

There are five factors which appear to be more significant than the others. The three most significant "technical" factors are study timing (i.e., studies were well timed so that study findings were available at key decision points); consideration of implementation (i.e., studies included an explicit consideration of political and administrative issues which might affect the implementation of study findings); and nature of problem studied (i.e., studies focused on well-defined problems rather than on broad or open-ended ones). The two most significant "bureaucratic" factors are immediate decision needed (i.e., issues which could not be deferred by policy makers); and decision maker interest (i.e., issues in which decision makers had shown clear interest).

In program analysis, care must be taken to avoid four common mistakes which occur as a result of an unrealistic desire to analyze for the sake of analysis. One mistake can be labeled "search under the lamp." A well-known story tells of the man who was searching at night for his lost watch under a street light. A friend comes by and offers to aid in the search. The friend asks where the man lost the watch and the man replies that the watch was lost half a block up the street. The friend then asks why the man is searching next to the street lamp. The man answers that the light is much better under the street light. In policy analysis situations, analysts often will concentrate their investigation on those aspects which are easy to measure and downplay the aspects difficult to measure. Thus they are looking under the street lamp instead of "up the street" where the watch was lost.

Another common mistake is to become fascinated by technique. An intellectual challenge for an analyst is to use and develop more sophisticated analytical—often mathematical—techniques. The normal desire is to select issues which require complex techniques or use more complex techniques when simpler ones would be adequate. Analysts should address the analytical problems and not techniques, otherwise there is means-ends confusion.

A third mistake is to delay reports and even policy decisions so that analyses can be performed for their own sake. Analysts can be consumed with interest in the analytical question, much as some people are consumed by crossword puzzles, mysteries, and good books. This consuming interest can overwhelm the original reason for the analysis. As was pointed out earlier, report timeliness is critical and sometimes analytical purity is sacrificed for timeliness.

The fourth mistake is to overanalyze. In some situations, a good analyst quietly thinking for a few hours may produce results equal to or better than an army of survey researchers. We automatically tend to use certain well-known approaches to analysis without appreciating their limitations and the tolerance for error implicit in the issue being studied. The advantage of the issue assessment mentioned earlier is to avoid such a mistake.

A final commentary of analysis is that there may be only "poor" solutions to problems. This commentary may seem obvious, but this realization is often difficult for decision makers to accept. If a program analysis is conducted and only "poor" solutions are cited, the decision maker can conclude either that solutions are indeed "poor" or that the analysis was bad. Thus, the analyst can be placed in an awkward position. The only professionally acceptable course of action is to be sure that no desirable answers exist and to explain this fact properly in the analyst's report.

Presentations of Results: Some Prescriptions

A common failure of program analysis is providing a poor presentation of study results. The work may be excellent, but the presentation is inadequate.

The first advice on presenting results is to review them carefully before they are distributed. The pressures of meeting a deadline and the distasteful chore of proofing combine to discourage proper review of papers before they are distributed. These final checks are essential if embarrassing mistakes or insensitive political statements are to be avoided.

Report findings should be in writing. Oral reports are useful but they should supplement or summarize written reports. Written reports provide the essential record which is often useful even years after a report was prepared.

Care must be taken to prepare compact, clear summaries. The summary is normally the first important portion of the report that is read—the other material may never be read. Long, vague summaries are counterproductive as they discourage use of the report.

In most program analysis reports, two or three options are discussed. If only one option were discussed, then the credibility of the report would be questioned. Many options only tend to confuse matters. Two or three options are adequate normally to illustrate the varieties of solutions. If the range of solutions is broad, the presentation of only two or three options is done to illustrate the types of solutions.

Studies must set out limitations and assumptions. Professional standards alone require such candor. On a more practical level, professional reputation and confidence are enhanced by frank, honest reports. A decision maker may not like the qualifications, but if something goes wrong the analyst is protected by that candor. Also, the decision makers are apprised fully of the risks inherent in their decisions.

Studies should discuss potential windfalls and pitfalls related to the issue. Windfalls are collateral benefits resulting from actions and decisions. Pitfalls are collateral hazards or disadvantages. Both can be easily overlooked in the analyses and by decision makers. The potential for oversight is the reason why this material should be in the report.

The studies should contain simple graphics where possible to communicate major findings and conclusions. Most readers will benefit from both written and graphic explanations. Graphics should not stand alone—reference should be made to them in the text. Complex graphics should be avoided because readers may not be able to understand them.

Clarity requires that jargon be avoided. If a special vocabulary is well known and used, then such jargon (e.g., piggyback containers, subsystem) can be used. Jargon is the shorthand means of communication. However, most program analysis reports are meant for managers and other decision makers unschooled in the jargon; thus it only makes the paper difficult to read.

Reports and studies should be written for the decision makers. Authors of reports and studies should know who are the intended and likely users of their work. What are the backgrounds, knowledge, and biases of the report and study users? If the users have extensive technical knowledge, then authors should use that fact in preparing the report. If the user has strong biases and the report finding runs counter to those biases, then greater care should be taken to explain and fully document the findings.

From the public budgeting perspective, one of the most obvious failures in the presentation of program analysis results is the omission of an explanation of how the recommendations should be translated to operational management direction. People working in budgeting are interested in policy debates and analysis, but their lives involve operational decisions. Study findings and recommendations must be translated to the operational before they can be treated as something more than a possibility. Exactly in what ways should the current program be changed? What specifically are the present and future budget implications? These questions should be addressed in the program analysis reports and studies if they are to be meaningful to the budget process.

Role of the Chief Executive

The product of program analysis is meant for decision makers, especially chief executives. If there is support from the chief executive and that person uses the products of program analysis, then there is a reasonable chance that program analysis will be significant in the government decision-making process. On the other hand, without top level support and use, program analysis as an activity is worthless. Detailed top level involvement is not needed, but the following types of involvement are essential. According to the Urban Institute, officials should:

1. participate actively in the selection of program and policy issues for analysis;
2. assign responsibility for the analysis to a unit of the organization which can conduct the study objectively;

3. ensure that participation and cooperation are obtained from relevant agencies;
4. provide adequate staff to meet a timely reporting schedule;
5. insist that the objectives, evaluation criteria, client groups, and program alternatives considered in the analysis include those of prime importance;
6. have a work schedule prepared and periodically monitored; and
7. review results, and if findings seem valid, see that they are used.[1]

BUDGET EXAMINATION

An important activity in the budget process is budget examination, which uses other forms of analysis and specific analyses to review agency budget requests and make staff recommendations to legislative and executive political leaders. This section explains how budget analysts can perform sophisticated budget examination within the context of democratic government, complex technology, and current analytical techniques.

Information Sources

Reviewers are not limited to the agency budget submission in forming their analysis and conclusions. Information can be obtained from the budget submissions, hearings, reports which may be available, other information such as newspaper stories, and answers to specific questions prior to and after budget hearings. The most important information source is normally the agency budget request because it directly addresses the information needs of the budget reviewer. Hearings are also a valuable information source as they can be used to focus upon specific inquiries. Hearings permit direct oral interchange between the agency and the reviewers. Reviewers should also make use of any available reports, such as special analytical studies and program evaluation reports. This type of information often is not organized well for budget analysis purposes, but studies and reports do provide useful insight and suggest areas of fruitful inquiry. Other information sources, such as national media reports and books, can also be extremely helpful in framing inquiries.

Specific questions by reviewers and answers by agency officials are valuable to budget reviewers. These questions and answers can occur before and after hearings. They can be oral or written depending upon the reviewers' request. The major limiting factor is time. Rarely are questions asked prior to budget submissions because the submissions may contain the answers. If there is a short time interval between the submission and the hearing, then written questions and answers may be impossible—normally at least five working days are needed to develop answers, have them approved by top agency personnel, and have them typed and transmitted. If there is an equally short time interval between the hearing and the central budget office decision on the budget, then again written questions may not be pos-

---

[1] Harry P. Hatry, Louis Blair, Donald Fisk, and Wayne Kimmel, *Program Analysis for State and Local Governments* (Washington, D.C.: Urban Institute, 1976), p. 11.

sible. Time pressures dictate that the answers must not require new analysis but use existing information.

The key to an outstanding budget review is for the reviewer to gain the necessary program information and insight. No one source of information is adequate and many inquiries can be tailored for the situation. The advocate wishes to anticipate inquiries so that confidence in the agency budget personnel can be enhanced. Both the examiner and the analyst preparing the submission have in common a set of information. One wishes to know the information and the other should be ready to supply the information. What can a good budget examiner look for and what should a good agency budget analyst be able to provide?

Code of Ethics

Ethical considerations are significant and do tend to be overlooked until a crisis occurs. The code of ethics described here is part of the handbook for budget analysts in the state of Florida and its purpose is to guide the professional conduct of state budget analysts. The role of budget examiners and the proper carrying out of their responsibilities is critical to a successful budget process. Improper conduct can mean fraud, impotent and frustrated policy, inefficiency, counterproductive management practices, and an inability on the part of the examiners to develop and grow as professionals and as members of an organization.

The following code of ethics and its implications should guide professional conduct.

1. *No gifts or favors may be accepted by a budget analyst beyond minor social courtesies which have little or no significant value.* This first ethical principle is obviously intended to prevent corruption and improper influence on analysts by actors in the political process. It is critical (1) if objectivity, as well as the confidence of others in that objectivity, is to be maintained; and (2) if the policy issues are to be determined through the democratic process. As stated, it does not require the analyst's total separation from influencing factors, but such a separation is not inconsistent with this principle. Some budget offices do require total separation because of the importance of the analyst's being free from the possibility of any improper influence.

2. *The role of the analyst does not extend to independent action which establishes government policy.* Analysts are expected to gather information, analyze it, and recommend policy with appropriate supporting data and documentation. Their purpose is to raise the level of debate associated with policy-making, not to make policy. Budget analysts are staff functionaries whose job is to help the true policy makers—the elected officials and their appointees. They are called on to provide useful information to help the political decision makers arrive at more enlightened decisions. Often, examiners judge their success by how much they shaped policy rather than by their role in creating an environment in which more enlightened decisions are more likely to occur. As long as the budget analyst is part of a political system in which overriding policy is established by elected officials, the examiner should view his or her role as advisory. If the examiner's advice is not taken, no professional failure occurred unless his or her presentation of that information tended to inhibit enlightened decision-making.

3. *Examiners must maintain their objectivity, which includes presenting all aspects of issues fairly and excludes advocating an agency's position for any purpose other than to clarify the issues.* Being emotionally committed to the agencies under review is one of the hazards of budget examination. Analysts must avoid becoming staff advocates of agency requests; instead, they must remain detached so that they can critically examine budget requests. This presents a staffing dilemma for budget offices. On the one hand, examiners must be involved with a line agency long enough to know the complexities of that agency; on the other hand, examiners must not be coopted, which does tend to occur over time. There is no simple way to deal with this ethical principle, but it is important that the spirit of the principle be respected.

4. *Every attempt must be made to ensure that managerial decisions are made by the proper line officials.* Managers must make their own decisions, whereas analysts must be free to comment on those decisions and to facilitate a more thoughtful decision-making process.

5. *Analysts must avoid acting in an arrogant manner to anyone, including other government officials.* Analysts may have their own strong opinions, but these opinions must be kept under control. Sensitivity and respect for feelings must be shown to all individuals who are part of the budget process. Examiners are staff advisors and not managers of line government units. A professional problem stemming from the examiner's unique access to high officials and role as overseer of the budget process is a tendency to substitute his or her own decisions for those of the line manager. Sometimes the examiner will arrogantly demand information on some policy change from the line manager. Sometimes a line manager, as a ploy to escape responsibility, will ask the staff budget analyst to make managerial decisions (e.g., whether to buy or lease equipment). In either situation, the examiner must recall that his or her responsibility is primarily advisory and should maintain a cordial working relationship with the line manager.

6. *In framing recommendations and in dealing with the bureaucracy, the examiner must make every effort to foster and improve the quality of government management.* Recommendations and accompanying information should be sensitive not only to policy considerations but also to the managerial environment needed to accomplish that policy.

7. *The professional development and growth of the examiners is important.* Budget analysts must continually strive to understand the substantive policy and management issues associated with the units being examined. Analysts must also strive to improve their budget examination skills and knowledge so that better work can be performed. Improved government quality does not occur automatically and improvement usually comes only after a struggle. Given other policy and management concerns, budget analysts can easily overlook or fail to emphasize the improvement of government management as a continuing priority. Ironically, examiners are in a unique position to foster and encourage those improvements. For example, funds for professional development tend to be ignored rather than treated as one of the fringe benefits associated with employment for a progressive organization. The budget analysts should insure that such matters are not overlooked. Professional development also applies to the examiner. The tendency is to become involved in the daily tasks and neglect one's own professional development. Thus, this ethical principle calls upon analysts to recognize the importance of their own professional growth and to pursue it by means of formal education, training, and professional conferences.

Services Performed

Results of services performed are important. The budget examiner determines services or types of services which are anticipated from the planned budget. Historical information can be used to illustrate the type of service likely to be provided as well as to establish the reliability of the agency to perform as planned. The budget submission often indicates objectives and states likely products of the agency. The examiner looks beyond specific outputs and tries to ascertain the likely impacts on society and individuals directly and indirectly due to the program. Also, unanticipated good and bad effects are considered. It is helpful if the information is available in the budget request. If not, the information may be available in speeches or program evaluation reports.

The agency normally has an excellent explanation of its likely outputs. Any budget is a plan requiring forecasting so every budget must be tentative, since there is no guarantee the events will evolve as planned. This is accepted; if something else were said, the budget examiner would question the realism of the agency. The character of explanation of output and projected benefits depends upon whether the program is demand responsive or directed. Demand responsive programs react to individuals and groups which meet the agency's general criteria of need and seek assistance. In contrast, directed programs are established to fulfill a specific need and are managed directly by government. Demand responsive programs are grants-in-aid and direct benefit (e.g., food stamps) programs. In demand responsive programs, the government cannot control the rate or type of demand; thus it is conditioned by outside factors. In directed programs, the government has a high degree of control over exactly what it will do.

Budget examiners can probe direct programs for the management plan of the agency. The agency normally has a detailed plan of how it will use its resources to achieve specific outputs. It should have a definite fix on the likely benefits and spillover effects of the program. The examiner's role is first to make sure such a plan exists, and secondly to see that the plan has a reasonable chance of being successful. The plan and management should be flexible enough to meet likely contingencies.

Budget examiners handle demand responsive programs differently. Budget examiners probe these programs in terms of anticipated demands and likely outputs and benefits. Agency management should have excellent forecasts of likely demand. The agency should have prepared an analysis of various likely funding scenarios and estimated the likely outputs and benefits of each scenario. To the extent that the agency can control its ability to meet the program demand, the agency should be able to explain what it can do and the significance of its action in terms of the scenarios and resulting outputs and benefits. If the agency cannot provide these explanations, then the agency's ability to manage the requested funds properly can be strongly questioned.

If the budget examiner ever sees vagueness in the information provided, this can serve as a red flag to the examiner. Vague subjects can be carefully isolated because vagueness indicates possibly serious managerial problems. If agency management does not know how to deal with a situation or there is serious internal conflict, then agency budget officers must be vague about those situations in the budget request because the uncertainty cannot, by definition, be resolved. Good budget officers may be able to minimize the problem but they cannot hide the use of a vague answer.

Budget examiners can carefully probe the exact reason for the vagueness. The explanation may be merely a poor presentation rather than management difficulties. If the vagueness is isolated early enough, questions and hearings can be used to determine the exact nature of the problem. This probing requires skill; but unless the agency budget officer directly lies, the budget examiner can isolate the problem, given enough time. Even in the rare cases where the agency personnel lie, a skillful examiner can normally isolate the problem because logical consistency is difficult for liars to maintain.

Program Inputs and Outputs

The budget examiner should determine key input, process, and output measures. These concepts are explained in more depth in chapter 5. Briefly, there are measures which tend to be more useful than other measures. These indicators show the resources going into the program, what activities are taking place, and the results attributable to the program. These measures are used for comparative and trend analytical purposes. By performing elementary analysis, the budget examiner can determine questionable program budget requests and poor management practices and can identify important changes in the program's environment which are not correctly reflected in the budget request.

Exhibit 6-2 is a checklist used by the city of Los Angeles to review performance reports. Notice how the budget examiner is sensitive to the interrelationship of input, process, and outputs. The examiner maintains a questioning, arm's length relationship with the agency.

The budget examiner can also check the accuracy of tables and data supplied by the agency. Exhaustive checks are not necessary, but any uncommon results, important statistics, and common places where errors occur can always be checked. Tables can be checked by observing if there is proper internal consistency among tables. Often totals of summary columns can be checked against other summary columns for internal consistency. Simple arithmetic errors do occur even in the most important budget requests. Commonly errors occur when incorrect pay rate scales are used or when personnel are placed into the wrong classification.

Budget examiners can carefully review the money requested and be sensitive to hidden revenue sources or "sleight-of-hand" tricks. This is a conventional spender's strategy and the diligent reviewer can determine when such strategy is being used. The examiner must be well versed in backdoor spending techniques and must know if any of them can be used by the agency. The examiner can profit from the use of accounting reports. Use of fund transfer, lag time among administrative reservations, obligations, expenditures, and closing of accounts can be significant in determining hid-

EXHIBIT 6-2   Checklist for Review of Performance Reports

GENERAL

1. Check total gross man-hours for department with the combined total standard hours plus paid overtime hours as shown for each pay period on the IBM Personnel Audit Reports of the Controller (on file in Budget Administration Division).

PERSONNEL

2. Have any new activities or sub-activities been added over those shown in original work program?
3. If so, how many positions are being used? Cost estimate?
4. Are any previous activities or sub-activities eliminated or curtailed?
5. If so, how many positions which were included in last year's work program have been eliminated? Cost estimate?
6. Net increase or decrease in cost as result of additions and deletions?
7. Are there any special projects on which work was performed on a one-time basis only?
8. If so, what sub-activities were affected and how many man-hours were devoted to such special projects?
9. How does the actual number of personnel utilized compare with the number of authorized positions?

MAN-HOURS

10. Where both net man-hours and gross man-hours are reported, what is the percentage of net total to gross total? Are there any sub-activities which have lower percentages than the overall average percentage? Which are they and how much variation from average is there? What are the causes? (Vacations, sick leave, other absences?)
11. How does actual work performed compare with the estimate for each sub-activity?
12. Has there been an increase or decrease in the number of personnel actually utilized over last month's figures?

MAN-HOURS PER UNIT

13. How does the gross man-hours per unit for each sub-activity compare with last month's figures?
14. How does the net man-hours per unit for each sub-activity compare with last month's figures?
15. What is the reason for any increase or decrease?
16. In sub-activities where work performed and work unit are comparable, what is the variation between gross man-hours per unit for such sub-activities?
17. What is the variation between net man-hours per unit for such sub-activities?

OVERALL APPRAISAL

18. Based on the above analysis, could any employees have been transferred temporarily during slack periods?
19. If so, how many and in what classes of positions?

(continued)

EXHIBIT 6-2   (continued)
OVERALL APPRAISAL

20. Based on the above analysis, were any additional employees required to handle peak loads?

21. If so, how many and in what classes of positions?

22. Were there any backlogs of work resulting from lack of sufficient personnel?

23. If so, how much?

24. What class of personnel and how many employees would be required to eliminate backlogs?

25. Are backlogs the result of seasonal variations? Of improper scheduling of vacations? Of greater than normal absences due to sickness? Of unfilled positions? If the latter, what is the recruitment situation?

26. At the end of each quarter, determine what percentage of last year's annual program has been completed for each sub-activity.

27. Will the remaining portion of the annual program be completed by the end of the current fiscal year if that rate of progress is maintained?

28. Will more or less personnel be required in each sub-activity to complete annual program?

29. If so, how many and in what classes of positions?

Source: Los Angeles, California, City Administrator's Office.

den revenue. Other types of hidden revenue or improper expenditure estimates require considerable knowledge of the programs, but examiners can sometimes find such savings. For example, possibly the program can use existing government facilities rather than rent or lease new property. Another possibility is interagency or intergovernmental cooperative management agreements which allow savings as a result of economy of scale.

For the budget examiner, detailed tables from agencies isolate personnel by grade, type, unit, and status (permanent, temporary, part- or full-time). A critical resource is always personnel. Does the agency have too many or too few personnel for the assigned task? Maybe the agency has enough people, but they are of the wrong grade or type, or are poorly distributed among the units. Two common problems occur when an agency overexpands its highest ranks and fails to reallocate its personnel once a major task has been accomplished. Examiners cannot address such questions without detailed information on personnel. Another problem occurs when the personnel hired are not properly trained to do upgraded and more complex work requirements. Judgments in this area must be predicated on a knowledge of the personnel as well as of the new challenges facing the agency.

Budget examiners can often profit by comparing the agency's overhead and direct costs. A common mistake in bureaucracies is to allow overhead (i.e., those people and costs which serve to make the agency operate) to grow at the expense of direct costs (i.e., those people and costs which perform the activities directly associated with the agency's mission). Examples of overhead are personnel, legal, housekeeping, and budget activities. The proper size of overhead and even the definition of overhead are topics subject to debate. Ideally, overhead would be large enough to facilitate agency effectiveness and efficiency. In some situations, the overhead activities can grow to a point where agency effectiveness and efficiency are actually decreased. The budget examiner can examine the facts and determine if overhead is becoming excessive.

The data can be used to identify relationships between program demands and work load. For example, there tends to be a positive identifiable relationship between the population under the age of 25 in an area and the number of parole officers needed. If such relationships can be verified, then the examiner is in a much better position to judge the budget request.

Trends on program inputs and outputs are valuable information for the budget examiner. For example, if resources have been increasing and outputs decreasing, then serious questions must be raised concerning the efficiency and possibly even effectiveness of the program. What are the causes underlying trends and deviations from the apparent natural trend? Does there appear to be any positive or negative relationship between and among trends? For example, does salt tend to be more effective than sand in alleviating snow conditions? This information can lead to suggestions resulting in the use of cheaper substances while maintaining the same level of service to the public.

Comparative data on program inputs and outputs are also valuable information. What do comparable cities spend for the same type of services? What levels of output do they achieve? What explains the differences? Can those positive advantages be achieved in the budget examiner's city?

Emphasis and Change

Whether the budget request is presented in incremental or zero-base format, the budget examiner needs information on yearly budget emphases and changes in emphases from prior years. Decision makers wish to know how much stress is being placed on a given program relative to other program efforts. Balance is a political consideration, thus it is useful information for decision makers. They also wish to know if the agency is shifting its policy from previous years. This can best be determined by comparing the budget request with previous budget requests and actual obligation/expenditure patterns.

Budgets can be categorized into various logical subdivisions. A single categorization is probably inadequate for the variety of analytical needs of the budget examiner. One categorization should reflect the major agency tasks, projects, and continuing activities. Another categorization may be necessary to relate the inputs (e.g., dollars requested) to agency goals and intended benefits. However, often one categorization may be sufficient for both purposes if the agency is not handicapped by multiple inconsistent objectives. A categorization using line-item information is normally not useful because various purposes can lie behind the use of the same items of expenditure.

Categorizations can provide comparative information over several fiscal years. Dollars requested and possible specific inputs and outputs can be presented in terms of the prior year, actual current year estimates, budget year estimates, and possibly budget year-plus-five estimates. Such a display of data permits comparative analyses by fiscal year. Thus program increases and decreases over time can be isolated.

Complex programs, involving contracts extending beyond the budget year, can be misleading in terms of increases and decreases. Obligations can be made for continuing, expanding, or starting programs. The decrease or increase in a given fiscal year only gives useful information on the rate of obligation, and says nothing about the use of the money. The categorization in such programs should indicate the changes in the funding level of programs divided into subcategories of continuing and expanded programs. Also any new programs can be identified as such. As noted in the previous chapter, the spender's strategy calls for the use of flexible definitions by the spender. The budget examiner can understand the nature of each program so that definitions and categorizations can be challenged.

The previous categorization and related work are all designed to help the budget examiner identify emphases and shifts. What programs, projects, activities, or tasks are receiving greatest stress? This is judged in the context of the available resource, the maximum effort which could be given, and the relative emphases among the programs. Each is important in judging "emphasis." What programs, projects, activities, or tasks are receiving increased or decreased support? To answer that question fully, the budget examiner discovers whether changes are addressed to existing or new programs. Also, the examiner relates the change to program outputs, including anticipated benefits or harm to society and individuals. This analysis helps answer the followup question: Is the change worth it? Budget examiners seek *hard data* and get *written responses* to this type of inquiry in order to avoid later misunderstandings between the examiner and agency officials.

Program and financial plans (PFP) are required periodically (quarterly or semi-annually). They are summary tables of the budget, categorized by major programs and activities. In the federal government, the PFP includes both obligations and disbursements; but obligations are normally sufficient for state and local government purposes. The information covers the past year, current year, budget, and budget year plus five.

The PFP should be analyzed by the examiner for patterns reflecting policy and consistency with previously established management policy. The PFP should reflect any changes in policy and it is particularly useful prior to the budget call to forecast possible agency requests. Quick comparisons against past PFP's can be made to see if an evolution in policy is occurring. If changes are not occurring, the agency should be questioned, because agency policy is rarely constant and lack of change reflects a neglect to update the PFP. The PFP is an advance warning and the examiner can encourage the agency to use the PFP in that manner.

Responsiveness

A major concern of a budget analyst is to be sensitive to the concerns of elected political leaders and appointees and insure that existing programs are carrying out established policy. In gathering information and examining programs and their issues, budget analysts seek useful data which reflect upon the policy matters significant to the legislators. Budget examiners should identify all major policy concerns in their area which pertinent political officials would wish to understand in terms of their budget decisions. Examiners should try to identify desired new programs, changes in existing programs, and desired analyst follow-through on programs and projects considered legislatively important.

Even in unusual years when tax receipts are particularly high, few funds are available for all desired improvements in existing programs and for new programs. Resources for new and improved programs are normally small, but that does not mean that new programs should automatically be disregarded. Improved programs are prime candidates for funding if:

1. they result in unit cost savings in those programs where growth is inevitable (use unit cost analysis and marginal cost analysis);
2. the improved program can be an alternative to other current programs (use cost-effectiveness analysis);
3. the improvements can generate benefits in the area economy over the cost of program (use benefit-cost analysis); or
4. a case is made that intended political outcomes are significant in terms of the values of pertinent political officials.

New programs are prime candidates for funding if:

1. they are mandated by current law to begin in the BY; or
2. a cost-effective alternative exists to current programs (use cost-effectiveness analysis).

If the above conditions exist, the budget examiner should bring them to the attention of the political appointee when new or improved programs are being considered. An examination should identify the likely program outcomes, the groups positively and negatively affected, and the effect on those groups. This is particularly true of new or improved programs; political officials should be apprised of the implications of such programs so that they can take intelligent positions on them. In addition, examiners should be able to explain the theoretical linkages between direct budget amounts and government action, services and products produced, and program outcomes on society and individuals.

Analysts must be convinced such linkages exist and any doubts should be shared with pertinent political officials. The desired outputs should lead to the desired outcomes in the BY and specified years beyond the BY. Programs should be reviewed for timeliness, appropriateness, and necessity.

The desired inputs and planned management activities should lead to the desired outputs in the BY and beyond. This requires the examiners to be sure each program is funded at least at the minimum level for viable operations. This is done by defining the minimum useful output level and by being sure the input level (e.g., salaries, expenses, and equipment) can produce that desired output level.

Examiners review current programs to determine outmoded, nonproductive, duplicative, overlapping, or very low priority programs or parts of programs. When this occurs, examiners should fully document and carefully justify recommendations because agency opposition is likely. If required, statutory, ordinance, or regulation revisions should also be recommended and all costs, including staff, should be deleted. Cost-effectiveness analysis might be especially useful here.

Effectiveness and Efficiency

A major concern of budget examination is program effectiveness and efficiency. The budget analyst's focus should be on the adequacy of the planned management processes to insure that the programs will be managed correctly. The examiner should be confident that intended outputs and outcomes will be achieved. The best evidence for this is the agency's established track record of achievement. Beyond that, the budget analyst should be confident that administrative or outside factors will not prevent the intended outputs and outcomes from occurring. Such confidence is normally acquired by site inspections and inquiries to agency officials to see if they have properly anticipated the likely administrative and outside factors which could interfere. Examiners should review programs for documented workload change. Was there unavoidable growth in workload which cannot be absorbed? Conversely, workload decreases should be noted. In both situations, adjustments in staffing, expenditures, and other resources should be considered. Unit cost and marginal cost analyses might be particularly useful. Input to output ratios (productivity measures) are very useful and can be of interest to political officials. Marginal analysis is particularly helpful in determining the optimal input level for the most effective program operation.

Normally, maximum use should be made of nongeneral revenue sources rather than the general fund. Examiners should examine user fees, grants, trust funds, and internal service funds to be sure that they cover the maximum amount of expenses permitted in order to take pressure off the general fund. Unit cost analysis is useful in determining proper user fee charges. At the state and local levels, analysts should seek full justification from former or reduced federally funded programs.

A common failure of government agencies is not to aggressively recruit and develop employees, especially professional employees. Specific sums of money should be earmarked for professional development, including education, training, and professional conferences. Care should be taken to document carefully how the professional development improves employees. Politically inappropriate travel must be carefully avoided.

Interagency staff harmony and interagency and intraagency cooperation can achieve efficiencies. Examiners should determine if agencies' support processes (e.g., budget, personnel, general services) work in harmony
and provide consistent management direction and control. This can be
done by site visit or by questioning agency personnel.

In this day of rapidly advancing technology, analysts should be sure
that each agency is taking advantage of modern technology to improve the
quality of government services and achieve greater efficiencies. Examiners
should determine if capital purchase or leasing can be used to improve
program output and efficiency.

Exploring Private Options

If a public activity can be transferred to the private sector, then taxes
are potentially less and another source of taxes has been created. Therefore,
one task of a budget examiner is to explore the possibility for policy makers
of using private approaches for the delivery of public services. The following actions can sometimes be taken to involve the private sector in public
programs in a useful way:

1. contracting out;
2. giving franchises;
3. giving grants and subsidies to help someone else do the job;
4. providing vouchers;
5. substituting volunteers for government employees;
6. encouraging self-help and do-it-yourself efforts;
7. altering regulations or tax policy;
8. encouraging private agencies to take over an activity;
9. otherwise reducing demand for services, through marketing;
10. obtaining temporary help from private firms;
11. using fees and charges to adjust demand; and
12. forming joint public-private ventures.

Each of the above actions has consequences for both service levels and
costs. If demand for government services can be reduced, then costs can be
cut. Altering regulations or tax policy as well as increasing fees can reduce
demand for government services. Another means to lower demand is to
confront the problem directly by a variety of marketing techniques. People
can be encouraged to alter their behavior in constructive ways. For example,
public education programs can be used to discourage unnecessary calls for
ambulances, to encourage water conservation, to encourage the use of car
pools, to reduce smoking, to dial "911" for emergency calls, and so on.

Sometimes the public services can be maintained but at a lower cost.
For example, contracting out a service (e.g., garbage collection) to a private
company can sometimes reduce taxpayer cost and still maintain service levels. Labor costs are usually a large cost item in government. If tasks can be
done by volunteers, then cost savings can be significant. Another device is

to get a temporary loan of help from a private firm. Hiring a permanent expert is more expensive than getting temporary assistance for a short period of time.

Another desirable consequence of private sector involvement is to reduce government service by transferring part of the demand to the private sector. One way to do this is for a local government to award a franchise to a private firm to provide service within a certain geographical area. This is often done with ambulance and mass transit service. A second approach is to provide a grant or subsidy to the private sector in order to have them provide a specific service. This approach is sometimes used by local government for social welfare services such as child care, assistance to the homeless, and so on. A third approach is to use vouchers. This is sometimes done for medical services. Instead of providing a hospital for the poor, government provides vouchers to poor citizens needing hospital services. They, in turn, can select their own hospital. A fourth approach is to encourage self-help. The government encourages individuals or groups, such as neighborhood associations, to undertake activities for their own benefit. Examples are the programs of Alcoholics Anonymous and neighborhood clean-up campaigns.

An excellent means to raise more money and take the burden off the major tax source is to apply or increase user fees. If that policy is adopted, there should be some means, such as a voucher policy, to deal with the question of economic equity when low-income people may be excluded from public services. Vouchers have the added advantage, in some circumstances, of often improving the quality and responsiveness of services to the public. If the service is publicly provided, the economy of scale or public pressure may result in minimum staff resources being used for an important purpose. If the service is privately provided with a voucher service, then the voucher user can take advantage of a much wider range of units that offer the needed service. The major problem with a voucher system is that an illegal secondary market (i.e., a black market) in re-sold vouchers can easily exist. This allows voucher holders to sell them and not receive the services contemplated by public policy. If care is not taken, voucher systems can easily be corrupted.

Forecasting

Budgeting is always future-oriented and predicting the future is important in terms of both revenues and expenditures (see chapter 5). Normally, a government has many revenue sources, of which the largest are usually forecasted by a central authority such as the chief state economist or county budget office. The smaller revenue sources tend to concern specific departments and are forecasted by them. Analysts should verify department forecast accuracy by comparing past forecasts and actual money received. In addition, the examiner should verify agency expenditure forecasts by checking past year accounting reports, developing comparative cost data, and checking to avoid improper inventory buildup. For demand responsive programs, analysts should normally use marginal utility analysis; but for one-time projects, analysts should review cost estimates, especially in relationship to construction time assumptions. Careful examination of Program Evaluation and Review Technique (PERT) time and PERT cost can be particularly useful in determining the reasonableness of the expenditure forecast. Care should be taken to review prior year nonrecurring expenditure summaries in order to ensure that CY projects and programs do not improperly extend into the BY. Care should also be taken to identify actual and potential nonplanned cost escalations.

An interesting approach to government forecasting is called "consensus forecasting" by the state of Florida. The legislature's Division of Economic and Demographic Research prepares revenue forecasts, recommends formula budgeting, and prepares expenditure forecast models for approximately 25 percent of the state's programs. In doing this, the unit uses a remarkably large database, extensive computer capability, and complex economic models. Economic data are acquired from major national economic forecasting organizations and are added to the unique data collected from state sources. In addition, data are gathered on state education, criminal justice, and social services. All these combine into a Florida database and are used with an econometric model containing 123 simultaneous equations. The result is a Florida economic forecast which is critical in developing forecasts for state revenues, education expenditures, criminal justice expenditures, and social service expenditures. The data are also used to develop education, criminal justice, and social service formula budgets.

Whenever possible, analysts should seek comparative program data. Often, other public or private agencies are doing something similar to the agency being examined. By contrasting input, process, output, and outcome data, the analyst is in a much better position to judge forecasting accuracy. If another agency in a comparable government is doing the same thing for less money, that fact is helpful.

A common mistake made by examiners is not to demand and receive an accurate analysis of future year operating expenditure implications of large capital and nonrecurring cost projects. Building a new facility is one consideration, but maintaining it properly is yet another matter. Budget examiners should seek such analyses, and fiscal implications should be carefully explained to the political decision makers.

Politically Sensitive Subjects

Both political and professional officials discover that there are sensitive management practices in which error can lead to serious political or managerial consequences. Examiners should identify those areas, check on the frequency of errors in those areas, and be sure that existing control procedures are adequate. Budget analysts should identify any occurrences of politically or managerially embarrassing or illegal actions, especially in such sensitive areas as travel (with special stress on out-of-state travel), energy use, authorized positions, capital outlays, consulting, and mainframe computers. An analysis of such matters should isolate inadequate control procedures and determine if existing or planned control procedures create a counterproductive management hardship on line officials.

Two expense items normally should be zero based and fully documented. Temporary employment and consulting are not meant to be a regular personnel expense, but that can occur. Careful attention should be paid to ensure that this line-item category is not being abused. Data processing is not only an expensive line-item category, but one which should be watched carefully. Early decisions tend to commit management to certain future hardware and software decisions. However, given the extreme rate of technological advancement, care must be taken to ensure that proper decisions are being made and reviewed each year.

Detailed Budget Examination

Detailed budget examination involves looking carefully at (1) salaries, benefits, and temporary employee expenses; (2) price level increases for expenditures; and (3) operating, capital outlays, and trust fund schedules. Normally, across-the-board cost-of-living expenses are calculated separately by the central budget office. Agencies are commonly asked to continue CY annual rates for authorized positions, modified for any appropriate productivity improvements. Budget analysts normally use agency information to calculate lapsed salaries rather than use an overall lapse factor. Care should be taken to examine vacancy rates as well as salary funds that have been transferred or have reverted to other line categories. Commonly, new positions are assumed to be at minimum current pay rates, with all necessary benefits included; benefits are calculated as percentages of the salary base. Examiners should confirm the rates and calculations. Budget analysts may find matrix algebra to be extremely useful in making these adjustments.

In calculating current program expenses, examiners normally start with CY levels and adjust them for program reductions and modifications. Care should be taken not to drop the input to levels below which desired output becomes impossible. Deductions from current estimated expenditures should include nonrecurring and nonessential terms, nonessential inventory buildups, and expenses for deleted or lapsed current positions. In normal years, inflation increases are allowed at the wholesale price index level, but these may not be at a flat percentage. If one or more categories dominate the expenses, price increases for those categories should be treated separately. If unusual price changes occur in significant items (e.g., insurance, telephone, travel), they should be calculated separately. Data processing expenses also must be carefully reviewed. Budget analysts should balance user unit costs against the data center's information. Examiners should use a general services schedule for rental space and the current market rate for private space. Rates can be unnecessarily high due to choice location or unnecessary co-location requests.

Budget analysts should be sure that each equipment item is justified. State or local contract prices should be used and additional equipment requests should be fully documented and verified. Equipment replacement should be done by means of standard rules unless specifically requested with full documentation. Examiners should be sure that inventory levels and practices are justified. Often governments use general and specific guidelines for commonly purchased items. These guidelines should be used in judging equipment requests.

Special attention should be given to grant and trust programs. Normally, policy makers prefer not to replace federal cuts with general revenue funds unless the basic intent of a necessary program is seriously jeopardized. State and local governments prefer funding "in kind" rather than "cash matching." Budget analysts should ensure that jointly funded programs maximize federal and trust (e.g., user fee) receipts as well as leave justifiable ending balances. All calculations which produce beginning and ending balances, including trust fund investments, should be carefully examined. Normally, small working capital amounts are allowed to cover cash flow requirements.

Automation

The budget preparation process can be automated, and various activities in that process are commonly automated. For example, revenue forecasting and preparation of budget allocation formulas are often automated. The former activity often involves a great deal of data, and the latter involves not only large data sets, but also "what if" types of analysis using those data sets. Some jurisdictions use computers to "roll up" the data from the lowest units to higher levels of aggregation. A few jurisdictions have a comprehensive automated budget preparation process. Normally, the weakest aspect of the system relates, not to computers, but to failure to acquire good performance (output or outcome) measures.

Regardless of the scope of automation, the keys to understanding automation are to use systems theory and to think backwards from the products of the automated system. A simple input-process-output system model is central to automation. One defines the products and then designs the process and inputs to get the desired outputs (products). In budget preparation, the most important output can be the appropriation act. However, it can be the revenue estimate report. Hardware (i.e., the computer and related equipment) and software (i.e., the instructions to the computer on how to manipulate the data) should be defined in relationship to the desired output reports. The input reports are the means to get the necessary data into the computer.

Automation can mean that "data crunching," consideration of "what if" possibilities, preparation of complex multiple consistent crosswalks, and even performance of various types of analysis can be done more accurately and faster with a computer. It permits much more sophisticated analysis and higher-quality budgeting. Automation also means a new set of complexities, including frustration when massive data sets are "lost" and computer breakdowns occur. Increasingly, automation will be more common as hardware becomes less expensive and more useful software is developed.

The microcomputer has particular relevance to the budget process and the electronic spreadsheet is especially significant software. Given the many tables employed in budgeting, commonly used tools are the multiple-column and row light-green paper, plus the calculator. The electronic spreadsheet is the modern replacement for those tools. The grandfather of the electronic spreadsheet is the VisiCalc® program which was conceived in 1978 by Daniel Bricklin and Robert Frankston. The VisiCalc program produces spreadsheets of 63 columns or more by 254 rows. However, the advantages go much beyond a very big sheet of data. The sheet is organized with A, B, C labels for columns and numbers for rows. Thus, one can iden-tify each cell of this very large matrix (e.g., A24, G2, M150, AA50). One of the strengths of the electronic version is that the user can use a formula to derive the answer for each cell and the formula can be stated with other cells as variables in the formula. Thus, a cell's value can be calculated by entering 7 + 13 or entering "add cell B24 (with a value of 7) to cell G177 (with a 13 value in it)." This permits use of complex interrelations of data which we commonly need for analysis and accounting. Analytical problems, such as purchasing decisions, often use sets of data arrayed by columns and rows. Thus, they are well suited for the electronic spreadsheet. Some analytical tools, such as the crosswalk, are ideally suited.

The major frustration with light-green ledger paper is the reality that mistakes are made, new ideas require major changes, and "what-if" analyses are often needed. The results are many erasures and versions of the first spreadsheet. The power of the electronic spreadsheet is the ease of making modifications. Rows and columns can be added even in the middle of the spreadsheet. Any data changes are automatically recalculated, saving time and eliminating mistakes. Thus, errors can be changed quickly and new ideas can be added easily. The most dramatic strength is that "what-if" anal-ysis becomes dramatically easier. Instead of preparing new sheets and run-ning the calculator on all the new numbers, the user merely finds the cells that contain the key variables, and makes the changes. Automatically and within seconds, all the numbers are recalculated. Some electronic spread-sheets, such as Lotus 1-2-3, can take a set of cells and convert them into graph, pie, and bar charts. More advanced software permits the user to link electronic spreadsheets. For example, in budgeting, let us assume we have a spreadsheet for each unit of government. In order to prepare aggregate information, some of the most important numbers must be "rolled-up" to the department and government level. This can be done by linking spread-sheets so that the entire set of spreadsheets can be updated when we enter changes in the unit's spreadsheet.

There are many software packages available that are especially helpful for forecasting. Three recommended by *PC Magazine* are 1, 2, 3 Forecast!, SmartForecasts II, and Forecast Master. They vary in price from $90 to $795 respectively. The 1, 2, 3 Forecast! requires you to also use Lotus 1-2-3. The forecast software is menu-driven and enables users without statistical expe-rience to create forecasts. It can handle 10 variables, 150 cases, and 1500

VisiCalc is a registered trademark of VisiCorp.

data points. It requires a 512 K (thousand) RAM (memory used to operate and to work the computer) and two disk drives (hardware data storage devices). SmartForecasts II is also menu driven with a command language that places your choices at the bottom of the screen at all times. It makes predictions automatically from your data and it automatically selects the best forecasting technique for you. It also shows the other methods and the percentages by which they were considered inferior. The information is presented in vivid color graphs complete with confidence intervals in different colors. It can handle 45 variables, 165 cases, and 7425 data points. It requires a 256 K RAM and two disk drives. Forecast Master uses a menu with defaults available to guide the beginners, but permits the entering of formulas for the more advanced user. The seven forecasting models available in the package are state space, Box-Jenkins, Bayesian vector autoregression, AUTOPRO regression, seasonal decomposition, exponential smoothing, and curve fitting. Forecast Master can handle 15 variables, 2000 cases, and 30,000 data points. It requires a 512 K RAM and one disk drive. All three require DOS 2.0 or later.

In a 1986 article in *Government Finance Review,* survey results on the use of microcomputers in local public finance organizations showed an explosive sevenfold growth from 1982 to 1986. Over 90 percent of the respondents reported using IBM personal computers or their clones. Secretarial and clerical employees tended to use word processing and file management software. The analytical and management employees tended to use spreadsheet, database management, and project management software. Senior management tended to use the computer less, and they preferred spreadsheet software. Few organizations used multiple-system units. About 67 percent used hard-disk storage systems and about 53 percent used graphics capability. The dominate software used was Lotus 1-2-3 and dBase II/III. Integrated software like Symphony and Framework had not achieved a significant following.

The survey results showed several popular applications. About 47 percent used it for budgeting and 22 percent for planning. About 35 percent used the microcomputer for modeling and forecasting. It was used less for billing, inventory, and payroll. In terms of planned future use, inventory, cash management, forecasting, and budgeting were areas of greatest growth potential. A trend seems to exist that will link microcomputers to mainframes with planned downloading from mainframe computers. Only 11 percent do not plan on such links. Local area networks (LANs) of microcomputers were not as popular since only 14 percent used them, but 40 percent planned on using them in the future.

Microcomputers are a big hit in budgeting and financial management. Exhibit 6-3 shows their positive influence on managerial concerns. There have been improvements in the areas of employee satisfaction, decisionmaking, the maintenance of schedules, and the meeting of budget limits. Exhibit 6-4 shows the remarkable effect on productivity in various tasks. Notice the improvements in budgeting, cash management, financial modeling, and forecasting. Clearly, the microcomputer is radically changing the manner in which public budgeting and financial management is done.

EXHIBIT 6-3   Microcomputer and Managerial Concerns

CONCERNS	VERY POSITIVE	POSITIVE	NO CHANGE	NEGA- TIVE	VERY NEGA- TIVE
Employee Satisfaction	23.9%	56.1%	18.6%	1.1%	.3%
Worker Health	2.0	7.1	89.8	.6	.6
Employee Communica- tions	4.5	29.4	65.0	.6	.6
Job Reductions	4.2	13.2	79.4	2.5	.6
Loss of Management Con- trol	2.4	10.1	84.6	1.7	1.1
Security of Information	3.9	17.9	73.1	4.5	.6
Quality of Decision	17.9	59.4	22.1	.3	.3
Maintenance of Schedules	14.1	45.4	40.0	.3	.3
Meeting Budget Limits	10.2	31.8	56.8	.6	.5

Source: John W. Ostrowski, Ella P. Gardner, and Magda H. Motawi, "Microcomputers in Public Finance Organizations: A Survey of Uses and Trends," *Government Finance Review,* February 1986, p. 26. Used by permission.

EXHIBIT 6-4   Productivity and the Microcomputer

TASK	SUBSTANTIAL INCREASE %	MODERATE INCREASE %	NO CHANGE %	DECREASE %
Accounting	44.9	41.9	12.1	1.0
Billing	35.3	39.7	23.5	1.5
Budgeting	51.2	41.8	5.5	1.6
Cash Management	50.0	39.4	10.1	.5
Financial Modeling	51.8	39.1	9.1	0.0
Forecasting	51.0	42.5	6.5	0.0
Inventory	34.7	39.6	24.8	1.0
Payroll	34.0	35.1	27.8	3.1

Source: John W. Ostrowski, Ella P. Gardner, and Magda H. Motawi, "Microcomputers in Public Finance Organizations: A Survey of Uses and Trends," *Government Finance Review,* February 1986, p. 27. Used by permission.

PROCESS ANALYSIS

Focus

The purpose of process analysis, in the context of public budgeting, is to help the line managers and the budget analyst understand the existing bureaucratic process between organization input and output. It is not an attempt to define the optimal process which will most effectively use available resources, although a by-product might be that determination. It does seek to determine if the existing process is an effective use of resources and to identify idle or poorly used resources.

This subtle stress in process analysis for public budgeting can be overlooked. When examining a budget, the analyst is seeking insight that will help higher-level decision makers and foster improved management within the organization. The budget analyst must always appreciate that a staff function is being performed and that the line-unit supervisor is responsible for managing his or her unit. The analyst is only an aid to the manager *and* other higher level managers and policy makers in the government. Thus, process analysis in the context of budget examination is not striving to necessarily find the optimal process as that task is really the responsibility of the line manager. Instead, process analysis here is used only to help others make reasonable judgments on the effectiveness of the existing process and the quality of management in that unit.

Steps

The steps in process analysis are as follows:

1. define programs within the organizational divisions of the government;
2. define the minimum level of service for each program; and
3. develop a flow chart for the process of each program.

Defining programs and minimum levels of service are difficult professional challenges. In order to foster greater managerial accountability, programs normally should be defined within specific lowest-level organizational units in a government. The defined programs should be the major sets of activities in an organizational unit which produces specific projects and services. If programs cut across organizational units, then both managerial and fiscal accountability are much more difficult to establish and maintain. A major problem in defining sets that are identified as programs and sometimes forcing such "fits" is that it may discourage needed managerial cooperation. Nevertheless, defining programs is very useful and managerially helpful for most administrative situations.

The problem of defining a program's "minimum level of service" is often a difficult challenge. "Minimum level of service," as notably used in ZBB, is the lowest amount of resources needed to conduct the program as a viable administrative undertaking. The professional challenge for the budget analyst is that line managers nearly always consider their present level minimum and they tend to refuse to consider the possibility of lesser amounts than what they are currently using. The best approach to take is to define with the manager the existing inputs and outputs. Then, the analyst starts posing "what if 5 percent less, 10 percent, and so on" situations to seek clarification of what would happen to the outputs. Next, the analyst should attempt to determine the impact of those smaller ouputs upon the program outcomes. This may become a problem because some managers have difficulty conceptualizing their program and program outcomes. Nor-

EXHIBIT 6-5 Daily Activities

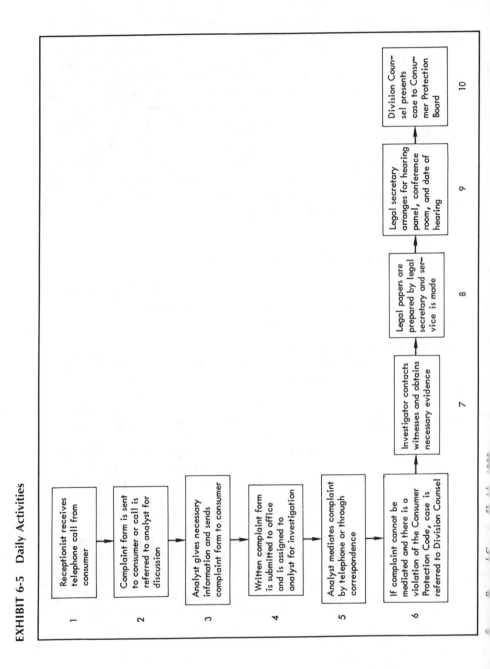

1. Receptionist receives telephone call from consumer

2. Complaint form is sent to consumer or call is referred to analyst for discussion

3. Analyst gives necessary information and sends complaint form to consumer

4. Written complaint form is submitted to office and is assigned to analyst for investigation

5. Analyst mediates complaint by telephone or through correspondence

6. If complaint cannot be mediated and there is a violation of the Consumer Protection Code, case is referred to Division Counsel

7. Investigator contacts witnesses and obtains necessary evidence

8. Legal papers are prepared by legal secretary and service is made

9. Legal secretary arranges for hearing panel, conference room, and date of hearing

10. Division Counsel presents case to Consumer Protection Board

mally, some reasonable minimum level of service becomes apparent after some discussions.

Flow charting the process of each program involves identifying, first, what activities take place in the unit, and secondly, who does what aspect of each activity. The latter should include an estimate of the percentage of time in a work week devoted to each activity by each person or class of employees in the unit. Flow charting gets the line manager away from broad superlatives about the virtues of programs and focuses on exactly what the unit does. The first document presents the unit's activities; normally, this is best defined by stating the trigger actions within the unit (e.g., a phone call from a client) and charting what follows until the unit produces a specific service or product. The chart, which can be done in several ways, should show the relationship of the steps to each other. The chart shows the activities done on a day-in and day-out basis. (See Exhibits 6-5 and 6-6.) The second document identifies who does what activity, the payload and position description of each person, and the percent of time on each activity (see Exhibits 6-7 and 6-8.)

The limitations of process analysis for the budget analyst are primarily those of time and organization size. The budget calendar forces the budget

EXHIBIT 6-6   Daily Veteran's Office Actiyities

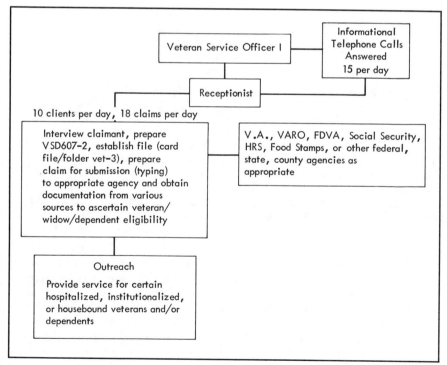

Source: Broward County, Florida, 1983.